AF891323

Tianyi Guan

Predictive energy-efficient motion trajectory optimization of electric vehicles

Karlsruher Schriften zur Anthropomatik
Band 42
Herausgeber: Prof. Dr.-Ing. habil. Jürgen Beyerer

Eine Übersicht aller bisher in dieser Schriftenreihe erschienenen Bände finden Sie am Ende des Buchs.

Predictive energy-efficient motion trajectory optimization of electric vehicles

by
Tianyi Guan

KIT Scientific Publishing

Karlsruher Institut für Technologie
Institut für Anthropomatik und Robotik

Predictive energy-efficient motion trajectory optimization of electric vehicles

Zur Erlangung des akademischen Grades eines Doktors der Ingenieurwissenschaften / Doktors der Naturwissenschaften von der KIT-Fakultät für Informatik des Karlsruher Instituts für Technologie (KIT) genehmigte Dissertation

von Dipl.-Ing. Tianyi Guan

Tag der mündlichen Prüfung: 18. Juni 2019
Referent: Prof. Dr.-Ing. habil. Jürgen Beyerer
Korreferent: Prof. Dr.-Ing. Michael Heizmann

Impressum

KIT Scientific Publishing

Karlsruher Institut für Technologie (KIT)
KIT Scientific Publishing
Straße am Forum 2
D-76131 Karlsruhe

KIT Scientific Publishing is a registered trademark of Karlsruhe Institute of Technology.
Reprint using the book cover is not allowed.

www.ksp.kit.edu

This document – excluding the cover, pictures and graphs – is licensed under a Creative Commons Attribution-Share Alike 4.0 International License (CC BY-SA 4.0): https://creativecommons.org/licenses/by-sa/4.0/deed.en

The cover page is licensed under a Creative Commons Attribution-No Derivatives 4.0 International License (CC BY-ND 4.0): https://creativecommons.org/licenses/by-nd/4.0/deed.en

Print on Demand 2019 – Gedruckt auf FSC-zertifiziertem Papier

ISSN 1863-6489
ISBN 978-3-7315-0978-3
DOI 10.5445/KSP/1000098619

Kurzfassung

Neben autonomem Fahren und Sicherheitsanwendungen sind umweltschonende Antriebstechnologien und energieeffizientes Fahren ebenfalls wichtige Aspekte der modernen Mobilität. Während Batterien, Brennstoffzellen sowie andere klimaneutrale Antriebstechnologien etablierte Antriebssysteme noch nicht ersetzen können, ist es bereits heute möglich, die Energieeffizienz durch energieeffizientes Fahren zu erhöhen. Energieeffizientes Fahren hängt von vielen Faktoren ab. Diese beinhalten unter anderem den fahrzeugspezifischen Antriebsstrang, die Straßentopografie und die Interaktion mit der dynamischen Umgebung wie beispielsweise Ampeln und andere Verkehrsteilnehmer. Darüber hinaus kann es weitere Kriterien geben, wie zum Beispiel Reisedauer und Komponentenverschleiß, die ebenfalls wichtig sind. Es existieren zwar generische Empfehlungen von staatlichen Institutionen und Forschungsinstituten zu diesem Thema, jedoch hat der normale Fahrer wenig Wissen über die genauen quantitativen Eigenschaften des Fahrzeugs und dessen Umgebung. Außerdem geht energieeffizientes Fahren über vereinfachte, isolierte und lokale Entscheidungen hinaus. Tatsächlich besteht es aus einer Kette von Entscheidungen.

Diese Arbeit verwendet eine Kombination aus existierenden und neuartigen Methoden, um die Bewegungstrajektorie eines Elektrofahrzeugs hinsichtlich der Energieeffizienz und anderer Kreiterien für eine vorgegebene Route zu optimieren. Obwohl ein Elektrofahrzeug als Beispiel verwendet wird, kann das vorgeschlagene Optimierungsverfahren auf eine große Bandbreite von verschiedenen Fahrzeugen angewendet werden. Viele existierende Ansätze konzentrieren sich auf isolierte Problemstellungen, während andere Aspekte vernachlässigt werden. Beispielsweise steht in manchen Untersuchungen die

Fahrsicherheit im Vordergrund, während die Energieeffizienz vernachlässigt wird. In anderen Untersuchungen steht wiederum die Energieeffizienz im Vordergrund, während die Interaktion mit anderen Verkehrsteilnehmern vernachlässigt wird. Im Gegensatz zur isolierten Problemlösung verwendet diese Arbeit einen ganzheitlichen Ansatz. Es wird eine einzige Kostenfunktion verwendet, die Energieeffizienz, Fahrsicherheit, physikalische Umsetzbarkeit und andere Kriterien beurteilt. Kostenterme werden in monetärer Form ausgedrückt, um eine direkte Vergleichbarkeit zu ermöglichen. Aufgrund möglicherweise langer Fahrstrecken und eines hohen Berechnungsaufwands, muss der Algorithmus die Optimierung innerhalb eines endlichen Berechnungshorizonts beschränken, der normalerweise viel kürzer als die gesamte Reise ist. Um eine bessere Einschätzung der optimalen Trajektorie jenseits des Horizonts zu erhalten, wird ein neuartiger Ansatz vorgestellt, der historisch akkumulierte Minimalkosten wiederverwendet.

Die Evaluation wird in einer simulierten Umgebung durchgeführt. Die Straßentopografie, Krümmung des Straßenverlaufs, Geschwindigkeitsbegrenzungen, Fahrstreifen, Ampelpositionen und andere zeitinvariante Eigenschaften der Route werden aus der Realität entnommen. Die Ampelschaltzeiten werden von Messungen in der realen Welt abgeleitet. Andere Fahrzeuge werden mit etablierten Fahrermodellen simuliert. Zahlreiche Ergebnisse demonstrieren die Fähigkeit des Algorithmus auf einheitliche Weise, energieeffizientes Fahren zu optimieren, physikalisch umsetzbare Entscheidungen zu generieren und Kollisionen zu vermeiden.

Abstract

Apart from autonomous driving and safety applications, environmental sustainability and energy efficiency are also important aspects of modern mobility. While long-range batteries and other zero-emission technologies have yet to replace established propulsion systems, it is already possible to increase energy efficiency through energy-efficient driving. Energy-efficient driving depends on numerous factors, including the specific vehicle powertrain, the static environment like road topography and road curvature, and interaction with the dynamic environment like traffic lights and other traffic participants. There can also be additional criteria like travel duration and component wear that are also important. While there are generic driving rules issued by the government and other institutions, the regular driver has little knowledge about the precise quantitative properties of the vehicle and the environment. Furthermore, energy-efficient driving goes beyond simplified, isolated, and localized decisions. In fact, it is a chain of decisions.

This thesis uses a combination of existing and novel methods to optimize the motion trajectory of an electric vehicle in order to improve the energy efficiency and other criteria for a predefined route. Although an electric vehicle is used as an example, the proposed optimization method can be applied to a wide range of different vehicles. Many existing approaches focus on travel safety but neglect energy-efficiency. Others focus on energy-efficiency but neglect interactions with other traffic participants. In contrast, this thesis uses a unified approach. It uses a single combined cost function incorporating energy efficiency, travel safety, physical feasibility, and other criteria. Cost terms are expressed in monetary form to enable direct comparison among them. Due to possibly long routes and high computational burden, the algorithm has to confine the optimization within a finite horizon that is usually much shorter than the entire journey. In order to give a better estimate of the optimal trajectory beyond the horizon, a novel technique is presented that reuses historically accumulated minimum costs.

The evaluation is conducted in a simulated environment. The road topography, speed limits, lanes, traffic light positions, and other time-invariant route properties used in the simulation are derived from real-world data. Traffic light phases are derived from real-world measurements. Other vehicles are simulated using established driver models. Numerous results demonstrate the algorithm's capability to optimize energy-efficient driving, make physically feasible decisions, and avoid collisions in a unified manner.

Acknowledgment

I would like to convey my gratitude to my advisor Prof. Dr.-Ing. habil. Jürgen Beyerer and my co-advisor Prof. Dr.-Ing. Michael Heizmann for their invaluable advice and expertise. I want to thank the head of my department Christian Frey for his unwavering support. I am most grateful to the students who have assisted me on numerous topics throughout the years. I would like to thank the partners of the REM-2030 research project for their technical assistance. I also want to thank all of my colleagues for their support and the amicable atmosphere they provided within the department. Finally, I would like to thank my parents and my girlfriend Wenting Sun for their moral support.

Contents

Acronyms

ABS	Anti-lock braking system
ACC	Adaptive cruise control and ACC model
BE	Bellman equation
CAN	Control area network
CAH	Constant acceleration heuristic
DP	Dynamic programming
ICE	Internal combustion engine
EDM	Extended driver model used by the ego-vehicle driver and the simulation
EE	Electric engine
ESP	Electronic stability program
EV	Electric vehicle
FBDP	Forward-backward dynamic programming
GLC	Gross labor cost
HMI	Human machine interface
HJBE	Hamilton-Jacobi-Bellman equation
IDM	Intelligent driver model
IIDM	Improved intelligent driver model
Lidar	Light detection and ranging
LRAHE	Long-range auxiliary horizon extension
MOBIL	Minimizing overall braking deceleration induced by lane changes
PEEMTO	Predictive energy-efficient motion trajectory optimization (the optimization developed in this thesis)

PEEO	Predictive energy efficiency optimization without lane changes (reference system used to compare to PEEMTO)
PO	Principle of optimality
Radar	Radio detection and ranging
REM-2030	Regional eco mobility 2030
LOS	Level of service
SDM	Simplified driver model used by PEEMTO and PEEO
SHE	Stationary horizon extension
SOC	State of charge
STD	Standard deviation
V2I	Vehicle-to-infrastructure communication
V2V	Vehicle-to-vehicle communication
U.S.	United States of America

Symbols

Notations

$*$	Optimality, e.g., J^* is the optimal accumulated cost
$\mathcal{O}$	Bachmann-Landau notation for the description of complexity
Scalar	e.g., t, s, v, G, Q
Vector	e.g., $\boldsymbol{x}$
Set	e.g., $\mathbf{X}$
Vector of scalars	e.g., $\boldsymbol{x} = [t, s, v, ...]$
Trajectory of discrete vectors	e.g., $\tilde{\boldsymbol{x}} = (\boldsymbol{x}_0, \boldsymbol{x}_1, ...)$
Set of discrete vectors	e.g., $\mathbf{X} = \{\boldsymbol{x}_0, \boldsymbol{x}_1, ...\}$
Tuple of discrete sets	e.g., $\tilde{\mathbf{X}} = (\mathbf{X}_0, \mathbf{X}_1, ...)$

Operators

$\dot{}$	Temporal derivatve, e.g., $\dot{v} = \frac{dv}{dt}$
∇	Gradient
$\min\limits_{\boldsymbol{x} \in \mathbf{X}}$	Minimization with respect to $\boldsymbol{x}$ within the set $\mathbf{X}$
$\arg\min\limits_{\boldsymbol{x} \in \mathbf{X}}$	Argument of $\min\limits_{\boldsymbol{x} \in \mathbf{X}}$

Coordinate system and environment

d	Lateral position
$\boldsymbol{P}_c$	Center of curvature
$\boldsymbol{P}_v$	Vehicle center of gravity
r	Road curvature radius
s	Longitudinal position

v_{max}	Speed limit
κ	Road curvature

Vehicle model

a	Acceleration
a_{lat}	Lateral acceleration
$A_{b,a}$	Main brake pressure cylinder area
$A_{b,w}$	Wheel brake cylinder area
A_{eff}	Effective cross sectional area
c_f	Cornering stiffness of the front wheel
c_r	Cornering stiffness of the rear wheel
c_w	Drag coefficient
C_b	Internal brake ratio
$f_{b,u}$	Brake force transition function
F_a	Acceleration resistance force
F_{air}	Air (drag) resistance force
F_b	Brake force
$F_{b,p}$	Brake pad force
$F_{b,u}$	Brake pedal force
F_c	Curve resistance force
F_g	Gravitational force
$F_{g,p}$	Normal force (gravitational force component perpendicular to the road)
F_{roll}	Rolling resistance force
F_{slope}	Slope resistance force
g	Gravitational acceleration
G	Gear level
$i_{b,a}$	Brake amplification ratio
$i_{b,u}$	Brake pedal ratio
i_f	Final drive ratio
i_s	Steering wheel ratio

i_t	Transmission ratio
I	Battery current
I_c	Battery cell current
$I_{c,max}$	Maximum battery cell discharge current
$I_{c,min}$	Maximum battery cell charge current
J_e	Engine inertia
J_w	Wheel inertia
l	Wheelbase
l_f	Front part of wheelbase
l_r	Rear part of wheelbase
m	Vehicle mass
$n_{bat,p}$	Number of parallel battery cells
$n_{bat,s}$	Number of serial battery cells
P_{bat}	Battery power
$P_{bat,c}$	Battery cell power
$P_{e,max}$	Maximum engine power
$P_{e,min}$	Maximum generator power
Q	Battery charge
Q_c	Battery cell charge
$r_{b,d}$	Effective brake disc radius
r_w	Dynamic wheel radius
R_i	Battery internal resistance
$R_{i,c}$	Battery cell internal resistance
T_b	Brake torque
$T_{c,in}$	Clutch torque on the engine side
$T_{c,out}$	Clutch torque on the transmission side
T_e	Engine torque
$T_{e,max}$	Maximum engine torque
$T_{e,min}$	Maximum generator torque
T_f	Final drive torque
T_t	Transmission torque

T_{w}	Wheel torque
u_{a}	Acceleration pedal position
u_{b}	Brake pedal position
u_{s}	Steering wheel angle
v	Velocity
V_{idle}	Battery idle voltage
$V_{\mathrm{idle,c}}$	Battery cell idle voltage
$V_{\mathrm{c,max}}$	Maximum battery cell voltage
V_{out}	Battery output voltage
$V_{\mathrm{out,c}}$	Battery cell output voltage
β	Side slip angle
$\Delta t_{\mathrm{shift}}$	Gear shift duration
ε_{b}	Progression of brake pad application
ε_{G}	Progression of gear level shift
ζ	Longitudinal jerk
ζ_{lat}	Lateral jerk
$\eta_{\mathrm{b,a}}$	Brake pressure efficiency of the amplifier
$\eta_{\mathrm{b,w}}$	Brake force efficiency at the wheels
η_{bat}	Battery efficiency
η_{c}	Clutch efficiency
η_{DCAC}	DC/AC converter efficiency
η_{DCDC}	DC/DC converter efficiency
η_{e}	Engine efficiency (map)
η_{t}	Transmission efficiency
μ_{b}	Ground adhesion coefficient
$\mu_{\mathrm{b,lin}}$	Linear ground adhesion coefficient
$\mu_{\mathrm{b,max}}$	Maximum ground adhesion coefficient
$\mu_{\mathrm{b,p}}$	Brake pad friction coefficient
μ_{r}	Rolling resistance coefficient
ρ_{air}	Air density
σ_{b}	Tire slip

$\sigma_{\mathrm{b,max}}$	Maximum acceptable tire slip
φ	Slope angle
ψ	Yaw angle
$\omega_{\mathrm{c,in}}$	Clutch (rotation) speed on the engine side
$\omega_{\mathrm{c,out}}$	Clutch (rotation) speed on the transmission side
ω_{e}	Engine (rotation) speed
$\omega_{\mathrm{e,max}}$	Maximum engine (rotation) speed
ω_{f}	Final drive (rotation) speed
ω_{t}	Transmission (rotation) speed
ω_{w}	Wheel (rotation) speed

Driver model

a_{ACC}	Acceleration of ACC model
a_{CAH}	Acceleration of CAH
a_{d}	Preferred acceleration
$a_{\mathrm{d,bias}}$	Lane bias
$a_{\mathrm{d,free}}$	Free acceleration
$a_{\mathrm{d,f}}$	Acceleration of front vehicle
a_{IDM}	Acceleration of IDM
a_{IIDM}	Acceleration of IIDM
b_{d}	Comfortable deceleration
$b_{\mathrm{d,safe}}$	Safe deceleration
F	Neighbor type symbol of front central neighbor
$\hat{\mathrm{F}}$	Neighbor type symbol of front left neighbor
$\check{\mathrm{F}}$	Neighbor type symbol of front right neighbor
$l_{\mathrm{d,goal}}$	Desired lane
$\hat{\mathrm{R}}$	Neighbor type symbol of rear left neighbor
$\check{\mathrm{R}}$	Neighbor type symbol of rear right neighbor
$\hat{\mathrm{S}}$	Neighbor type symbol of left adjacent neighbor
$\check{\mathrm{S}}$	Neighbor type symbol of right adjacent neighbor
$v_{\mathrm{d,goal}}$	Desired velocity

$v_{d,f}$	Velocity of front vehicle
δ_{d}	Acceleration exponent
$\Delta a_{d,min}$	Lane change incentive
Δs_{d}	Distance to front vehicle
$\Delta s_{d,evasion}$	Evasion activation distance
$\Delta s_{d,goal}$	Desired distance to front vehicle
$\Delta s_{d,min}$	Acceptable minimum distance to front vehicle
Δt_{d}	Desired time gap to front vehicle (reaction time)
$\Delta t_{d,evasion}$	Evasion activation time gap
Δv_{d}	Velocity difference compared to front vehicle
$\lambda_{d,c}$	Coolness factor
$\lambda_{d,p}$	Politeness factor

Optimization

e	Energy consumption
j	Transition cost (function)
j_{b}	Average brake wear (transition) cost
j_{G}	Average transmission wear (transition) cost
j_{e}	Energy consumption (transition) cost
j_{t}	Travel duration (transition) cost
J	Accumulated cost (function)
t_{0}	Start time of the optimization
s_{0}	Current longitudinal position of the ego-vehicle
s_{end}	End position of the route
ζ_{min}	Minimum for comfortable longitudinal jerk
ζ_{max}	Maximum for comfortable longitudinal jerk
$\zeta_{lat,max}$	Maximum for comfortable lateral jerk
λ_{b}	Brake wear weight
λ_{e}	Energy consumption weight
λ_{G}	Transmission wear weight

λ_t	Travel duration weight

Continuous optimization

$\dot{\boldsymbol{x}}(t) = f(\boldsymbol{x}(t), \boldsymbol{u}(t))$	System equations
t	Continuous time
$\boldsymbol{u}(t)$	Control (trajectory)
$\boldsymbol{u}^*(t)$	Optimal control (trajectory)
$\boldsymbol{x}(t)$	State (trajectory)
$\boldsymbol{x}^*(t)$	Optimal state (trajectory)
Υ	Admissible control space

Discrete optimization

$a(t_i)$	Acceleration of state $\boldsymbol{x}(t_i)$
a_i	Acceleration of state $\boldsymbol{x}_i$
$a_{b,i}$	Acceleration of state $\boldsymbol{x}_{b,i}$
$a_\mathrm{lat}(t_i)$	Lateral acceleration of state $\boldsymbol{x}(t_i)$
$a_{\mathrm{lat},i}$	Lateral acceleration ofstate $\boldsymbol{x}_i$
$a_{\mathrm{lat},b,i}$	Lateral acceleration of state $\boldsymbol{x}_{b,i}$
$d(t_i)$	Lateral position of state $\boldsymbol{x}(t_i)$
d_i	Lateral position of state $\boldsymbol{x}_i$
$d_{b,i}$	Lateral position of state $\boldsymbol{x}_{b,i}$
$G(t_i)$	Gear level of state $\boldsymbol{x}(t_i)$
G_i	Gear level of state $\boldsymbol{x}_i$
$G_{b,i}$	Gear level of state $\boldsymbol{x}_{b,i}$
n_a	Number of different discrete acceleration values
n_{a_lat}	Number of different discrete lateral acceleration values
n_d	Number of different discrete lateral position values
n_G	Number of different gear levels
n_lane	Number of different lanes
n_Q	Number of different discrete battery charge values

n_t	Number of different discrete time
n_v	Number of different discrete velocity values
$n_{\boldsymbol{x}}$	Number of states in decision stages
n_κ	Number of different discrete road curvature values
n_φ	Number of different discrete road slope angle values
$Q(t_i)$	Lateral acceleration of state $\boldsymbol{x}(t_i)$
Q_i	Battery charge of state $\boldsymbol{x}_i$
$Q_{b,i}$	Battery charge of state $\boldsymbol{x}_{b,i}$
s_i	Position with index i
t_i	Time with index i with reference to s_i
$t_{i,\text{toa}}$	Time of arrival with reference to t_i
$t_{i,\text{tod}}$	Time of departure with reference to t_i
$t_{\text{b,i}}$	Time of a state $\boldsymbol{x}_{b,i}$
$t_{b,i,\text{toa}}$	Time of arrival with reference to $t_{\text{b,i}}$
$t_{b,i,\text{tod}}$	Time of departure with reference to $t_{\text{b,i}}$
$\boldsymbol{u}(t_i)$	Control vector with respect to t_i within control trajectory
$\tilde{\boldsymbol{u}}(t_i)$	Control trajectory from t_0 to t_i
$\boldsymbol{u}_i$	Control vector with respect to s_i within control tuple
$\tilde{\boldsymbol{u}}_i$	Control tuple from s_0 to s_i
$u_{\text{a},i}$	Acceleration control of $\boldsymbol{u}_i$
$u_{\text{b},i}$	Brake control of $\boldsymbol{u}_i$
$u_{\text{s},i}$	Steering wheel control of $\boldsymbol{u}_i$
$v(t_i)$	Velocity of state $\boldsymbol{x}(t_i)$
v_{i}	Velocity of state $\boldsymbol{x}_i$
$v_{\text{b,i}}$	Velocity of state $\boldsymbol{x}_{b,i}$
$\boldsymbol{x}(t_i)$	State vector with respect to t_i within state trajectory
$\tilde{\boldsymbol{x}}(t_i)$	State trajectory from t_0 to t_i
$\boldsymbol{x}_0$	Start state
$\boldsymbol{x}_i$	State at s_i within state tuple
$\tilde{\boldsymbol{x}}_i$	State tuple from s_0 to s_i
$\boldsymbol{x}_{b,i}$	State with state index b at stage X_i within $\tilde{\mathbf{X}}$

$\tilde{\mathbf{X}}$	Regular state graph
$\mathbf{X}_i$	Decision stage of $\tilde{\mathbf{X}}$ at position s_i within $\tilde{\mathbf{X}}$
$\breve{\boldsymbol{x}}_{b,i}$	Auxiliary state with state index b at stage $\breve{\mathbf{X}}_i$ within $\breve{\tilde{\mathbf{X}}}$
$\breve{\tilde{\mathbf{X}}}$	Auxiliary state graph
$\breve{\mathbf{X}}_i$	Decision stage of $\breve{\tilde{\mathbf{X}}}$ at position s_i within $\breve{\tilde{\mathbf{X}}}$
ΔG_i	Gear change of $\boldsymbol{u}_i$
$\Delta Q(\boldsymbol{x}_{b,i}, \boldsymbol{x}_{c,k})$	Change in battery charge from $\boldsymbol{x}_{b,i}$ to $\boldsymbol{x}_{c,k}$
Γ	Admissible control space using time discretization
Γ_s	Admissible control space using position discretization
Δs	Position discretization interval
$\Delta s_{\tilde{\mathbf{X}}}$	Horizon (length) of $\tilde{\mathbf{X}}$
$\Delta s_{\breve{\tilde{\mathbf{X}}}}$	Horizon (length) of $\breve{\tilde{\mathbf{X}}}$
Δt	Time discretization interval
$\Delta t_{\text{gap,min}}$	One second time gap
$\Delta t_{\text{gap,max}}$	Two second time gap
Θ_s	Admissible state space using position discretization

1 Introduction

1.1 Motivation

The development of electric vehicles (EV) greatly accelerated during the price hike of crude oil during 2007 and the first half of 2008. Although the price and the demand for a great variety of different commodities including oil have heavily decreased during and after the financial crisis of 2008 and 2009, the development of EVs has not lost momentum. Another observation is that the transportation of goods and passengers is overall increasing around the globe despite temporary recessions. Thus, decreasing transportation cost is an important topic for the world economy. While zero-emission vehicles are not yet able to replace traditional vehicles with internal combustion engines (ICE) on a large scale, it is already possible to increase energy efficiency through energy-efficient operation of existing vehicles.

Several optimization strategies regarding energy-efficient driving already exist. But certain aspects of autonomous driving that can further improve the results, especially lanes changes, are omitted from the energy-efficiency evaluation. Meanwhile, autonomous driving does not truly consider energy-efficient driving or the physical feasibility during the computation of motion trajectories. Another problem is the limited horizon used in many model predictive optimization applications. Due to the finite length, the horizon may not be able to capture the full extent of mountainous roads even if the information is available. This thesis will address these outstanding issues among other topics.

1.2 Predictive energy-efficient motion trajectory optimization (PEEMTO)

The objective of this work is to create a unified model predictive optimization strategy that increases the energy efficiency of a given electric vehicle and also find improvements regarding other important criteria by adopting an optimal driving behavior. The trajectory optimization developed in this thesis shall be called the *predictive energy-efficient motion trajectory optimization*. The acronym shall be PEEMTO.

Let the *ego-vehicle* be the vehicle that is guided by PEEMTO. In general, the term ego-vehicle is used to describe the vehicle connected to the employed optimization or control system. Apart from the ego-vehicle, there are other vehicles in the environment that are not directly connected to the proposed system. The motion trajectory computed by PEEMTO is primarily composed of time, position, velocity, and gear choice. Once computed, the optimal trajectory can be used by a controller to control the ego-vehicle.

PEEMTO includes multiple aspects that can have an impact on energy efficiency:

- Energy consumption cost.
- Travel duration cost.
- Vehicle model and physical feasibility of the decisions.
- Static environmental influences, e.g., road slope, road curvature, and speed limits.
- Dynamic environmental influences, e.g., traffic lights and other vehicles.

It is very important to note that energy consumption is only one optimization criterion of PEEMTO. Indeed, the goal of PEEMTO is to find the optimal solution to several different optimization criteria.

1.3 Scientific contributions

The first contribution is a unified optimization that combines certain aspects of energy-efficient driving and autonomous driving that have been, so far, treated separately.

The second contribution addresses the optimization horizon and its finite length. This thesis introduces a long-range auxiliary horizon that uses historically accumulated minimum costs in order to help the optimization make better decisions at the end of the regular horizon.

The third contribution is the first ever model predictive energy-efficient driving optimization of an electric vehicle that has a transmission.

1.4 Scope of this thesis

Autonomous driving is a highly complex task and has to overcome a vast number of different problems in order to function. These problems can be highly complex individually. The task only becomes more challenging if the optimization of energy-efficient driving is added to the existing problems. This thesis cannot cover all aspects that may be relevant to autonomous driving. In fact, the focus of this thesis is energy-efficient driving while incorporating certain aspects of autonomous driving (e.g., lane changes) to further enhance the optimization result. There are several problems that are not covered or only partly covered and could be potential research topics in future work:

- PEEMTO assumes there is a predefined route. Route planning and route changes during the journey are not considered.
- Obstacle detection and tracking is not part of this thesis. It is assumed that obstacles can be reliably detected.
- Traffic lights broadcast their phases to the ego-vehicle, but there is otherwise no cooperation.
- Highly complex questions regarding travel safety, e.g., choices made during unavoidable accidents with pedestrians, are not discussed. Nevertheless, PEEMTO will always try to avoid accidents if physically possible.
- PEEMTO is not the same as model predictive control. Typical control applications [Lun10a] [Lun10b] assume that the reference trajectory is already available as an input to the controller. The optimization task is usually to compute the necessary controls to follow the reference trajectory under certain optimization criteria and constraints. However, the purpose of PEEMTO is to compute the optimal reference trajectory.

1.5 Thesis structure

Chapter 2 provides an overview of existing concepts regarding energy-efficient driving, autonomous driving, and optimization. Chapter 3 describes the different models used in the optimization. Chapter 4 contains the optimization problem formulation and the description of the optimization algorithm. Chapter 5 presents the results obtained with PEEMTO. Chapter 6 summarizes what has been created in this work. It also provides an outlook on how the system could further evolve in the future. Finally, the appendix contains optional information to further improve the understanding of this thesis, e.g., details about the simulation environment and parameters.

2 Existing work

During the past decades, a vast number of authors have proposed solutions in the fields of autonomous driving, energy-efficient driving, motion trajectory planning, and model predictive optimization. This chapter provides an overview of state-of-the-art research relevant to this thesis. The numerous different publications can be viewed from different perspectives: application, employed technologies, different levels of abstraction, and the optimization method used to obtain the solution. While applications are problem specific, e.g., energy-efficient driving or obstacle avoidance, the employed optimization method can often be used for a wide range of different problems. Employed technologies may include perception sensors, communication infrastructure, and digital maps.

2.1 Different levels of abstraction

Especially from the point of view of transportation engineering, one can distinguish between the microscopic and the macroscopic level of abstraction [TK13]. While the microscopic analysis distinguishes between individual vehicles at a certain position and time, macroscopic analysis evaluates overall traffic flow consisting of a large number of vehicles over a long period of time. The research focus of this work is primarily energy-efficiency optimization on a microscopic level.

2.2 Robotic applications

Mobile robotic applications like path planning in combination with simultaneous digital map construction of the environment are an active field of research. These tasks also form a major difference to the field of automotive safety applications of vehicles on urban roads, which usually operate in well-structured environments, e.g., on well-defined roads.

A well-known series of robotic research contests, the DARPA Grand Challenges, are documented in [Def04] [Def05] [Thr+06] [Def07] [Urm+07] [ZW08]. One of the most reputable approaches is the method of simultaneous localization and mapping (SLAM) that is widely used beyond the DARPA Challenges. In general, the problem is to create and update a digital map of the robot's surrounding while tracking the robot's own position within the map at the same time [SC86a] [SC86b] [Thr+06] [EU12]. Based on the current map information and its position, a robot can plan its own path through unstructured and previously uncharted territory [Thr+06] [ZW08] [PEF13a] [PEF13b] [PEF13c] [Pet16]. Once the map is constructed or even before the entire map is available, a common task for robots is to find a feasible path towards a predefined goal while avoiding different kinds of obstacles on the map. Dijkstra related A*, D*, and other forms of discrete planning algorithms with directional heuristics are popular optimization methods that are used to construct a feasible path for the robots to follow. An overview can be found in [LaV06]. Real-world applications include reconnaissance, security, rescue, and catastrophe management systems [Kun+12]. Mobile robots may even venture into the depth of the ocean, measuring and creating digital maps of the ocean floor [Woo16].

Robots can also be constrained within a very small area of operation. Industrial robotics, for example, often relies on stationary robots or mobile robots that only travel short distances. Regarding subtle motion optimization of robots, human and robot interaction is a novel field of research [ZF15] that requires a high degree of precision within a usually spatially confined environment.

2.3 Autonomous driving and safety in automotive applications

Modern driver assistance systems, autonomous vehicles, and robots can be highly complex. Automotive systems in structured environments, e.g., roads and highways, have a heavy focus on object detection, situation interpretation, travel safety, driver comfort, and overtaking maneuvers. Extensive research has been conducted in all of these important areas.

The first step in autonomous driving is the perception of the environment, including static elements and the prediction of the behavior of other traffic participants.
In [AW11] [ACK12], the researchers use laser scanners, radars, cameras, and ultrasonic sensors to create a 360° perception coverage of the vehicle's surrounding. A linear prediction of other vehicles is developed. The general assumption is that other vehicles will maintain their current speed, and there will be no lane changes unless lane changes are mandatory.
In [Koh+13], speed limits, traffic light phases, and road curvatures are considered. A detailed map of the vehicle's surrounding is created using the SLAM method. The authors also conduct extensive research in the area of object detection and situation interpretation. In [NGZ11] [Nie14], methods for environment perception and situation interpretation are presented. After characteristic static traffic elements are recognized, hierarchical support vector machines and active learning methods are used to subsequently classify, track, and fuse the most important types of traffic elements. A Markov logic networks framework is used to cope with various situation interpretation tasks. The complementary research with the focus on dynamic traffic elements is conducted in [Sch14] [Koh+14]. A semantic scene representation of traffic scenes and an ontology that describes the relationships among traffic elements are developed among other approaches.

Once the surrounding environment is sufficiently interpreted, motion trajectories are computed to guide the vehicle through the dynamic environment. Some scientists put emphasis primarily on perception and scene interpretation in autonomous driving, whereas trajectory planning is based on heuristic rules and analytical Newtonian mechanics. In [Sch14] [Koh+14], for example, threshold functions, rules, and analytical considerations are used to plan trajectories on urban roads based on knowledge about the environment. In the end, P and I controllers are used to realize the planned trajectories.

Other researchers are more heavily focused on trajectory planning and control by assuming that the behavior of other vehicles can be sufficiently described through deterministic or stochastic models. For model predictive trajectory optimization, both local and global approaches are employed.
In [ZS09], spatiotemporal state lattices are used in a dynamic programming optimization approach. It is assumed that obstacles are already successfully detected. State transitions that are blocked by obstacles are removed offline before the actual optimization, i.e., the interaction between the autonomous vehicle and the obstacles is not evaluated. The states within the lattice refer to the driven distance and the lateral position on the road. Quintic polynomials and quintic splines are used to describe state trajectories. The cost functional is designed to prefer low jerk and therefore high travel comfort. In subsequent publications [Wer+10] [Wer+12], the cost functional is defined using the Euler-Lagrange formulation. A set of terminal states, called terminal manifold, is defined that should be reached eventually. A feasible set of continuous quintic and quartic polynomials is precomputed as the solution space for the unconstrained movement. A discretization within the terminal manifold is used to obtain a finite number of trajectories. Each trajectory is additionally discretized into a finite number of states. All feasible solutions eventually align with a trajectory in the terminal manifold. Finally, the lowest cost trajectory among the remaining solutions is selected. Due to high computational complexity, the optimization strategy changes to a local

continuous iterative approach in [Zie+14a] [Zie+14b], called BERTHA. A real-world demonstration of an autonomous vehicle is conducted. In the experiment, the vehicle moves along a historically important route from Mannheim to Pforzheim in Southern Germany. A non-linear optimization problem with non-linear inequality constraints is formulated. Model simplifications enable the formulation of a quadratic cost function. The initial solution only applies to the unrestricted case, i.e. no obstacles are initially incorporated. Once obstacles are included, the final solution can become suboptimal. In an alternative approach to address computational complexity [Ben+15], the authors decide to systematically enumerate maneuver variants in structured environments. The original solution space is partitioned into discrete solution classes. In each class, a possibly local optimum is found. By using the initial local minima, the chance of finding the global optimum is increased.

In [Ruf+14a] [Ruf+14b], a predictive optimization approach called SPARC is presented. A Kumaraswamy distribution is used to estimate the position distribution and behavior distribution of other vehicles. Bayesian networks are proposed to learn the dependencies among different vehicles. Due to problems created by local optima, the original local iterative optimization changes to a dynamic programming approach [Zie+15] [Ruf+15b]. The original Euler-Lagrange problem formulation remains unchanged. But in order to use a discrete global optimal solver like the Viterbi algorithm without changing the original problem formulation, the correspondence between variational methods and hidden Markov models needs to be established [Zie+15]. The correspondence enables the transformation from the original continuous Euler-Lagrange formulation to its discrete hidden Markov form. In [Ruf+15a], the benefit of the proposed dynamic programming approach is presented in comparison to local iterative optimization strategies. While in some scenarios the local iterative optimization has difficulties with local optima, dynamic programming is still able to find the global optimum. In [Zie+16], the authors incorporate the interaction between other vehicles and the ego-vehicle during the optimization process. This extension is called progressively interacting trajectories (PITRA).

In [Fun+12], the researchers test the physical vehicle handling limits during autonomous vehicle operation. A variety of different roads are chosen for the experiment, including the Pikes Peak Hill Climb in Colorado. The optimized trajectories are precomputed for the preselected route, i.e., the autonomous vehicle merely follows the precomputed path to reach its destination. Other vehicles are barred from the test route during the experiment. The vehicle is equipped with a highly accurate differential GPS to identify its exact position. The onboard real-time control system operates at 200 Hz. The feasibility study shows that an autonomous vehicle is technically able to operate at high velocities even under extreme circumstances, although the motion trajectory is entirely precomputed offline.

In [Kuh+16] [Zof+16], the authors focus on robust algorithms in autonomous driving, including sensor and algorithm failures. A probabilistic hierarchical road perception algorithm using compositional hierarchical models and system performance assessment methods is developed to enable robust autonomous driving in an artificial urban setting. The final system is demonstrated during the Audi Autonomous Driving Cup in the form of miniature cars.

Finally, modern communication technologies in the form of vehicle-to-infrastructure communication (V2I) and vehicle-to-vehicle communication (V2V) can further increase the possibilities of autonomous driving. In [SZ12] [Plo+12], the autonomous vehicle AnnieWAY and its cooperative algorithm are presented. During the Grand Cooperative Driving Challenge 2011, the participants communicate with other vehicles within the platoon and with certain infrastructure elements along the route. Additional emphasis is put on situation recognition as well as geometrical and topological reasoning using Markov logic networks. The creation of temporary optimal platoons is the focus in [Fre11]. By computing cooperative trajectories, complex safety-related problems can be resolved that would have been significantly more challenging if communication and cooperation had not been used.

2.4 Energy-efficient driving in automotive applications

Several authors have published solutions in the field of energy-efficient driving. The approaches range from passive driver assistance systems to active systems.

2.4.1 Heuristic energy efficiency recommendations

In the most simplistic case of energy-efficient driving, macroscopic fuel or energy efficiency recommendations are used. Government bodies and non-government organizations are possible sources for further information [Por+13] [Ene17] [Nat17] [US 17]. The guidelines include:

- Anticipation of the future development of the surrounding traffic.
- Avoidance of unnecessary acceleration and deceleration.
- Coasting or engine brake utilization instead of utilization of brake pads.
- Early gear shifts to higher gear levels.
- Avoidance of high velocities.
- Avoidance of engine idling.

These recommendations are based on statistics of numerous road vehicles over long travel distances. Naturally, they ignore the unique fuel or energy consumption properties of a specific vehicle. Furthermore, the driver is only given a rough guideline.

2.4.2 Driver assistance systems for energy efficiency improvement

This section discusses different driver assistance systems that support energy-efficient driving. Several representative examples are presented.

Passive driver assistance systems are the most basic technical systems that can further increase energy efficiency by assisting the driver. Passive driver assistance systems do not actively control vehicle operation. They usually collect a certain amount of measurement data during the journey. Based on the measurements and the internal algorithm, fuel or energy-efficient driving suggestions are presented to the driver through visual or acoustic means.
The most basic form of technical energy efficiency assistance systems is usually based on knowledge, rules, and heuristics. For example, a set of threshold functions, based on the previously described basic energy efficiency guidelines, can be used to warn the drivers of inefficient driving behavior. The most rudimentary solutions use commonly available sensors in smartphones to estimate the velocity, the acceleration, the deceleration, and the position of the vehicle [Joy16] [FCA17] [Eas17]. More advanced apps can additionally incorporate current control area network (CAN) bus data from the vehicle sent via CAN bus reading devices [Gar10] [Eff16].
One may also attempt to learn the powertrain properties of unknown vehicles by using recorded and current CAN bus data in order to tailor the energy efficiency suggestions to specific vehicles [GF12a] [GF12b] [GF12c] [GF14].

Other passive driver assistance systems focus on adaptation to traffic light phases. In the most simplistic V2I setup, the traffic light signal control broadcasts future phases to all vehicles that are able to receive the infor-

mation without cooperating with the vehicles. In [RK11] for example, a microscopic fuel consumption model is used to analytically compute an improved velocity profile in front of a single traffic light. Basic Newtonian mechanics are used as the underlying model foundation. Decisions are made according to predefined rules. Disadvantages of commonly used simplified cost functions are discussed in comparison to the proposed microscopic model. In a subsequent publication [KR13], the authors use a multistage A* approach in order to make the optimization less dependent on rules.
In [SMB11], the authors go beyond traffic light phase information by combining it with vehicle queue length estimation. They show in simulations that additional benefits can be obtained compared to methods only using traffic light phase information.
In [Tie+12], different rule-based strategies are investigated for electric vehicles approaching traffic lights. The optimization parameters are manually chosen. Lane changes are not included in the optimization.
In [Xia+12], the authors create a fuel efficiency assistant that is evaluated in the real world. Using the V2I communication and the current speed limit, the optimization plans a predictive velocity profile that guides the vehicle through the green phase of a single traffic light. The optimization procedure mainly consists of rules, prescribed velocity profiles, and thresholds. A graphic display provides a speed recommendation to the driver based on the optimization results.
Similarly, the authors of [Als+12] compute a recommended reference speed based on traffic light phase information. The trajectory consists of acceleration, deceleration, and constant cruise phases.

There are also systems that try to address several distinct issues. One example is the research project called Energieeffizientes Fahren 2014 (EFA 2014) [Wil12] [Sma+14]. Numerous technologies and resources are used for the EFA 2014 system: CAN bus data from the ego-vehicle, communication with traffic lights, digital maps with information about speed limits, object detection using cameras, radars, and ultrasonic sensors. The energy efficiency optimization consists of three main systems: energy efficient route selection, driver assistance, powertrain control, and energy management optimization. The passive driver assistance system developed in the project is called the Anticipatory Energy Saving Assistant (ANESA) [Koh+11] [Bär+11] [Sch12] [Nie+12] [Wil12] [Sch14]. A vehicle model is formulated to compute the velocity profile to a specific velocity at a certain distance relative to the ego-vehicle. Speed limits, road curvature, road elevation, traffic lights, and other vehicles are included in the rule-based optimization. Lane changes are not evaluated. The system defines different operation modes including braking, coasting, cruising at constant speed, and acceleration. Several threshold functions in combination with vehicle model and situation analysis decide which mode should be selected. The vehicle operation suggestions are presented on a graphical display to the driver. The main fuel saving rule is coasting. In order to adapt the driver assistance system to individual drivers, the authors in [Bär+11] identify the most probable driving style of the current driver by analyzing internal data from the vehicle, the environment, and the driver's eye gaze through fuzzy logic. Although multiple sources of information are available, the system of [Sma+14] [Sch14] does not truly compute a unified solution to energy-efficient driving. For example, the velocity profile computation is not used by the powertrain control.

Active driver assistance systems that support energy-efficient driving are primarily force feedback instruments, which actively try to persuade the driver to perform other actions through gentle resistance forces. Examples include the force feedback acceleration pedals [Con15] [Bos16] that discourage excessive acceleration among other functionalities.

2.4.3 Autonomous systems for energy efficiency improvement

In partial autonomous systems, energy-efficient driving is only partly automated. In the vast majority of vehicles, only a few powertrain components can act without direct control of the driver. Examples include automatic transmissions [CPR10], energy power-supply systems [Wil12] [Sma+14], and energy management in hybrid vehicles [Mok+16].

There are also more comprehensive partial energy-efficiency autonomous systems that support many tasks commonly found in autonomous driving. But as they are often extensions to existing Adaptive Cruise Control (ACC) systems, lane changes are not regarded. If there is a front vehicle (i.e., another vehicle ahead of the ego-vehicle) on the same lane, the partial autonomous vehicle merely stays behind it. The driver still has to manually change the lane.

In [Sah+07], the authors present a longitudinal cruise control using digital maps containing information about road curvature, road slopes, and speed limits. The appropriate vehicle velocity preferably does not exceed the driver defined reference speed, the speed limit, or the maximum safe speed in curves. Fuel saving is primarily achieved through coasting, engine brake utilization, and avoidance of brake pad utilization.

In [Keu+09] [Keu+10], the authors present a predictive ACC system used for hybrid vehicles. The authors divide the upcoming road with respect to new speed limits, and roughly constant sections of curvature and slope. The admissible velocity trajectory is predefined to have a certain shape, split into three phases: acceleration, constant cruise velocity, and deceleration. By analyzing longitudinal vehicle dynamics using Newtonian mechanics based on a complete hybrid powertrain model formulation, the precise shape of the different phases is computed. The goal is to minimize energy consumption,

maximize energy recuperation, and avoid braking in the sense of brake pad utilization.
There are also less rule-based and more flexible approaches. In [Hel10], the objective is to compute a model predictive optimization using dynamic programming for heavy-duty vehicles with respect to fuel efficiency. Road slope and speed limit information along the driven route are necessary system inputs. A complete manufacturer specific inverse powertrain model is formulated. The state transition cost function primarily penalizes fuel consumption, braking, gear shifts, deviation from a certain manually set reference velocity, and acceleration. Optimal velocity and optimal gear choice trajectories are computed. Similar optimization goals, constraints, and prerequisites are used in [Ter09] [Wah15].

As in driver assistance systems, V2X communication can also be beneficial for autonomous and partial autonomous systems.
The authors of [Ask+17] compare the traffic flow of regular vehicles and platoon forming vehicles that are additionally communicating with each other. Simulation results show that overall traffic flow can be increased through V2X communication at signalized intersections.
Aforementioned V2V systems like [Fre11] [SZ12] can also improve energy efficiency to some extent, even if energy efficiency is not evaluated in detail. For example, a dense platoon can be formed that reduces the air drag on vehicles behind the lead vehicle.

2.5 Optimization methods

Different from problem-specific applications, optimization algorithms can often be applied to many application domains. This section reviews different existing optimization strategies used in energy-efficient driving applications.

2.5.1 Cost formulation

If cost formulations are used in the optimization, the vast majority of authors use manually weighted costs. This approach offers great flexibility. But it can be highly subjective, and the description of the optimization problem may be oversimplified. The possibly greatest disadvantage is tied to the fact that the results of multi-criteria optimization problems often cannot lead to improvements regarding all criteria. Thus, it is difficult to gauge if the optimization has lead to an improvement or how significant the improvement is.
Alternatively, there is also the possibility to convert all optimization criteria into a unified form, e.g., monetary costs using a fiat currency. The author is only aware of one example in energy-efficient driving that has used such an approach. In [PKS09], a profit-maximizing energy efficiency system is developed. Income with respect to driven distance, cost of travel duration, and cost of fuel consumption are converted into Euro.

2.5.2 Knowledge and rule-based optimization

The most rudimentary form of energy-efficient driving assistance systems is based on knowledge, rules, and heuristics. In the most rudimentary cases, threshold functions can be used to generate binary decisions [Gar10] [Joy16] [Eff16] [FCA17] [Eas17].
More advanced techniques combine analytical Newtonian mechanics with knowledge and rule-based decision making to compute motion trajectories. In some cases, predefined shapes of acceptable velocity profiles, e.g., acceleration, constant cruise velocity, and deceleration, are used. Examples include [Keu+10] [Als+12] [Sch14] [Koh+14].
Fuzzy inference methods are also used to make energy-efficient driving decisions. One common approach is to convert comparatively imprecise human experience and expertise to membership functions in order to compute the optimal decision [Ros10]. Additional knowledge about the vehicle can be

used to further enhance the results. Examples in the field of energy-efficient driving include [SFY07] [Pér+10] [Ros10].

2.5.3 Optimization through data mining and machine learning

Although data mining and machine learning are usually associated with classification and data analysis problems, these strategies are also used in the context of energy-efficient driving.

Regression analysis

Regression analysis is a commonly used method to analyze data using preselected analytical model assumptions. Through regression, the optimal parameters of (often simplified) functions are computed based on the available data. In transportation engineering, for example, macroscopic models are often used to describe traffic in general. As there is a vast amount of different vehicles, specific vehicle models cannot be used. Through regression, a macroscopic model can be created using a large data set of numerous vehicles. The simplified generic model can then be used to describe the overall behavior and conduct approximate evaluations.

Alternatively, the problem formulation may initially be based on a precise vehicle model but is subsequently transformed into a generic polynomial form through regression in order to simplify the optimization.

Many publications have at least used regression at some point to reduce model complexity. Sometimes the model simplification is essential for the feasibility of the proposed optimization. Examples include [Hel10] [MA12] [GF12c] [Zie+14a] among numerous others. In [Hel10] certain characteristic maps are converted to avoid time-consuming interpolation. In [GF12c], different polynomials are adapted with respect to recorded

CAN bus data. Together, they form a spline to estimate the characteristic map of a truck's engine. In [MA12], a dynamic vehicle model is created but eventually simplified to a quadratic polynomial with respect to fuel consumption, velocity, and acceleration. This eventually makes efficient quadratic programming optimization possible. The fuel efficiency system tends to prefer low velocity and no acceleration because the polynomial model promotes this kind of behavior. But in reality, if dynamic scenarios are regarded, it can sometimes be beneficial to temporarily choose a high acceleration in order to increase engine efficiency.

Neural networks and reinforcement learning

Artificial neural networks are one of the oldest artificial intelligence concepts in computer science that gained attention through the back-propagation algorithm and again in recent years through the formulation of deep learning. An artificial neural network tries to reproduce the construction of the human brain through artificial neurons. During training, the network is presented with different data samples that are accompanied by the corresponding class memberships. Reinforcement learning is sometimes regarded as a special training strategy of neural networks, complementing supervised learning and unsupervised learning. Training samples are not a priori provided but generated through interaction with the environment. The basic principle is to make a software agent take actions in a previously unknown environment with the goal to maximize some form of expected overall reward. The learning procedure is usually separated into an exploration phase and an exploitation phase. During the exploration or training phase, new knowledge is acquired which may require the removal of older, possibly less important experience. During the exploitation phase, the learned experience is used to make decisions based on the current situation. Reinforcement learning can use data tables or neural networks to conduct training and store the outcome. For further background information, the reader can turn to [Sug15].

An example of reinforcement learning used for energy-efficient driving is [Qi+17]. A deep reinforcement learning method is used to learn the fuel-efficient operation of the onboard energy management system of a plugin hybrid vehicle. The neural networks are trained using real-world data obtained from inductive loop detectors. The formulation of a vehicle model is not necessary.

In [Pér+10], the authors primarily use fuzzy control. But the rules are obtained through training of an artificial neural network. The motivation lies in the possible imprecision of manual interpretation of human expertise. Therefore, learning the optimal membership functions from historical data can be an efficient and automated procedure. The system learns from several expert drivers for a predefined route. In general, gradual acceleration and deceleration are deemed as preferable, whereas braking is discouraged. Naturally, the underlying assumption of thc authors is that the invited expert drivers truly drive efficiently.

Despite the presented advantages of neural networks and reinforcement learning, there can also be disadvantages. Regarding training, there can be theoretically an infinite number of relevant scenarios to learn and the feature vector dimension can also increase if more complicated situations should be described. If truly long-range predictive energy-efficient driving should be optimized, the distinction of numerous different scenarios can drastically increase training complexity and the number of neurons or table entries. Alternatively, if the number of neurons or table entries is restricted, the system can only compute an approximate solution to a previously unseen scenario. Indeed, the research conducted in works like [Pér+10] [Qi+17] does not investigate long-range predictive energy-efficient driving. Instead, the focus is on the imminent next decision.

Evolutionary algorithm

Evolutionary algorithms are inspired by biological evolution. The goal is to find the optimal solution by applying processes commonly found in evolution, e.g., mutation, crossover, and survival of the fittest. Due to an often large number of possible outcomes, some predefined heuristics is often chosen in practice. As in the case of neural networks, a possible advantage is the independence from precise analytical models. A possible drawback is the uncertainty regarding local optima. For further background information, the reader can turn to [PB17]. An example, in which evolutionary algorithms are used for energy-efficient driving, is [CPR10]. The authors combine fuzzy logic with genetic algorithms, which are a type of evolutionary algorithm, in order to make fuel-efficient gear shift decisions depending on current measurements from the engine and the current driver intention. While the rules are defined through fuzzy logic, the precise layout of the fuzzy membership functions is obtained using genetic algorithms.

2.5.4 Calculus of variations

Calculus of variations involves the utilization of subtle changes (variations) in functionals to find minima or maxima. A necessary but not sufficient condition for an extremum is the Euler-Lagrange equation that is often used to solve optimization problems in the sense of calculus of variations. In practice, it may be necessary to subsequently show that the optimization result is truly globally optimal. An example in energy-efficient driving optimization that uses the Euler-Lagrange formulation is [Ter09].

2.5.5 Pontryagin's maximum/minimum principle

Pontryagin's maximum/minimum principle is primarily used in optimal control problems and is derived from the maximization/minimization of a Hamiltonian using optimal states, controls, and Lagrange multipliers. Just like the Euler-Lagrange equation, the Pontryagin's principle is a necessary but not a sufficient condition for an optimum. In practice, it may be necessary to subsequently show that the optimization result is truly globally optimal. Examples in energy-efficient driving optimization that use Pontryagin's maximum/minimum principle, include [SL77] [PKS09] [ZXL16].

2.5.6 Local numeric optimization

In the most ideal case, mathematical problems can be solved analytically. But in practice, it is often not possible. Therefore, a numeric approximation of the solution may sometimes be the only option. Many numeric solvers that are based on gradient descent require the optimization problem to be convex in order to find the globally optimal solution. Otherwise, it is possible that the result is merely a local optimum. Calculus of variations is often realized through iterative local optimization, i.e., an iterative sequence of local optimization computations that approaches the global optimum with every new computation step. For further background information on numeric optimization theory, the reader can turn to [NW06].

Linear programming and sequential linear programming

Linear optimization problems have a linear cost function that is subject to linear equality and linear inequality constraints. Especially, if there are no constraints, linear optimization problems can be solved using linear algebra. This leads to precise analytical solutions obtained with little computational complexity. But if the constraints consist of numerous stringent inequality constraints, linear programming algorithms may be necessary. Well established examples include the simplex algorithm, the criss-cross algorithm, and the interior point methods. Difficulties emerge if the optimization problem or the constraints are not linear, or if the feasible solution space is not a convex polytope. In these cases, a problem simplification may be necessary to reestablish a linear formulation. Alternatively, sequential linear programming can be used, i.e., iteratively computing the solution starting at an initial position in the solution space. This can lead to suboptimal results. Examples of linear programming used in the context of energy-efficient driving are [Jin+16] [VB16].

Quadratic programming and sequential quadratic programming

An extension to linear optimization problems is quadratic optimization. While equality and inequality constraints still have a linear form, the cost function itself can have a quadratic form. Well established solution methods include interior point methods, active set methods, and conjugate gradient methods. If the original optimization problem does not comply with the prerequisites of quadratic programming, sequential quadratic programming can iteratively solve the problem given a feasible initial solution. The original cost function is approximated by a quadratic function, and the constraints are linearized. Examples of quadratic programming used in the context of energy-efficient driving are [Hua+08] [Ter09] [MA12].

Both linear programming and quadratic programming can have high computational efficiency, even if a sequential local iteration method is used. In favorable cases, the iteration quickly converges towards ever smaller costs, and good solutions are found with little computation duration. But there can be major problems especially if the solution space is non-convex and has numerous local minima. In practice, local iterative solution methods like sequential linear programming and sequential quadratic programming can lead to suboptimality, convergence difficulties, and difficulties to obtain optimality in mixed integer problems [Ter09] [Ruf+15a] [Ruf+15b]. Furthermore, a start solution needs to be provided, which can be difficult to define itself.

2.5.7 Global numeric optimization

As previously discussed, if an iterative approach is used, the optimization algorithm has greater difficulties in finding the globally optimal solution if the cost function is non-convex and if there are numerous constraints. An alternative to local iterative optimization is global optimization, which often involves searching for the optimal solution and efficiently evaluating all feasible solutions within certain constraints. Apart from avoiding local optima, there also other advantages. For example, it is not necessary to simplify the model, the constraints, or the cost formulation. There are no convergence problems. An initial solution is not necessary. But there are also disadvantages. The discretization of the original continuous problem is generally a requirement, which inherently introduces imprecision. Thus, the global optimization of a discretized problem only finds the global optimum within the given discrete search space, and the discrete solution is actually only an approximation of the original continuous problem. Arguably, the greatest challenge is that the search space and the computation time can be too long for real-time applications.

Enumeration

For problems that only have a comparatively small solution space, enumeration can be a feasible approach. As all possible state trajectories have to be evaluated one by one, it is one of the simplest forms of discrete optimization but can be highly inefficient for problems with many continuous state dimensions. It is mostly used for rule-based approaches that only use a small search space. Examples include [SMB11] [GF12b] [GF12c].

Stagewise dynamic programming

An efficient form of discrete search algorithms is dynamic programming (DP). The term dynamic programming was first used by Richard Bellman, who created its theoretical and practical foundation [Bel54]. Two of the most important theoretic contributions are the formulation of the Hamilton-Jacobi-Bellman equation (HJBE) for continuous problems and the formulation of the Bellman equation (BE) for discrete problems. The discretization of the Hamilton-Jacobi-Bellman problem leads to the corresponding Bellman formulation in the discrete case. More importantly, solving the problem in the discrete case for ever finer discretization will eventually solve the original continuous Hamilton-Jacobi-Bellman problem in theory. The globally optimal solution of the Bellman equation is found by using dynamic programming. Instead of solving the entire problem in one single step, dynamic programming computes the optimal decisions for partial problems. The entire optimal solution is then composed of the partial solutions. For further information on dynamic programming, the reader can turn to chapter 4 and [Bel54] [Ber05] [Ber07]. Examples of dynamic programming used in the context of energy-efficient driving include [Hel10] [Wah15].

Dijkstra and path planning algorithms guided by heuristics

From a historical point of view, the dynamic programming formulation by Bellman [Bel54] and the Dijkstra algorithm [Dij59] are created independently from each other. Nevertheless, Dijkstra and its subsequent extensions, e.g., A*, D*, and ARA*, actually use Bellman's principle of optimality [Sni06]. Using A* or one of its modifications can be difficult to apply to energy-efficient driving. The primary reason is that a simple, yet effective, and at the same time monotonic heuristic cannot be chosen as easily as in classic path planning, which often uses the linear Euclidean distance heuristic. Nevertheless, there are a few authors who attempt such an approach [KR13] [CGF14]. In [CGF14], the vehicle model is heavily simplified. Due to the simplification, the model can be incorporated into a monotonic heuristic. Numerous simulation results show that the heuristic can reduce the computation duration by more than 50 % compared to the corresponding Dijkstra algorithm. A drawback is that whenever a different model is introduced, the monotony of the heuristic has to be mathematically proven in order to ensure global optimality. This can be difficult and may sometimes even be impossible in practice, especially if the vehicle model consists of numerous data tables like characteristic maps. Another drawback stems from the sequential nature of the Dijkstra algorithm and the internal sorting algorithm along different search paths. These procedures make parallelization during implementation difficult. For further information on the background of Dijkstra, A*, and associated algorithms, the reader can turn to [LaV06].

Computational complexity

The major drawback of global discrete search algorithms is computational complexity for problems with numerous continuous state dimensions, which Richard Bellman called the curse of dimensionality [Bel54].

One commonly used complexity reduction strategy is model simplification, which reduces the computation duration and possibly also reduces memory demand. It can also reduce the number of state dimensions and therefore the number of evaluated state transitions. [HRR83] [HRR85] [Hoo88] [MG93] are among the first authors to use dynamic programming to optimize energy-efficient driving. Due to the limited computational capabilities of computers at that time, the optimization is conducted in offline simulations with significant model simplifications and state dimension reduction.

It is also possible to reduce the search space by reducing the discretization precision, the number of state dimensions, the number of decision stages, etc. Dynamic programming strategies that deliberately attempt to reduce the search space as a trade-off to optimality are known as approximate dynamic programming.
One possible strategy is iterative dynamic programming. The first optimization iteration uses a less precise discretization than actually required.

Subsequent optimization iterations confine their search area to the vicinity of the result obtained from the previous iteration. Discretization precision is increased for later iterations until the final result is obtained. Examples that employ iterative dynamic programming are [BZK05] [HT08] [JSV08] [HT09].
Another form of iterative dynamic programming is to group several states to unified state groups and initially evaluate transitions among the state groups [BZK05] [Wah15].
It is also possible to omit certain state transitions. In [Hel10], a heuristic simplification is used that removes crossing state transitions from the search.

Computational complexity can also be addressed by the horizon length. The task of predictive optimization is often to find a sequence of optimal decisions from a start state to an end state. In practice, it is often not possible to find the entire solution in real-time. Therefore, only the solution within a finite horizon is computed. In general, both optimization precision and computation duration increase with the horizon length. Simple heuristics are often used to adapt the terminal behavior of the solution to the liking of the developer.
The most common approach is to perform the regular optimization within the horizon and add a terminal cost to its end. For example, [Ter09] uses a deviation penalty from a carefully chosen stationary state. [Hel10] advocates for high velocity at the end of the horizon to increase the kinetic energy. Definitions of terminal costs are also found in model predictive control applications like [ZF15].

In order to increase horizon length, while keeping computational complexity in check, some authors develop strategies that deal with long-range optimization. The general idea is to decrease optimization precision for distant decisions in the future. Examples include [Wah15] [Pet16]. In [Pet16], fine discretization and evaluation of dynamic obstacles are confined within a very short horizon of only a few seconds. For low maximum velocity, this effectively only leads to horizons of a few meters. For mid-range and long-range optimization, dynamic obstacles are no longer considered and discretization precision is reduced. Similarly, [Wah15] computes additional approximate solutions for distant decisions beyond the regular horizon with reduced precision. In general, if the problem truly refers to a long distance, this type of optimization approach can only offer a rough estimate for distant decisions.

Model simplification and search space reduction usually lead to a trade-off between computational complexity and optimization precision. But the reduction of computation time can also be decreased through implementation. Apart from compiler and code optimization, it is possible to precompute state transition costs before the real optimization begins and save the results for later use [Pet16]. Naturally, this increases memory demand. It is also possible to reduce computational complexity by distributing the computation across several threads. This approach is especially effective for stagewise dynamic programming because the algorithm inherently consists of numerous parallel processes. Modern CPUs and GPUs generally consist of numerous cores, and the overall trend is to further increase the number of cores. Thus, software implementations that make use of parallelization benefit from the development in the semiconductor industry. A drawback is that the demand regarding computation hardware is increased.

2.6 Unresolved issues

Various different applications and optimization strategies are discussed in previous sections. This section addresses some of the unresolved issues that this thesis attempts to confront.

Obstacle avoidance and lane changes in autonomous driving have been thoroughly investigated. Examples include [ZS09] [Wer+12] [Bah+14] [Ruf+14b] [Ben+15]. Generally, there is a heavy focus on passenger comfort and safety related issues, whereas energy-efficient driving is not thoroughly investigated. Speed limits or the recommended speed on highways are often chosen as the reference speed [Wer+12], although truly energy-efficient driving may require a different choice. Furthermore, these systems do not evaluate gear shifts and purely rely on the existing automated transmission within the vehicle. The arguably biggest deficiency is the often ignored uncertainty if the planned trajectory is even physically feasible. Many autonomous systems are focused on highway scenarios with little road slope and road curvature. The controller tries to follow the reference trajectory to the best of its capability. Therefore, deviations from the planned trajectory may not appear as catastrophic. But, in fact, there are also publications involving overtaking on the opposite lane with oncoming traffic (e.g., [ZS09]). These scenarios clearly do not refer to highways. But the physical feasibility of the overtaking maneuver is still ignored. This can lead to dangerous outcomes if the road involves strong slopes and curvatures.

In contrast to typical autonomous driving applications, microscopic energy-efficient driving optimization uses detailed models of the powertrain. Therefore, both energy-efficiency and physical feasibility can be evaluated in detail. Model predictive optimization examples include [Ter09] [Hel10] [Wah15]. Gear shifts are fully incorporated into the optimization. Apart from speed limits, road slope and road curvature are also included in the optimization. But the evaluation of the dynamic environment, especially other vehicles and lane changes, is limited or not considered all. Optimal longitudinal movement is the main focus of these approaches. If there is a front vehicle on the same lane, the optimization simply follows the front vehicle. This can be inefficient if the front vehicle is extremely slow.

This thesis combines detailed model predictive optimization strategies for physically feasible, energy-efficient driving with certain aspects of autonomous driving like lane changes. Additionally, traffic light phases are evaluated. An optimization strategy is presented that computes a uniform solution with regard to all theses relevant aspects.

Another topic is the finite optimization horizon often used in predictive optimization. Due to computational complexity, the horizon usually cannot evaluate the entire problem but only a small part of it. Approaches that try to mitigate the problem are discussed in previous sections. Their precision beyond the horizon is usually low.
This thesis proposes an approach that provides a cost estimate beyond the regular horizon using an additional long-range auxiliary horizon. The auxiliary horizon grows during the journey until it reaches the final destination. The discretization precision within the auxiliary horizon is the same as in the regular horizon. The intermediate results can already be used before the auxiliary horizon reaches the final destination.

3 Models

The proposed model predictive optimization PEEMTO depends on several models to fulfill its tasks. These models describe the vehicle model, the static environment, the dynamic environment, and the driver model.

3.1 Vehicle model

In general, PEEMTO is not only confined to one specific vehicle. In fact, the underlying optimization strategy can be applied to a wide range of different vehicles, no matter if they have electric or conventional propulsions. The vehicle model used in this thesis primarily serves as an example. It is based on the REM-2030 powertrain, developed in the project REM-2030 [REM15]. The model is formulated in an inverse manner similar to the formulations suggested in [GS05] [KN10]. The model inputs are the vehicle's desired acceleration, its current velocity, and the external resistance forces. Their propagation through the model ultimately lead to an energy consumption in the battery. A schematic illustration is shown in Figure 3.1. The different REM-2030 vehicle parameters are given in Tables A.2 to A.4 in the appendix.

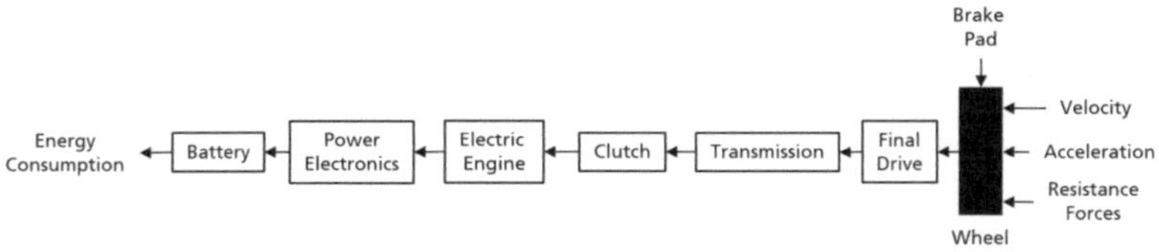

Figure 3.1: Vehicle powertrain.

3.1.1 Longitudinal vehicle model

The longitudinal properties of the vehicle model are primarily focused on the powertrain, the vehicle's longitudinal movement, and the longitudinal external resistance forces. The model formulation is based on [GS05] [KN10] [Hak14].

External resistance forces and vehicle acceleration

The external resistance forces are the forces from the external world applied to the vehicle's wheels and its hull. They consist of the air drag resistance F_{air}, the slope resistance F_{slope}, the rolling resistance F_{roll}, and the acceleration resistance F_{a}.

F_{air} is dependent on the air density ρ_{air}, the effective cross sectional area A_{eff}, the drag coefficient c_{w}, and the vehicle velocity v:

$$F_{\mathrm{air}} = \frac{1}{2}\rho_{\mathrm{air}} c_{\mathrm{w}} A_{\mathrm{eff}} v^2. \tag{3.1}$$

The gravitational force F_{g} is dependent on the vehicle mass m and the gravitational acceleration g:

$$F_{\mathrm{g}} = mg. \tag{3.2}$$

The slope resistance F_{slope} is composed of F_{g} and the slope angle φ:

$$F_{\mathrm{slope}} = F_{\mathrm{g}} \sin(\varphi). \tag{3.3}$$

The normal force $F_{\mathrm{g,p}}$, i.e., the gravitational force perpendicular to the road, is only a portion of F_{g} if there is a slope:

$$F_{\mathrm{g,p}} = F_{\mathrm{g}} \cos(\varphi). \tag{3.4}$$

The rolling resistance F_{roll} is primarily dependent on $F_{\text{g,p}}$ and the rolling resistance coefficient μ_{r}:

$$F_{\text{roll}} = \mu_{\text{r}} F_{\text{g,p}}. \tag{3.5}$$

According to [Hak14], the rolling resistance can increase with the fourth power of the velocity for extremely high velocities. This is due to the thermal changes in the tires. Precise numeric values are not provided in [Hak14]. The vehicle model as formulated in this thesis does not consider these extreme cases.

The acceleration resistance F_{a} is the force needed to accelerate the entire vehicle:

$$F_{\text{a}} = m\dot{v}. \tag{3.6}$$

Braking

If the braking capabilities of the electric engine (EE) during recuperation is insufficient to slow down the vehicle as demanded, the brake pads at the wheels have to be used. More explanations regarding braking and recuperation with an EE are provided in the discussion of the EE model.

According to [BB12], the brake force F_{b} between tire and road depends on $F_{\text{g,p}}$ and the ground adhesion coefficient $\mu_{\text{b}}(\sigma_{\text{b}})$:

$$F_{\text{b}} = \mu_{\text{b}}(\sigma_{\text{b}}) F_{\text{g,p}}. \tag{3.7}$$

The ground adhesion coefficient itself is dependent on the tire slip σ_{b}. The tire slip is a measure for the difference between the vehicle velocity v and the velocity at the wheel derived from the wheel rotation speed ω_{w} and the dynamic wheel radius r_{w}:

$$\sigma_{\text{b}} = \frac{v - \omega_{\text{w}} r_{\text{w}}}{v}. \tag{3.8}$$

The dynamic wheel radius is the wheel radius during driving, which is slightly different from the original geometric radius of the wheel due to subtle deformations.

According to [BB12], $\mu_\text{b}(\sigma_\text{b})$ initially increases for small slip values until the maximum ground adhesion coefficient $\mu_\text{b,max}(\sigma_\text{b,max})$ is reached for the maximum acceptable tire slip $\sigma_\text{b,max}$. Thus, F_b also reaches its maximum at $\sigma_\text{b,max}$. Beyond $\sigma_\text{b,max}$, μ_b starts to decrease. For $\sigma_\text{b} = 100\,\%$, the tires completely slide out of control. On a dry asphalt road, $\mu_\text{b,max} = 1.18$ and $\sigma_\text{b,max} = 15\,\%$ can be expected [BB12]. Within the slip interval $[0, \sigma_\text{b,max}]$, the slip can be approximated by a linear function [Ter09] with respect to σ_b. The linear approximation for the braking force uses a linear ground adhesion coefficient $\mu_\text{b,lin}$:

$$F_\text{b} = \mu_\text{b}(\sigma_\text{b})F_\text{g,p} \approx \mu_\text{b,lin}\sigma_\text{b}F_\text{g,p}. \tag{3.9}$$

Using the linear approximation, it is possible to estimate the tire slip for a certain demanded brake force F_b:

$$\sigma_\text{b} \approx \frac{F_\text{b}}{\mu_\text{b,lin}F_\text{g,p}}. \tag{3.10}$$

Within PEEMTO, the tire slip during braking must not exceed $\sigma_\text{b,max}$:

$$\sigma_\text{b} \leq \sigma_\text{b,max}. \tag{3.11}$$

The maximum tire slip also confines the brake force:

$$F_\text{b} \leq \mu_\text{b,lin}\sigma_\text{b,max}F_\text{g,p}. \tag{3.12}$$

The corresponding brake torque T_b at the wheels can be computed with F_b and r_w:

$$T_\text{b} = F_\text{b}r_\text{w}. \tag{3.13}$$

The restriction of brake force and tire slip is also a functionality commonly found in anti-lock braking systems (ABS) [BB12].

As discussed in section 4.1, the trajectory optimization does not compute the brake controls. It only includes the previously stated brake force constraints. If required, the necessary controls can be computed using more detailed models of the braking system. A short overview shall be provided to explain how the brake controls could be computed using F_{b} from the trajectory optimization. But these additional model components are not further used in the optimization.
According to [BB12], the braking system consists of the brake pedal, the brake amplifier, the brake pads, and the brake discs in the case of a disc brake system. If the driver steps on the brake pedal, a certain brake pedal force $F_{\mathrm{b},u}$ is generated depending on the brake pedal position u_{b}. $F_{\mathrm{b},u}$ is amplified by the brake amplifier, which generates the brake pad force $F_{\mathrm{b,p}}$ that presses the brake pads against the brake disc. This slows down the wheel rotation.
If only the brake pad force $F_{\mathrm{b,p}}$ at the wheels is needed instead of the brake pedal position u_{b}, it can be directly computed using the brake pad friction coefficient $\mu_{\mathrm{b,p}}$ and the relation:

$$F_{\mathrm{b,p}} = \frac{F_{\mathrm{b}}}{\mu_{\mathrm{b,p}}}. \tag{3.14}$$

According to [BB12], the average brake pad friction coefficient $\mu_{\mathrm{b,p}}$ is between 0.35 and 0.5. If the necessary brake pedal position u_{b} needs to be constructed from the demanded brake force F_{b}, the procedure is more complex. The relation between the brake force F_{b} at the wheels and the brake pedal force $F_{\mathrm{b},u}$ can be described using the brake pedal ratio $i_{\mathrm{b},u}$, the brake amplification ratio $i_{\mathrm{b,a}}$, the brake pressure efficiency of the amplifier $\eta_{\mathrm{b,a}}$, the main brake pressure cylinder area $A_{\mathrm{b,a}}$, the wheel brake cylinder area $A_{\mathrm{b,w}}$, the brake force efficiency at the wheels $\eta_{b,w}$, the internal brake ratio C_b, the effective brake disc radius $r_{b,d}$, and the dynamic wheel radius r_w:

$$F_{b,u} = \frac{F_b}{i_{b,u} i_{b,a} \eta_{b,a} \frac{A_{b,w}}{A_{b,a}} \eta_{b,w} C_b \frac{r_{b,d}}{r_w}}. \tag{3.15}$$

The relation between the brake pedal position u_b and the brake pedal force $F_{b,u}$ is defined by a manufacturer specific brake force transition function $f_{b,u}$, which is primarily designed from the perspective of HMI:

$$u_b = \frac{F_{b,u}}{f_{b,u}}. \tag{3.16}$$

Alternatively, characteristic maps are often used to describe the different ratios, efficiencies, pressures, and forces. Finding a feasible solution is assured as long as only feasible operation points within the characteristic maps are considered. More detailed explanations and examples are given in [BB12].

Wheels

The external resistance forces and the acceleration resistance in combination with the brake torque T_b can be used to derive the wheel torque T_w applied to the wheels:

$$T_w = J_w \dot{\omega}_w + r_w (F_{air} + F_{roll} + F_{slope} + F_a) + T_b. \tag{3.17}$$

Furthermore, let ω_w be the wheel rotation speed:

$$\omega_w = \frac{v}{r_w} \tag{3.18}$$

and let J_w be the wheel inertia.

Final drive

The final drive is assumed to be stiff [KN10]. The final drive ratio is denoted by i_f. The wheel torque T_w is transformed by i_f to the final drive torque T_f:

$$i_\mathrm{f} T_\mathrm{f} = T_\mathrm{w}. \tag{3.19}$$

The wheel rotation speed ω_w is transformed by i_f to the final drive rotation speed ω_f:

$$\omega_\mathrm{f} = i_\mathrm{f} \omega_\mathrm{w}. \tag{3.20}$$

Transmission and clutch

It is assumed that the transient behavior between the transmission and the final drive can be neglected [KN10]. The transmission rotation speed ω_t is the same as ω_f:

$$\omega_\mathrm{t} = \omega_\mathrm{f}. \tag{3.21}$$

The transmission torque T_t is the same as T_f:

$$T_\mathrm{t} = T_\mathrm{f}. \tag{3.22}$$

The clutch controls the connection between the engine and the transmission. The REM-2030 transmission uses a dry clutch. The clutch rotation speed $\omega_\mathrm{c,in}$ on the engine side is the same as the engine rotation speed ω_e:

$$\omega_\mathrm{c,in} = \omega_\mathrm{e}. \tag{3.23}$$

The clutch rotation speed on the transmission side $\omega_\mathrm{c,out}$ depends on the transmission rotation speed ω_t, the selected gear level G and the gear ratio $i_\mathrm{t}(G)$:

$$\omega_\mathrm{c,out} = i_\mathrm{t}(G)\omega_\mathrm{t}. \tag{3.24}$$

It is assumed that in reality, the gear level G cannot instantly change. There is always a continuously differentiable gear shift $\dot{G}$ in the transmission mechanics although the duration may be very short. It is assumed that a shift in gear level requires a certain gear shift duration Δt_{shift} (e.g., one second) to complete. If there is no gear shift ($\dot{G} = 0$), the clutch is assumed to be stiff, i.e., there is no rotation speed difference in the clutch:

$$\omega_{\text{c,in}} = \omega_{\text{c,out}} \quad \text{if} \quad \dot{G} = 0. \tag{3.25}$$

Furthermore, the clutch torque on the engine side $T_{\text{c,in}}$ is the same as the clutch torque $T_{\text{c,out}}$ on the transmission side $T_{\text{c,out}}$:

$$T_{\text{c,in}} = T_{\text{c,out}} \quad \text{if} \quad \dot{G} = 0. \tag{3.26}$$

If there is a gear shift ($\dot{G} \neq 0$), the clutch efficiency formulation of [NBL07] is used. It describes the temporary inefficiency due to the temporary rotation speed difference between $\omega_{\text{c,in}}$ and $\omega_{\text{c,out}}$. The clutch efficiency η_{c} is described by:

$$\eta_{\text{c}}(G) = \begin{cases} \frac{\omega_{\text{c,in}}}{\omega_{\text{c,out}}} & \text{if} \quad \omega_{\text{c,in}} \leq \omega_{\text{c,out}} \\ \frac{\omega_{\text{c,out}}}{\omega_{\text{c,in}}} & \text{if} \quad \omega_{\text{c,in}} > \omega_{\text{c,out}} \end{cases} \tag{3.27}$$

during a gear shift. Apart from the clutch efficiency, the transmission has a gear level dependent efficiency $\eta_{\text{t}}(G)$. $T_{\text{c,in}}$ is transformed to the transmission torque T_{t} via the previously described ratio and efficiencies:

$$\eta_{\text{c}}(G)\eta_{\text{t}}(G)i_{\text{t}}(G)T_{\text{c,in}} = T_{\text{t}}. \tag{3.28}$$

If there is no transmission and clutch, the engine torque and engine rotation speed are directly transformed to the final drive torque and final drive rotation speed.

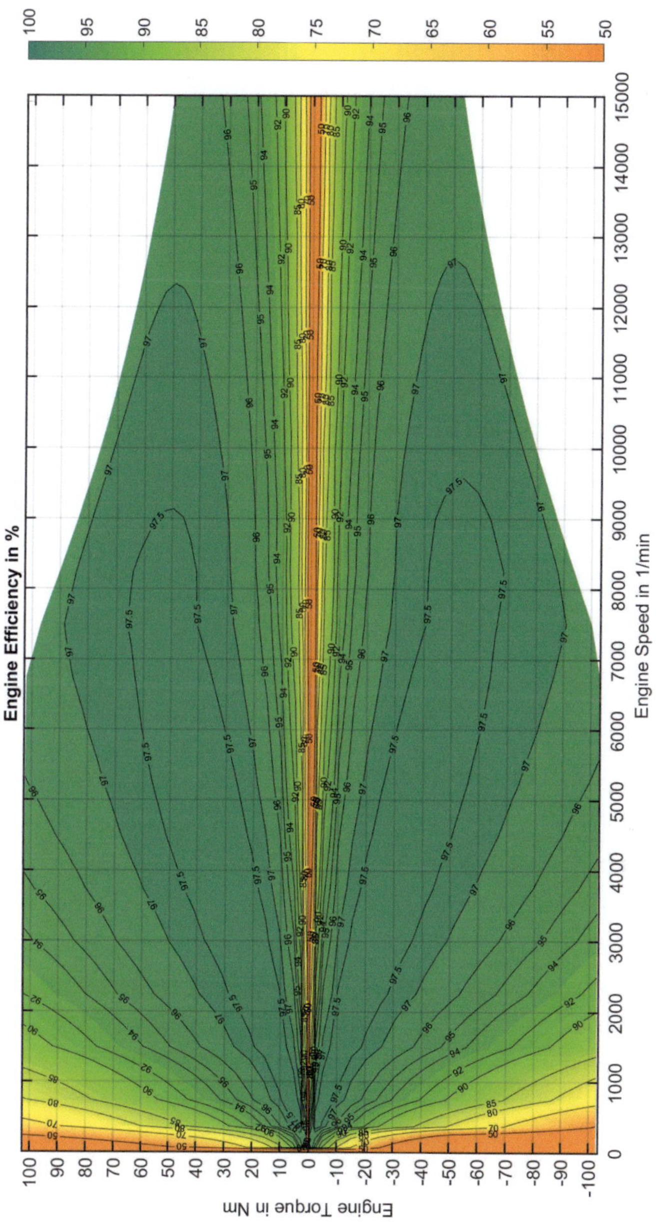

Figure 3.2: REM-2030 electric engine efficiency map.

Electric engine

The engine torque T_e is influenced by $T_{c,in}$ and the engine inertia J_e if the engine rotation speed ω_e is changing:

$$T_e = T_{c,in} + J_e \dot{\omega}_e. \tag{3.29}$$

The engine efficiency of the electric engine (EE) can be described by an engine efficiency map $\eta_e(\omega_e, T_e)$ depending on the engine torque T_e and the engine rotation speed ω_e. This thesis defines positive engine torque demand as propelling torque that the engine has to provide. In case of negative engine torque demand, energy is provided to the engine. The engine then becomes a generator that charges the battery. In the case of the REM-2030 EE, the maximum engine and generator torque magnitude are both 103 Nm and remain constant until approximately 7,500 $\frac{1}{\text{min}}$ before gradually decreasing to 55 Nm at 15,000 $\frac{1}{\text{min}}$. The engine efficiency map is displayed in Figure 3.2. Apart from engine efficiency, it also shows the physical boundaries of the engine.

There are several differences between an electric engine (EE) and an internal combustion engine (ICE). The EE can provide the maximum torque even if ω_e is very low. The average efficiency and the peak efficiency are much higher than in the case of ICEs. In the REM-2030 EE, the maximum efficiency reaches almost 98 %. In comparison, the peak efficiency for an ICE is usually below 50 %. An EE can maintain high efficiency over a vast operation area in the engine efficiency map, while the maximum efficiency for ICEs is only concentrated in a small operation area. In the case of the REM-2030 EE, low efficiency is only present for very low torque demand or for very low engine rotation speed. Due to high efficiency over a large operation area, an electric vehicle (EV) can use strong acceleration and still maintain relatively high engine efficiency.

Additional advantages of the EE compared to the ICE are energy recuperation and continuous brake torque control. When the driver steps off the acceleration pedal, an ICE can use fuel-cutoff and apply a specific engine brake torque dependent on the engine rotation speed. Other than changing the gear level and therefore the engine rotation speed, the brake torque of ICEs cannot be changed by the driver. Alternatively, coasting can be used. In this case, the clutch opens and separates the ICE from the rest of the powertrain. The resistance is then dictated by external forces and additional fuel is needed to keep the ICE running. In contrast to the ICE, the EE can control how much energy is recuperated and how much is used to propel the vehicle. Even in generator mode, every feasible operation point in the efficiency map can be adopted. In the case of the REM-2030 EE, the maximum engine brake torque or rather generator torque is as large as the maximum propelling torque. In an ICE, the maximum brake torque is usually significantly smaller than the maximum propelling torque.

The flexibility in adjusting the brake torque leads to a human machine interface (HMI) design question not encountered in ICEs. When stepping off the acceleration pedal in an electric vehicle, it is unclear how much brake torque the EE should generate. In an ICE, there is only one brake torque for a given engine rotation speed. One design option is to "brake with the acceleration pedal" in the sense that a low acceleration pedal position u_a (for example 0 % to 50 % depression) actually takes the EE into generator mode and therefore creates a brake torque. Thus, only a high acceleration pedal position (for example 50 % to 100 % depression) generates a propelling torque. This design can be unfamiliar for drivers who only have experience with ICE propelled vehicles. To address this issue, it is possible to indirectly simulate traditional brake control by controlling the generator mode with the brake pedal. For low brake pedal positions u_b (for example 0 % to 50 % depression), only the EE is used for braking. The brake pads at the wheels are only used for higher brake pedal positions (for example 50 % to 100 % depression). An example of this kind of brake control is the Audi e-tron.

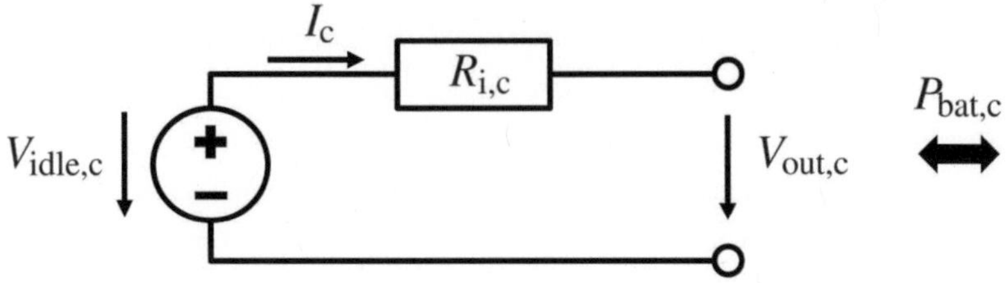

Figure 3.3: Battery cell equivalent circuit. The rest of the powertrain can demand power from the battery or provide power to the battery.

Similar to the previously discussed braking model, the acceleration pedal position u_a can be computed with the engine efficiency map, given a feasible pair of engine torque and engine rotation speed. As discussed in section 4.1, the optimization does not consider the computation of u_a or u_b. The design of the brake control HMI is not further discussed. Instead, PEEMTO makes use of all feasible operation points within the engine efficiency map.

Power electronics

The REM-2030 power electronics between the EE and the battery consists of a DC/DC and a DC/AC converter. The DC/DC converter increases the intermediate circuit voltage, while the DC/AC converter transforms the DC current from the battery to the AC current used in the EE [KVD13]. The efficiency of both DC/DC converter η_{DCDC} and DC/AC converter η_{DCAC} is approximated by a constant efficiency of 98 % in the REM-2030 powertrain model.

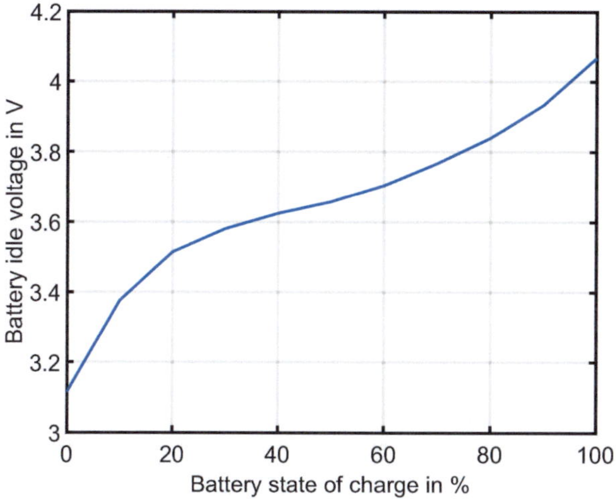

Figure 3.4: REM-2030 battery cell idle voltage depending on the battery state of charge.

Battery

An overview of battery models of different degrees of complexity can be found in [HB11] [MN14]. Complex models use equivalent electric circuits that consist of multiple voltage sources, resistors, capacitors, and diodes, which may dependent on the temperature and the state of charge (SOC). The battery model used in this work does not describe transient and polarization effects. For the purpose of this thesis, the equivalent circuit of a single battery cell only consists of a voltage source, which represents the battery cell idle voltage $V_{\mathrm{idle,c}}$, and the battery cell internal resistor $R_{\mathrm{i,c}}$. The equivalent circuit is illustrated in Figure 3.3. The battery cell output voltage $V_{\mathrm{out,c}}$ is computed from $V_{\mathrm{idle,c}}$, $R_{\mathrm{i,c}}$, and the battery cell current I_{c}:

$$V_{\mathrm{out,c}} = V_{\mathrm{idle,c}} - R_{\mathrm{i,c}} I_{\mathrm{c}}. \tag{3.30}$$

The powertrain can demand or provide a certain battery cell power $P_{\mathrm{bat,c}}$ from or to each battery cell:

$$P_{\mathrm{bat,c}} = V_{\mathrm{out,c}} I_{\mathrm{c}} = V_{\mathrm{idle,c}} I_{\mathrm{c}} - R_{\mathrm{i,c}} I_{\mathrm{c}}^2. \tag{3.31}$$

This leads to a certain amount of electric current flowing from the battery to the engine. Vice versa, if the electric engine is in generator mode, the battery receives a charging current. The same battery model is used for both charge and discharge scenarios. With the constraint $I_{\mathrm{c}} = 0$ for $P_{\mathrm{bat,c}} = 0$, the battery cell current I_{c} is the temporal derivative of the battery cell charge Q_{c}:

$$I_{\mathrm{c}} = \dot{Q}_{\mathrm{c}} = \frac{V_{\mathrm{idle,c}}}{2R_{\mathrm{i,c}}} - \sqrt{\frac{V_{\mathrm{idle,c}}^2}{4R_{\mathrm{i,c}}^2} - \frac{P_{\mathrm{bat,c}}}{R_{\mathrm{i,c}}}}. \tag{3.32}$$

$V_{\mathrm{out,c}}$ can be described by the power demand of the powertrain, the idle battery cell voltage, and the internal cell resistor:

$$V_{\mathrm{out,c}} = V_{\mathrm{idle,c}} - R_{\mathrm{i,c}} I_{\mathrm{c}} = \frac{V_{\mathrm{idle,c}}}{2} + \sqrt{\frac{V_{\mathrm{idle,c}}^2}{4} - P_{\mathrm{bat,c}} R_{\mathrm{i,c}}}. \tag{3.33}$$

$V_{\mathrm{idle,c}}$ increases with higher Q_{c}, while $R_{\mathrm{i,c}}$ decreases with higher battery temperature. The REM-2030 electric vehicle uses lithium battery cells provided by Leclanché. An illustration of the idle voltage depending on the SOC (charge in percentage of full charge) in the case of the REM-2030 battery cell is provided in Figure 3.4. In general, the voltage cannot completely drop to zero. Simulation of the battery temperature or temperature management is not done in this thesis but can be part of future work. In this thesis, a constant temperature of 20°C is assumed, which leads to a $R_{\mathrm{i,c}}$ of 5 mΩ.

According to the specifications of the battery manufacturer, the REM-2030 battery is recommended to be used within a SOC operation range of 20 % to 95 %. As discussed in section 5.3.4, the impact of SOC on the optimization is small as long as the vehicle does not need to recharge. The battery idle voltage does, however, decrease with decreasing SOC. Following the equivalent circuit model, this leads to higher currents if the power demand from the battery does not change. Furthermore, the battery cell current must not exceed the maximum charge and discharge current of 20 A.

The idle voltage V_{idle} of the entire battery is increased by the number $n_{\text{bat,s}}$ of battery cells connected in series:

$$V_{\text{idle}} = n_{\text{bat,s}} V_{\text{idle,c}}. \tag{3.34}$$

The output voltage V_{out} of the entire battery is also increased accordingly:

$$V_{\text{out}} = n_{\text{bat,s}} V_{\text{out,c}}. \tag{3.35}$$

The charge and discharge current of the entire battery I is increased by the number $n_{\text{bat,p}}$ of battery cells connected in parallel configuration:

$$I = n_{\text{bat,p}} I_{\text{c}}. \tag{3.36}$$

The charge of the entire battery Q is also increased accordingly:

$$Q = n_{\text{bat,p}} Q_{\text{c}}. \tag{3.37}$$

The battery power P_{bat} is composed of the power of all battery cells:

$$P_{\text{bat}} = n_{\text{bat,s}} n_{\text{bat,p}} P_{\text{bat,c}}. \tag{3.38}$$

The battery efficiency η_{bat} is defined by the ratio between the battery output voltage V_{out} and the battery idle voltage V_{idle}. The definition is:

$$\eta_{\text{bat}} = \begin{cases} \frac{V_{\text{out}}}{V_{\text{idle}}} & \text{if } I \geq 0 \\ \frac{V_{\text{idle}}}{V_{\text{out}}} & \text{if } I < 0 \end{cases} \tag{3.39}$$

for the discharge mode $I \geq 0$ and the charge mode $I < 0$ respectively.

The REM-2030 battery in its original configuration arranges the cells in two rows, each with 84 cells in series. For the purpose of this thesis, the battery is extended to 12 rows each with 84 cells in series to match the maximum power of the EE.

3.1.2 Lateral vehicle model

The lateral properties of the vehicle model describe the lateral acceleration, the lateral vehicle stability, and the curve resistance among other topics.

Lateral dynamics

In this thesis, the linear stationary single track model is used to evaluate the lateral dynamics of the vehicle. The model is possibly best known for its employment in the electronic stability program (ESP). An illustration of the single track model is shown in Figure 3.5. In the single track model, the vehicle is reduced to a single front wheel and a single rear wheel. When discussing the single track model, a vehicle that is moving in a circle is often used. Let there be a vehicle that is revolving around a point $\boldsymbol{P}_c$. Let $\boldsymbol{P}_v$ be the point that represents the vehicle's center of gravity. Let r be the distance between $\boldsymbol{P}_c$ and $\boldsymbol{P}_v$. If a vehicle is moving on a bent road, r represents the road curvature radius. Let $\dot{\psi}$ be the yaw rate of the vehicle (i.e., temporal derivative of the yaw angle ψ) with respect to $\boldsymbol{P}_v$. The vehicle velocity v is tangential with respect to the circular trajectory. The lateral acceleration of

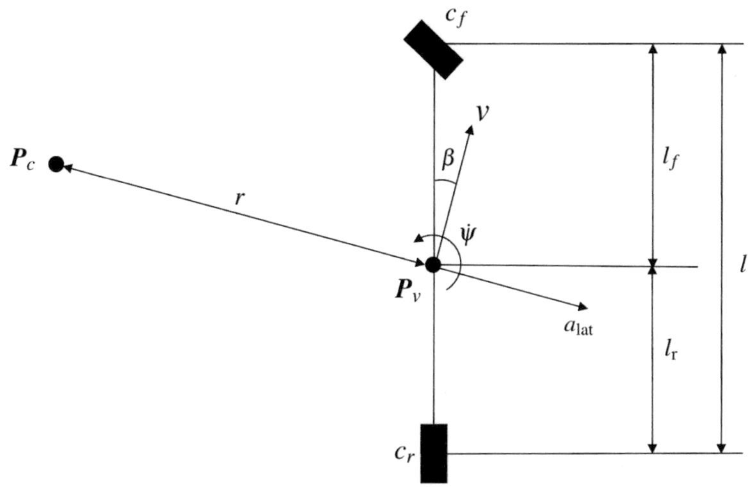

Figure 3.5: Single track model.

the vehicle a_{lat} refers to $\boldsymbol{P}_v$. During a circular movement, the longitudinal axis of the vehicle's body frame does not exactly match the direction of the vehicle velocity. The angle difference is the vehicle side slip angle β. Let l be the vehicle's wheelbase. Let l_{f} be the front part of the wheelbase. Let l_{r} be the rear part of the wheelbase. Therefore, the wheelbase is:

$$l = l_{\text{f}} + l_{\text{r}}. \tag{3.40}$$

Furthermore, let c_{f} be the cornering stiffness of the front wheel, and let c_{r} be the cornering stiffness of the rear wheel. The lateral acceleration a_{lat} depends on the change rate of the vehicle yaw angle ψ, the change rate of the vehicle side slip angle $\dot{\beta}$, and β itself. For small angle changes and small β, a_{lat} is approximately the same as the vehicle's lateral acceleration if the entire vehicle is reduced to its center of gravity [SHB10] [MW15]:

$$a_{\text{lat}} = v\left(\dot{\psi} + \dot{\beta}\right)\cos(\beta) \approx \frac{v^2}{r}. \tag{3.41}$$

For stationary cases or small angle changes [SHB10] [MW15], β can be described as:

$$\beta \approx \frac{l_\mathrm{r}}{r} - \frac{ml_\mathrm{f}}{c_\mathrm{r}l} a_\mathrm{lat}. \tag{3.42}$$

The single track model parameters used in this thesis are obtained from a Mercedes C280. They are presented in Table A.4 in the appendix.

Lateral stability

In modern vehicles, the electronic stability program (ESP) is commonly used to address lateral vehicle stability. One of the primary goals is to prevent lateral instability due to excessive lateral acceleration a_lat and side slip angle β of the vehicle. A typical scenario of lateral instability is the loss of control of the front wheels or the rear wheels. According to [BB12], the ESP system must ascertain that the magnitude of β is kept below 5°. This threshold value is also used in this work to represent lateral stability.

Curve resistance

During a circular movement of the vehicle, the direction of resistance from the ground acting on the tires does not entirely match the longitudinal movement direction of the tires. The lateral forces have a component that acts against the propelling force, which leads to the curve resistance F_c. The curve resistance model follows the formulation of [Hak14]. The different tire velocities are approximated by the vehicle velocity. Furthermore, the same curvature radius is used for all tires. Thus, F_c can be approximated by:

$$F_\mathrm{c} \approx \frac{m^2 l_\mathrm{r}^2 v^4}{2c_\mathrm{f} l^2 r^2} + \frac{m^2 l_\mathrm{f}^2 v^4}{2c_\mathrm{r} l^2 r^2}. \tag{3.43}$$

Steering wheel control

As discussed in section 4.1, PEEMTO does not compute the controls. But it is generally possible to compute the controls from the motion trajectories. If the

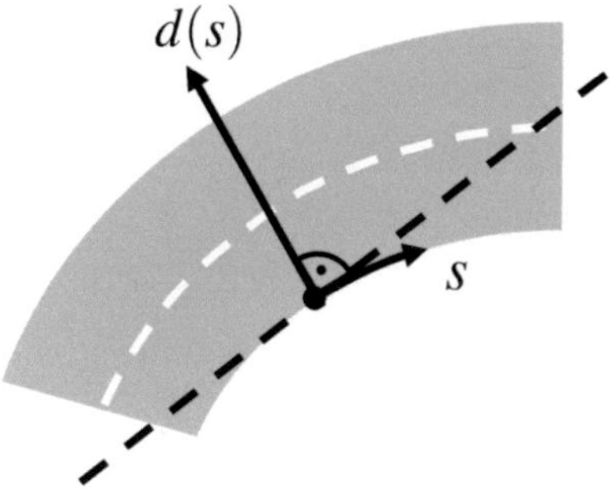

Figure 3.6: Parametric coordinate system.

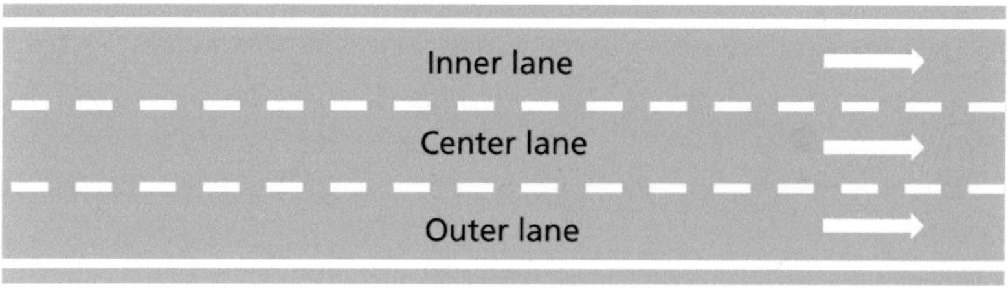

Figure 3.7: Route with three lanes.

steering wheel angle u_s is required, it can be computed using the single track parameters, a_lat, r, m, and the steering wheel ratio i_s according to [SHB10] [MW15]:

$$u_\mathrm{s} = i_\mathrm{s}\left(\frac{l}{r} + \frac{m(c_\mathrm{r}l_\mathrm{r} - c_\mathrm{f}l_\mathrm{f})}{c_\mathrm{f}c_\mathrm{r}l}a_\mathrm{lat}\right). \tag{3.44}$$

3.2 Coordinate system

In automotive and robotic applications, cartesian coordinate systems are widely used. An alternative coordinate system formulation is a special type of parametric coordinate system that focuses on longitudinal position, i.e., driven distance. Examples that use this kind of coordinate system include [ZS09] [Ter09] [Hel10]. The advantage is simplicity. Points beyond the road are inherently excluded. Furthermore, the points on the road have a clear order with respect to driven distance.

A descriptive illustration is given in Figure 3.6. Let s be the longitudinal position along the route. In this thesis, it shall always refer to the rightmost edge of the route. Let $d(s)$ be the lateral position of points on the route that have the same longitudinal position s. A point with $d(s) = 0$ refers to the rightmost edge of the route. Furthermore, let $\varphi(s)$ be the road slope at s, let $\kappa(s)$ be the road curvature, and let $r(s)$ be the road curvature radius at s. The road curvature and road curvature radius have an inverse relationship:

$$\kappa(s) = \frac{1}{r(s)}. \tag{3.45}$$

Apart from the lateral position, there are also lanes. An example of three lanes is given in Figure 3.7. The rightmost lane in the direction of travel is called the *outer lane*. The leftmost lane in the direction of travel is called the *inner lane*. The lane in between is called the *center lane*. If the route has more than three lanes, there are several center lanes. A lane has a certain width. For the purpose of this thesis, a universal lane width of 3 m is used.

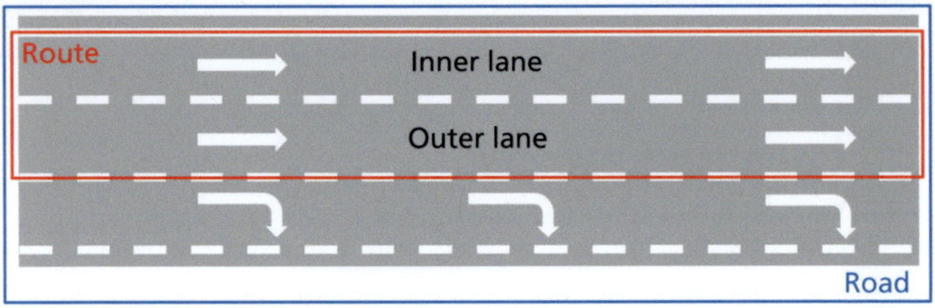

Figure 3.8: Route with two lanes. Lanes of the road that diverts the ego-vehicle from the route are not part of the route.

In this thesis, there is a distinction between *road*, *route*, and *journey*. A journey describes the entire track the ego-vehicle has to travel, from the very beginning to the final destination. A route can incorporate the entire journey or only a part of it. The optimization only considers the route. If the route is only a part of the journey, a human driver has to take over control at the end of the route. A road refers to the entire physical road with a single road name and includes opposite lanes, acceleration lanes, exit lanes, etc. The route is sometimes only a part of the road and may sometimes consist of several different roads. The lanes of the road that would divert the ego-vehicle from the route are not part of the route. An example is given in Figure 3.8. The route only has two feasible lanes. The exit lane is not part of the route because the progression of the route is straight ahead in the example.

The lanes and lane directions used in this thesis are obtained from Google Maps. Route choice selection is not considered in this thesis. It assumed that the route is already predefined prior to any optimization. Within the scope of this thesis, only a limited amount of road compositions is considered. Roundabouts, lane closures (i.e., road sections with lane number reduction), and areas without roads like parking lots are not evaluated.

3.3 Static influence from the environment

Static influence from the environment refers to road characteristics that do not change over time.

3.3.1 Speed limits

The speed limits of real-world routes used in this thesis are either obtained from Open Street Map or directly observed in reality. If there is no speed limit, the recommended maximum speed of 130 $\frac{\mathrm{km}}{\mathrm{h}}$ according to German traffic rules is used as a reference. German traffic rules also require drivers not to drive too slowly to prevent disruptions in the traffic flow. There is no precise definition of a specific minimum speed and drivers need to make individual decisions in practice. In this thesis, the optimization uses speed limits up to 80 $\frac{\text{km}}{\text{h}}$ as references for the choice of the minimum cruise velocity.

3.3.2 Road topography

Gravitation on road slopes can act as a significant resistance or a significant propelling force on the vehicle. Road altitude or road slope information can be obtained through existing elevation data, e.g., [Nat00] [Ger10] [Goo17] [Her17] [Int17]. Alternatively, it is also possible to directly measure the road slope in the real world using angle measurement tools. In this thesis, elevation data from the Google Elevation API [Goo17] is used for highway scenarios. Google does not publish the precision of its elevation data. Studies conducted in [Wan+17] suggest that the root-mean-square error is 2.27 m for roadways. Slope angle information for urban roads is directly measured along the real roads using a Bosch Professional GIM 60 inclinometer with a measurement precision of 0.2°. Once the data is collected, B-Splines are used to smooth the slope and elevation data along the route.

3.3.3 Road curvature

In this thesis, the points along the given route in geographic coordinates are used to estimate the road curvature. The road curvature radius of the road can be estimated using at least three neighboring points or more on the arc that describes the curvature. The Kasa method [Rus+03] is used to estimate the radius. The estimated curvature is subsequently smoothed using B-Splines before putting to use.

3.4 Dynamic influence from the environment

Dynamic influence refers to obstacles that change their state over time. In this thesis, traffic light phases and other vehicles on the same route as the ego-vehicle are considered.

3.4.1 Traffic lights

From the perspective of PEEMTO, a traffic light has a certain longitudinal position along the route. For a certain point in time, a traffic light is in a certain phase, i.e., yellow, green, or red. A traffic light provides PEEMTO with the schedule of its time-dependent phases. PEEMTO is independent of the exact nature of traffic light phase shift mechanics. From the perspective of PEEMTO, the red phases are dynamic obstacles that can appear and disappear dependent on time and at specific locations. The reaction of PEEMTO to traffic light phases is discussed in section 4.11. The simulation of traffic lights is described in section A.3.1.

3.4.2 Other vehicles and driver model

Estimating the behavior of other traffic participants is an active field of research. As this thesis is primarily about energy-efficient driving, the creation of novel driver behavior models or driver behavior estimation are not the goal of this work. For the purpose of this thesis, the evaluation is confined to other vehicles on the same route as the ego-vehicle, while anomalies like accidents are not investigated. Pedestrians, cyclists, etc. are not included.

This section describes the driver model that is used by PEEMTO. It shall be called the *simplified driver model* (SDM). The driver model used in the simulation environment is more extensive and is further described in section A.3. The SDM is based on the well-established *intelligent driver model* (IDM) from transportation engineering [Str06] and its extensions [TK13], the *improved intelligent driver model* (IIDM) and the *adaptive cruise control model* (ACC). Parameter recommendations are provided in [TK13], which are also used in this thesis. They are also listed in Table A.5 in the appendix and form the default driver parameters of the SDM.

IDM model

In its original form, the IDM tries to reach the desired velocity $v_{\mathrm{d,goal}}$ and tries to keep a certain distance to the closest front vehicle in the same lane as the ego-vehicle. In this thesis, the speed limit serves as a reference for $v_{\mathrm{d,goal}}$. Let v be the velocity of the ego-vehicle controlled by the driver. Let a_{d} be the preferred acceleration. Let b_{d} be the comfortable deceleration. Let δ_{d} be the acceleration exponent. Let $\Delta s_{\mathrm{d,goal}}$ be the desired distance to the front vehicle. Let $\Delta s_{\mathrm{d,min}}$ be the acceptable minimum distance to the front vehicle. Let Δt_{d} be the desired time gap to the front vehicle, which can also be interpreted as the reaction time of the driver. Let Δs_{d} be the distance to the front vehicle. Let Δv_{d} be the current velocity difference to the front vehicle. The desired distance $\Delta s_{\mathrm{d,goal}}$ to the front vehicle can then be described by:

$$\Delta s_{\mathrm{d,goal}} = \Delta s_{\mathrm{d,min}} + \max\left(0, v\Delta t_{\mathrm{d}} + \frac{v\Delta v_{\mathrm{d}}}{2\sqrt{a_{\mathrm{d}}b_{\mathrm{d}}}}\right). \tag{3.46}$$

The acceleration of the driver is described by the IDM acceleration a_{IDM}:

$$a_{\mathrm{IDM}} = a_{\mathrm{d}}\left(1 - \left(\frac{v}{v_{\mathrm{d,goal}}}\right)^{\delta_{\mathrm{d}}} - \left(\frac{\Delta s_{\mathrm{d,goal}}}{\Delta s_{\mathrm{d}}}\right)^2\right). \tag{3.47}$$

IIDM model

The IDM has several deficiencies, which include the infinite deceleration if $v_{\mathrm{d,goal}} = 0$. The first extension of IDM is the IIDM. First, the free acceleration

$$a_{\text{d,free}} = \begin{cases} a_{\text{d}}\left(1 - \left(\frac{v}{v_{\text{d,goal}}}\right)^{\delta_{\text{d}}}\right) & \text{if } v \leq v_{\text{d,goal}} \\ -b_{\text{d}}\left(1 - \left(\frac{v_{\text{d,goal}}}{v}\right)^{\frac{a_{\text{d}}\delta_{\text{d}}}{b_{\text{d}}}}\right) & \text{otherwise} \end{cases} \tag{3.48}$$

is defined. It is the preferred acceleration if the driver is not constrained by any front vehicles. The IIDM acceleration

$$a_{\text{IIDM}} = \begin{cases} a_{\text{d}}\left(1 - \left(\frac{\Delta s_{\text{d,goal}}}{\Delta s_{\text{d}}}\right)^{2}\right) & \text{if } \frac{\Delta s_{\text{d,goal}}}{\Delta s_{\text{d}}} \geq 1 \ \wedge \ v \leq v_{\text{d,goal}} \\ a_{\text{d,free}}\left(1 - \left(\frac{\Delta s_{\text{d,goal}}}{\Delta s_{\text{d}}}\right)^{\frac{2a_{\text{d}}}{a_{\text{d,free}}}}\right) & \text{if } \frac{\Delta s_{\text{d,goal}}}{\Delta s_{\text{d}}} < 1 \ \wedge \ v \leq v_{\text{d,goal}} \\ a_{\text{d,free}} + a_{\text{d}}\left(1 - \left(\frac{\Delta s_{\text{d,goal}}}{\Delta s_{\text{d}}}\right)^{2}\right) & \text{if } \frac{\Delta s_{\text{d,goal}}}{\Delta s_{\text{d}}} < 1 \ \wedge \ v > v_{\text{d,goal}} \\ a_{\text{d,free}} & \text{if } \frac{\Delta s_{\text{d,goal}}}{\Delta s_{\text{d}}} \geq 1 \ \wedge \ v > v_{\text{d,goal}} \end{cases} \tag{3.49}$$

is defined by using several case distinctions.

ACC model

A further improvement is the ACC model that prevents safety related overreaction of the driver model for low-speed differences and small gaps between the driver and the closest front vehicle in the same lane. The ACC model introduces the constant acceleration heuristic. The underlying assumption is that the front vehicle will not significantly change its current behavior. Let $v_{\text{d,f}}$ be the velocity of the closest front vehicle in the same lane. Let $a_{\text{d,f}}$ be the acceleration of the closest front vehicle in the same lane. The acceleration according to the constant acceleration heuristic

$$a_{\text{CAH}} = \begin{cases} \frac{v^2 \min(a_{\text{d,f}},a)}{v_{\text{d,f}}^2 - 2\Delta s_{\text{d}} \min(a_{\text{d,f}},a)} & \text{if } v_{\text{d,f}}(v - v_{\text{d,f}}) \leq -2\Delta s_{\text{d}} \min(a_{\text{d,f}},a) \\ \min(a_{\text{d,f}},a) - \frac{(v - v_{\text{d,f}})^2}{2\Delta s_{\text{d}}} & \text{if } v_{\text{d,f}}(v - v_{\text{d,f}}) > -2\Delta s_{\text{d}} \min(a_{\text{d,f}},a) \ \wedge \ v \geq v_{\text{d,f}} \\ \min(a_{\text{d,f}},a) & \text{if } v_{\text{d,f}}(v - v_{\text{d,f}}) > -2\Delta s_{\text{d}} \min(a_{\text{d,f}},a) \ \wedge \ v < v_{\text{d,f}} \end{cases} \tag{3.50}$$

is defined by using several case distinctions. The ACC model does not abandon the IIDM model. In fact, it is actually a combination of the IIDM model and the constant acceleration heuristic. The combination is governed by a so-called coolness factor $\lambda_{\mathrm{d,c}}$. The acceleration compromise

$$a_{\mathrm{ACC}} = \begin{cases} a_{\mathrm{IIDM}} & \text{if } a_{\mathrm{IIDM}} \geq a_{\mathrm{CAH}} \\ (1-\lambda_{\mathrm{d,c}})a_{\mathrm{IIDM}} + \lambda_{\mathrm{d,c}}\left(a_{\mathrm{CAH}} + b_{\mathrm{d}} \tanh\left(\frac{a_{\mathrm{IIDM}}-a_{\mathrm{CAH}}}{b_{\mathrm{d}}}\right)\right) & \text{otherwise} \end{cases} \tag{3.51}$$

is computed by using both a_{IIDM} and a_{CAH}.

Reaction to traffic lights

If there is a red traffic light ahead, the driver model treats it as an idle vehicle and decelerates accordingly. A decision becomes more complicated if the initial green phase changes to the yellow phase. According to [TK13], the driver should decelerate if the vehicle is able to come to a full stop in front of the traffic light and if the deceleration does not exceed the maximum safe deceleration $b_{\mathrm{d,safe}}$. If a safe deceleration is not possible, the driver should ignore the traffic light and move past it even if it turns to the red phase.

Desired velocity, desired lane, and lane changes

The basic assumption of the authors in [AW11] [ACK12] is that other vehicles do not change their current velocity and lane. The SDM makes a similar assumption. It assumes that the current velocity and the current lane of a vehicle are identical to its desired velocity and desired lane. If a vehicle changes the velocity or the lane, the SDM adapts its assumptions accordingly. If the ego-vehicle observes another vehicle that is in the process of changing lanes, i.e. already occupies two lanes, the SDM assumes that the vehicle will continue to occupy both lanes until the ego-vehicle observes the completion of the lane change. Learning the behavior of other drivers and predicting future lane changes remain challenging topics within the scientific community and is not investigated in this thesis.

Restrictions

The SDM is based on the driver model of [TK13] and uses several restrictions:

- Lane closures and vehicle cooperation are not considered.
- Lane change predictions are not considered.
- Slopes and curvatures are not considered.
- Drivers do not estimate the behavior of other drivers. They all use the default driver parameters as specified in Table A.5 in the appendix.
- The vehicles do not make simultaneous decisions. The vehicle that is furthest ahead, i.e., has the highest longitudinal position makes the first decision. The vehicle with the second highest longitudinal position makes its decision based on the decision of the leading vehicle. This process is repeated for all vehicles one by one.

The extended driver model (EDM) used by the simulation environment is more extensive than the SDM and is described in the appendix.

4 Optimization

This chapter formulates the optimization problem of energy-efficient driving. It is very important to note that energy consumption is only one optimization criterion of PEEMTO. Indeed, the goal of PEEMTO is to find the optimal solution to several different optimization criteria. These optimization criteria are further described in the cost formulation in section 4.3. The cost formulation leads to the corresponding continuous Hamilton-Jacobi-Bellman equation (HJBE) and the discrete Bellman equation (BE). The discrete problem is solved through dynamic programming (DP). Among numerous topics, it is shown how lane changes and traffic lights can be combined with energy efficiency optimization, and how long-range horizons can improve the optimization result. These two topics are the main contributions of this thesis. Additional publications of the author regarding PEEMTO can be found in [GF13] [Gua15] [GF15] [GF16c] [GF16b] [GF16a] [GF17].

4.1 System overview

The system architecture of PEEMTO is illustrated in Figure 4.1. PEEMTO is an on-board component of the ego-vehicle. It is notified about the state of the ego-vehicle $\boldsymbol{x}(t)$ and the state of the environment with t being the continuous time. The environment consists of time-invariant elements like speed limits, road slope, road curvature, and dynamic elements like traffic lights and other vehicles.

PEEMTO tries to maximize the energy efficiency of the ego-vehicle along the predefined route through optimized energy-efficient driving. The definition of energy-efficient driving is discussed in section 4.3. The goal of

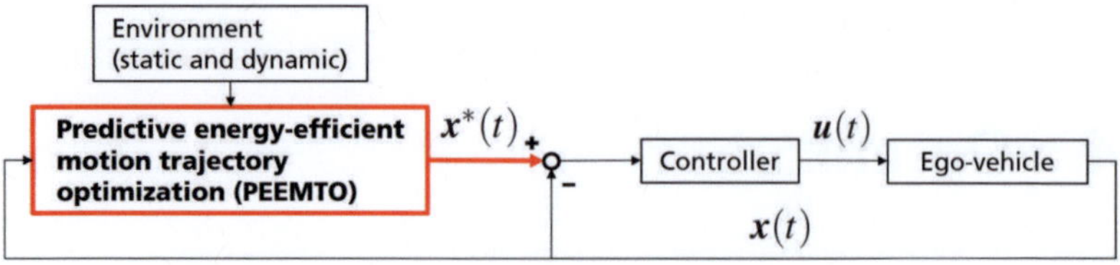

Figure 4.1: System architecture of the *predictive energy-efficient motion trajectory optimization* (PEEMTO). $\boldsymbol{x}^*(t)$ is the computed optimal state trajectory. $\boldsymbol{x}(t)$ is the state of the ego-vehicle. $\boldsymbol{u}(t)$ is the control generated by the controller. The elements marked in red are part of PEEMTO. The optimization is primarily focused on trajectory optimization. The design of the controller and the environment perception are not part of this thesis.

PEEMTO is to compute the optimal energy-efficient state trajectory $\boldsymbol{x}^*(t)$ of the ego-vehicle along a predefined route. The most important components are the optimal velocity trajectory and the optimal gear level trajectory.

The computation of the optimal control trajectory $\boldsymbol{u}^*(t)$ is regarded as optional in PEEMTO and is not evaluated in further details. Once $\boldsymbol{x}^*(t)$ is computed, $\boldsymbol{u}^*(t)$ can be additionally retrieved through the vehicle model if required. Alternatively, if position related information is needed, it is also possible to compute $\boldsymbol{x}^*(s(t))$ and $\boldsymbol{u}^*(s(t))$ instead, which are dependent on the longitudinal position $s(t)$. For further information on the coordinate system used in this thesis, the reader can turn to section 3.2. Indeed, as is shown in section 4.5.2, the underlying discrete optimization seeks out the position related optimal motion trajectory first and subsequently constructs the time-dependent trajectory from the position related result if required.

PEEMTO receives all necessary information about the state of the ego-vehicle and the environment. The system requires different sources of information:

- Predefined route.
- Knowledge about the ego-vehicle, e.g., power-train components, vehicle mass, etc.

- Access to all relevant vehicle internal measurement data, e.g., velocity, gear level, etc.
- Knowledge about the road slope angle $\varphi(s)$ along the route.
- Knowledge about the road curvature radius $r(s)$ along the route.
- Knowledge about speed limits along the route.
- Knowledge about the lane configuration along the route, i.e., number of lanes, direction of lanes, etc.
- Vehicle-to-infrastructure communication (V2I) with traffic lights to obtain current and future phases.
- Reliable capability to detect other vehicles in the vicinity.

Additional explanations are given in the other sections of this chapter.

4.2 Continuous optimization problem formulation

The Hamilton-Jacobi-Bellman equation (HJBE) was formulated by Richard Bellman [Bel54] as a generalization of the Hamilton-Jacobi equation from classical physics. It was created as part of the theory on dynamic programming (DP), which was also formulated by Richard Bellman.

The corresponding discrete equation to the HJBE is the Bellman equation (BE), which can be solved through DP. Thus, DP yields the optimal discrete approximate solution to the corresponding HJBE. Furthermore, the optimization problem must not contradict the principle of optimality (PO) [Bel54]: "An optimal policy has the property that whatever the initial state and initial decision are, the remaining decisions must constitute an optimal policy with regard to the state resulting from the first decision." Typical problems that maintain the PO are problems in which a decision only depends on the outcome of the previous decision.

Different from the Euler-Lagrange equation and the Pontryagin maximum/minimum principle, the HJBE is both a necessary and sufficient condition for the existence of a globally optimal solution [Ber05]. Another advantage is the direct correspondence to the BE and the discrete DP algorithm, which yields the globally optimal discrete solution with respect to the employed discretization.

4.2.1 States, controls, trajectories, and costs

In order to formulate the HJBE, several definitions are needed. Let $\boldsymbol{x}(t)$ be the continuous state dependent on the continuous time t. It consists of the longitudinal position of the ego-vehicle $s(t)$, its lateral position $d(t)$, its velocity $v(t)$, its longitudinal acceleration $a(t)$, its lateral acceleration $a_{\text{lat}}(t)$, its gear level $G(t)$, and its battery state of charge $Q(t)$:

$$\boldsymbol{x}(t) = [s(t), d(t), v(t), a(t), a_{\text{lat}}(t), G(t), Q(t)]. \tag{4.1}$$

Let $\boldsymbol{u}(t)$ be the continuous control dependent on the continuous time t. In a vehicle that can also be controlled by the driver, it consists of the acceleration pedal position $u_{\text{a}}(t)$, the brake pedal position $u_{\text{b}}(t)$, the gear change $\dot{G}(t)$, and the steering wheel angle $u_{\text{s}}(t)$:

$$\boldsymbol{u}(t) = [u_{\text{a}}(t), u_{\text{b}}(t), \dot{G}(t), u_{\text{s}}(t)]. \tag{4.2}$$

Note that in many established optimization textbooks (e.g., [Ber05] [NW06] [Ber07]), a clear distinction between state and state trajectory is not made, and only $\boldsymbol{x}(t)$ is used to describe both the state and the state trajectory. The same applies to control and control trajectory. Furthermore, t represents the continuous time and not one specific point in time. This thesis follows the same notation for the formulation of continuous state, control, and trajectories. In the continuous domain, the term “trajectory” shall only be used to explicitly stress out the entire progression of the state or control over time. No additional symbols are defined to describe continuous trajectories, i.e., only $\boldsymbol{x}(t)$ and $\boldsymbol{u}(t)$ are used. Both $\boldsymbol{x}(t)$ and $\boldsymbol{u}(t)$ should be ideally continuously differentiable with respect to time to simplify real-world applicability. It is assumed that even gear level changes cannot be instantly completed in reality.

Let $j(\boldsymbol{x}(t),\boldsymbol{u}(t))$ be the transition cost function, which is dependent on $\boldsymbol{x}(t)$, $\boldsymbol{u}(t)$, and the state transition governed by the system equations $\dot{\boldsymbol{x}}(t) = f(\boldsymbol{x}(t),\boldsymbol{u}(t))$. Note that the system equations usually use the state and an admissible control to compute the change of the state. But as discussed in section 3.1, the vehicle model used in this thesis is actually formulated in an inverse fashion. The system equations in their original form are not explicitly formulated. The vehicle model of section 3.1 is used instead.

Furthermore, let $J(\boldsymbol{x}(t))$ be the accumulated cost function, which is the integral of $j(\boldsymbol{x}(t),\boldsymbol{u}(t))$ with respect to the integration time variable τ:

$$J(\boldsymbol{x}(t)) = \int_{\tau=t_0}^{t} j(\boldsymbol{x}(\tau),\boldsymbol{u}(\tau))d\tau. \tag{4.3}$$

This also means that the accumulated cost $J(\boldsymbol{x}(t))$ refers to the entire trajectory $\boldsymbol{x}(t)$ starting with the start time of the optimization t_0.

4.2.2 Hamilton-Jacobi-Bellman equation

Let $\boldsymbol{\Upsilon}$ be the admissible control space. Let $V(\boldsymbol{x}(t))$ be a certain function. With the previous definitions, the HJBE can be formulated as a minimization problem with respect to $\boldsymbol{u}(t)$ in the form of:

$$0 = \min_{\boldsymbol{u}(t)\in\Upsilon} \Big(j(\boldsymbol{x}(t),\boldsymbol{u}(t)) + \dot{V}(\boldsymbol{x}(t)) + \nabla V(\boldsymbol{x}(t)) f(\boldsymbol{x}(t),\boldsymbol{u}(t)) \Big). \tag{4.4}$$

Additional equality constraints are imposed if the initial cost or the terminal cost for the beginning or the end of the solution trajectory must have a specific value.

If $V(\boldsymbol{x}(t))$ is continuously differentiable with respect to t and $\boldsymbol{x}(t)$, solves the equation over the entire state space for all t and $\boldsymbol{x}(t)$, and if the corresponding control trajectory is piecewise continuous with respect to t, then $V(\boldsymbol{x}(t))$ is the globally optimal solution of the optimization problem, i.e., $V(\boldsymbol{x}(t))$ is the minimum accumulated cost $J^*(\boldsymbol{x}^*(t))$. In this case, let the corresponding $\boldsymbol{x}^*(t)$ be the optimal state trajectory, and let the corresponding $\boldsymbol{u}^*(t)$ be the optimal control trajectory. Together, they constitute the optimal solution of the HJBE. For further information, the reader can turn to [Ber05].

4.3 Problem-specific monetary cost formulation

Many studies conducted in the area of energy-efficient driving use a weighted trade-off between low energy consumption and short travel duration [Hel10] [Ter09] [Hua+08] [Wah15]. These weighting parameters often have to be manually adjusted to reach the desired outcome. Furthermore, it can be difficult to decide if there is a net improvement, e.g., if energy consumption is reduced, but travel duration increases.

In order to make different types of cost terms directly comparable, all cost terms are converted into a monetary form in this thesis. This also means that the cost formulation becomes problem specific and is directly derived from the financial aspects of individuals or the business model of a company. There is no universal definition of costs. Instead, the specific problem at hand dictates the definition of the cost formulation. Additionally, the cost terms are made HJBE compliant, i.e., the cost formulation is in continuous form and the cost terms are continuously differentiable with respect to time t and the state components of $\boldsymbol{x}(t)$. Note that the cost terms presented here primarily serve as an example of the definition of monetary costs. In general, there is a vast amount of different problems that can greatly differ from each other. The author is only aware of one other approach, namely [PKS09], in which monetary cost formulation is applied to energy-efficient driving.

In this work, costs are positive, while gains are negative. The cost parameters are directly taken or derived from different government statistics, surveys, and scientific studies. As these sources are not published at the same time, the data has to be synchronized to the same year. The reference year used in this thesis is chosen as 2014. The cost terms describe continuous processes, which are converted to monetary cost. Neither t, $\boldsymbol{u}(t)$, $\boldsymbol{x}(t)$, or anything used in the cost terms can instantly change. Even braking and gear changes need some form of continuous transition, no matter how brief they may be. The different monetary cost terms are presented as follows.

4.3.1 Energy

Energy consumption $e(\boldsymbol{x}(t),\boldsymbol{u}(t))$ can be converted to monetary cost through the price of electricity λ_{e}. The cost term incorporates both energy consumption and energy generation through recuperation. If energy is recuperated, energy consumption is negative. According to [Bun18], the average electricity cost for German households in 2014 was 0.2953 € for each kWh, which shall be the default value used in this thesis. The energy consumption cost is described as:

$$j_{\mathrm{e}}(\boldsymbol{x}(t),\boldsymbol{u}(t)) = \lambda_{\mathrm{e}} e(\boldsymbol{x}(t),\boldsymbol{u}(t)). \tag{4.5}$$

4.3.2 Travel duration

Apart from energy consumption, time consumption is the other major cost component in PEEMTO. The cost of time $j_{\mathrm{t}}(\boldsymbol{x}(t),\boldsymbol{u}(t))$ is highly problem specific, and there can be a large number of different possible scenarios. This thesis uses a *business trip scenario* as an example, which includes a corresponding *holiday trip scenario* as a special case. Alternative scenarios are, e.g., delivery services and taxi companies. The creation of additional use cases can be part of future work.

Business trip scenario

In the business trip scenario, one or several employees are traveling in a vehicle to a destination. If they cannot be productive or if their productivity is reduced during the journey, the business trip causes additional cost for the employer. In this case, the time cost can be defined using the travel duration with respect to the start time t_0 and the gross labor cost (GLC) of the passengers in the vehicle λ_t. According to [Sta17], the 2014 gross minimum wage in Germany was 8.5 € per hour. The overall average GLC was 16.97 € per hour. The average GLC of the upper 10 % income class was 31 € per hour. The travel duration cost is described as:

$$j_t(t) = \lambda_t(t - t_0). \tag{4.6}$$

Holiday trip scenario

As a special case of the business trip scenario, the holiday trip scenario refers to business unrelated travels or business trips that do not lead to additional costs. The passengers simply want to reach the destination. In this case, there is theoretically no travel duration cost. This can lead to the practical problem that the optimization chooses extremely low velocities. EVs are especially prone to this kind of optimization result because EEs have significantly higher and more homogeneous efficiency than ICEs. Traveling at extremely low velocities can disrupt the traffic flow if there are other vehicles. Thus, the optimization actually has to choose a minimum amount of λ_t in order to prevent extremely low cruise velocities. In this thesis, it is assumed that the ego-vehicle should at least choose the speed limit as the long-time cruise velocity on even, straight roads. If the speed limit is above the speed limit of trucks (i.e., 80 $\frac{\mathrm{km}}{\mathrm{h}}$) or if there is no speed limit, a minimum long-time cruise velocity of 80 $\frac{\mathrm{km}}{\mathrm{h}}$ is chosen as reference. In order to achieve this, PEEMTO conducts internal simulations to adjust λ_t. Examples are given in section 5.3.

4.3.3 Vehicle component wear

Repair of vehicle components can be costly for private individuals and companies. In this thesis, the overhaul and replacement costs for transmission and brakes are considered. Attrition of other vehicle components, warranty, insurance policies, and malfunction probabilities are not discussed but can be part of future work. The data on the service life of vehicle components, their replacement costs, and overhaul costs used in this work are largely based on a wide-ranging study conducted by the United States (U.S.) Department of Transportation and Federal Transit Administration in 2007 [Lav+07]. The study contains numerous data sets on the service life and maintenance costs of fleet vehicles provided by transportation agencies and manufacturers.

Transmission wear

The first component to consider is the transmission. For the purpose of this thesis, an estimate is computed regarding how much average attrition cost is caused through a single gear shift. According to [Lav+07], the service life of a transmission is 75,000 miles - 100,000 miles (approximately 120,000 km - 160,000 km). According to [NBL07], the service life of transmissions should be 150,000 km. This thesis assumes that overhaul becomes necessary after 160,000 km. In order to estimate the average transmission attrition for each gear shift, the distance limit of 160,000 km is transformed to the maximum number of gear shifts before the transmission should be overhauled.

The first step is to estimate the number of gear shifts performed over each kilometer. To the best knowledge of the author, there is no study that investigates of how many gear shifts drivers make in electric vehicles. In fact, many electric vehicles do not have transmissions. For the purpose of this thesis, a study on vehicles with ICEs [SR09] [SRD09] is used to compute an estimate. The REM-2030 transmission only has two gears, while vehicles with ICEs have significantly more. In [SR09] [SRD09], the studies include the investigation of how many gear shifts untrained drivers perform on average. Naturally, if one transmission has significantly more gear levels than another transmission, the frequency of gear shifts will be different. In order to apply the study of [SR09] [SRD09] to the REM-2030 transmission, this thesis makes the simplified assumption that the ratio of the number of gear levels of two different transmissions can be directly applied to the average number of gear shifts over the same driven distance. In the case of [SR09] [SRD09], the studies are conducted on diesel-powered trucks with 18 gear levels. Therefore, the assumption is that the average number of gear shifts is 9 times smaller for the REM-2030 transmission, which only has 2 gear levels, over the same driven distance. This leads to 0.31 shifts per kilometer on average for the REM-2030 vehicle.

Another assumption is that a transmission has to be overhauled after a driven distance of 160,000 km for average gear shift behavior. This leads to a maximum number of 49,600 gear shifts before the REM-2030 transmission should be overhauled. According to [Lav+07], the average overhaul cost for transmissions in 2007 is approximately 2000 \$. The monetary costs used in this thesis all refer to the year 2014 and the Euro currency. With the average U.S. inflation rate of 1.85 % from 2007-2014 and a Euro exchange rate of 1.3 in 2014, the overhaul cost would be 1749 € in 2014. Distributed over 49,600 gear shifts, the average transmission wear cost $j_{\mathrm{G}}(\boldsymbol{x}(t), \boldsymbol{u}(t))$ amounts to $\lambda_{\mathrm{G}} = 0.035$ € for each gear shift with λ_{G} being the transmission wear weight.

In this thesis, the transmission wear is only relevant if there is a gear shift, i.e., $\dot{G}(t) \neq 0$. Let $\varepsilon_{\mathrm{G}}(t)$ be the continuous change in gear level from 0 (no change) to 1 (change completed). It is assumed that the gear level cannot instantly change in the real world, i.e., there is still a short continuous mechanical progression. In the discrete case, the gear level can only be completely changed from one discrete point in time until the next.

Thus, the average transmission wear cost is described by:

$$j_{\mathrm{G}}(\boldsymbol{x}(t), \boldsymbol{u}(t)) = \lambda_{\mathrm{G}} \varepsilon_{\mathrm{G}}(t). \tag{4.7}$$

In reality, gear shifts that lead to higher rotation speed differences in the clutch lead to higher attrition. Very high rotation speed differences also lead to a sudden rise in powertrain resistance and passenger discomfort. Detailed transmission wear models are not investigated in this thesis but can be part of future work.

Brake wear

The second component to consider are the brakes at the wheels. Braking using the brake pads causes attrition to the brakes. Similar to the case of transmission wear, driver behavior statistics are used to estimate the average number of braking for each kilometer. The data of [SR09] [SRD09] leads to an average braking frequency of slightly more than one time for each kilometer. According to [Lav+07], the service life of brakes is 15,000 miles to 30,000 miles (approx. 24,000 km - 48,000 km). In this thesis, the service life is assumed to be 36,000 km for a regular driver. By combining the statistics of [Lav+07] [SR09] [SRD09], it can be assumed that the brakes have to be replaced after 51,648 brake actions on average.

According to [Lav+07], the average replacement cost for all four brakes is approximately 1,000 \$ in 2007. With the average U.S. inflation rate of 1.85 %

from 2007-2014 and a Euro exchange rate of 1.3 in 2014, the equivalent replacement cost is 875 € in 2014. Distributed over 51,648 brake actions, the average brake wear cost $j_\mathrm{b}(\boldsymbol{x}(t),\boldsymbol{u}(t))$ amounts to $\lambda_\mathrm{b} = 0.017$ € for each brake action with λ_b being the brake wear weight. As discussed in section 3.1.1, the EE already has strong braking capabilities. The utilization of brake pads is only necessary if the EE is insufficient.

Similar to the transmission wear description, let $\varepsilon_\mathrm{b}(t)$ be the continuous change that describes the application of the brake pads from 0 (not applied) to 1 (fully applied to the wheels). In the discrete case, the brake pads can only be fully applied or not applied at all.

Thus, the average brake wear cost is described by:

$$j_\mathrm{b}(\boldsymbol{x}(t),\boldsymbol{u}(t)) = \lambda_\mathrm{b}\varepsilon_\mathrm{b}(t). \tag{4.8}$$

If the EE is able to bring the vehicle to a complete stop on its own according to the vehicle model, no braking cost is used. In reality, one may have to use the brake pads to ascertain that the vehicle truly comes to a complete stop and remains in that state. This kind of stabilizing braking at velocities close to zero is not further considered. Detailed brake wear models are not investigated in this thesis but can be part of future work.

4.3.4 Combined cost function

The combined cost function is composed of the previously introduced cost components:

$$j(\boldsymbol{x}(t),\boldsymbol{u}(t)) = j_\mathrm{e}(\boldsymbol{x}(t),\boldsymbol{u}(t)) + j_\mathrm{t}(t) + j_\mathrm{G}(\boldsymbol{x}(t),\boldsymbol{u}(t)) + j_\mathrm{b}(\boldsymbol{x}(t),\boldsymbol{u}(t)). \tag{4.9}$$

4.4 Constraints and regulations

The optimization considers several constraints and regulations. They range from vehicle internal physical constraints to traffic regulations. In this thesis, German traffic regulations are used. For further information on all existing regulations, the reader can turn to [Jan18].

In general, there are numerous rules and regulations in the real world, e.g., cooperative zipper merging in the case of lane closures (i.e., lane number reduction), or decisions about the right of way at small intersections and in traffic circles. This thesis only performs evaluations on a limited number of road configurations. The optimization shall only consider the constraints and regulations as described in the following sections. The inclusion of additional constraints, regulations, and road configurations can be part of future work.

4.4.1 Vehicle internal constraints

The vehicle internal constraints are discussed in section 3.1.1 and section 3.1.2. It is assumed that a gear shift requires a short time period Δt_{shift} to complete. The optimization shall not initiate a new gear shift before the previous gear shift is completed.

4.4.2 Travel comfort and jerk

Travel comfort is often associated with jerk [Wer+12]. The longitudinal jerk $\zeta(t)$ is the derivative of the longitudinal vehicle acceleration $a(t)$. The lateral jerk $\zeta_{\text{lat}}(t)$ is the derivative of the lateral acceleration $a_{\text{lat}}(t)$. One possibility to avoid strong jerk is to define an additional cost term. As this thesis uses monetary cost, a precise definition is difficult. Generally, there is no direct correspondence between monetary cost and travel comfort. Furthermore, the continuous range from "no discomfort" to "extreme discomfort" can be highly subjective. Thus, this thesis uses constraints instead of costs to avoid high amounts of jerk. In [Liu15] extensive studies are conducted regarding the longitudinal acceleration, deceleration, and jerk of a vast number of drivers. The longitudinal jerk during acceleration and deceleration are concentrated within the domain of -1.5 $\frac{\mathrm{m}}{\mathrm{s}^3}$ to 1.5 $\frac{\mathrm{m}}{\mathrm{s}^3}$. According to [TK13], longitudinal jerk up to a magnitude of 1.5 $\frac{\mathrm{m}}{\mathrm{s}^3}$ can be regarded as comfortable. According to recommendations of the American Association of State Highway and Transportation Officials [Ame01], roads should be constructed to keep the lateral jerk below a maximum lateral jerk $\zeta_{\mathrm{lat,max}}$ of 0.9 $\frac{\mathrm{m}}{\mathrm{s}^3}$. Therefore, the travel comfort constraints are

$$\zeta_{\mathrm{min}} \leq \zeta(t) \leq \zeta_{\mathrm{max}} \tag{4.10}$$

$$\zeta_{\mathrm{lat}}(t) \leq \zeta_{\mathrm{lat,max}} \tag{4.11}$$

for the longitudinal and lateral jerk respectively. While constant acceleration and deceleration do not produce any jerk, some jerk is unavoidable if the vehicle starts to accelerate from a stationary state, e.g., constant velocity. The jerk estimation in PEEMTO is described in section 4.8.4.

4.4.3 Speed limit

The ego-vehicle velocity should not exceed any speed limits if possible. If the optimization is not able to find any feasible solution, the speed limit can be relaxed.

4.4.4 Minimum velocity directive

Vehicles should not proceed too slowly in order to avoid disruption in the traffic flow. There are no precise definitions of the minimum velocity. In practice, drivers are expected to make decisions at their own discretion. The realization of a minimum cruise velocity in PEEMTO was already discussed in section 4.3.2. Despite having a reference minimum velocity, the ego-vehicle is, of course, allowed to choose lower velocities including full stop.

4.4.5 Lane change regulations

The lane change regulations used in this thesis consider the following rules:

- Keep-right directive: The regulation demands that drivers should try to change to the outer lane if they only plan on cruising. The purpose of the regulation is to create sufficient opportunities for overtaking maneuvers in the inner and center lanes.
- Left-side overtaking directive: Overtaking is only allowed left of the slower front vehicle.
- Multiple lane changes: Lane changes over several lanes without interruption are not allowed.
- Lane changes close to traffic lights: Changing lanes and overtaking in close proximity to traffic lights may enable a driver to catch the green phase of a traffic light. Although lane changes in front of traffic lights are not explicitly forbidden, these maneuvers may increase the chance of an accident. In this thesis, the optimization shall not plan any lane changes in close proximity to traffic lights, e.g., within a distance of 50 m.

4.4.6 Full intersection

The ego-vehicle shall not enter an intersection if the intersection or the lanes on the other side of the intersection are occupied by other vehicles and do not offer sufficient space for the ego-vehicle.

4.4.7 Velocity-dependent safety gaps

Sufficiently large spatial gaps between vehicles are of great importance to prevent accidents. Commonly used recommendations are the *one-second rule* and the *two-second rule*. On roads with speed limits below 80 $\frac{\text{km}}{\text{h}}$, the driver should keep a *one-second distance* $\Delta t_{\text{gap,min}}$ to the front vehicle. The one-second distance refers to the distance that the vehicle would traverse at the current velocity in one second. On roads with speed limits at or above 80 $\frac{\text{km}}{\text{h}}$, the driver should keep a *two-second distance* $\Delta t_{\text{gap,max}}$ to the front vehicle. The two-second distance refers to the distance that the vehicle would traverse at the current velocity in two seconds. The utilization of the safety gaps in PEEMTO is described in section 4.9.

4.4.8 Traffic lights

The ego-vehicle must not pass by a traffic light during its red phase. The length of the ego-vehicle body is not considered. The only part of the vehicle that shall be considered is the front bumper. The yellow phases are incorporated into the closest green phase.

4.4.9 Strict and optional constraints

Numerous strict constraints in combination with extremely difficult scenarios may leave the optimization without a feasible solution. In general, travel safety is more important than travel comfort and certain traffic regulations in emergency situations. Indeed, as previously mentioned, some regulations are not strictly followed by drivers in practice.

In this thesis, the physical limits of the ego-vehicle (i.e., braking, lateral stability, and the maximum battery current), traffic light phases, and collision avoidance are treated as strict constraints. All other constraints and regulations shall be followed unless the optimization is unable to find a solution.

More discussions are conducted in section 4.13.

In general, it is also possible to define additional costs instead of constraints. But it is often difficult to find objective formulations. Safety-related costs can be especially difficult to formulate in monetary form as the monetary cost of human injury and human life is hard to define from an ethical point of view.

4.5 Discrete optimization problem formulation

The HJBE is rarely directly used to compute the optimal solution in practice because retrieving the analytical solution is often infeasible. Instead, the corresponding discrete solution can be obtained through the corresponding discrete BE, which is solved through DP. With ever increasing discretization precision, the globally optimal discrete solution converges towards the corresponding HJBE solution. It is important to note that the globally optimal solution in the discrete case is only globally optimal with respect to the employed discretization. In general, the discrete solution can only be an approximation of the continuous solution and is therefore inherently suboptimal in that respect.

4.5.1 Bellman equation

The discretization with the time interval Δt uses the discrete time t_k with the index k with t_0 being the start time of the optimization:

$$t_k = t_0 + k\Delta t. \tag{4.12}$$

The discretization leads to the discrete state trajectory $\tilde{\boldsymbol{x}}(t_k)$ and the discrete control trajectory $\tilde{\boldsymbol{u}}(t_k)$ from t_0 to t_k. Let $\boldsymbol{x}(t_i)$ be a certain discrete state within $\tilde{\boldsymbol{x}}(t_k)$ at a certain discrete time t_i. It consists of the longitudinal position of the ego-vehicle $s(t_i)$, its lateral position $d(t_i)$, its velocity $v(t_i)$, its longitudinal acceleration $a(t_i)$, its lateral acceleration $a_{\text{lat}}(t_i)$, its gear level $G(t_i)$, and its battery charge $Q(t_i)$:

$$\boldsymbol{x}(t_i) = [s(t_i), d(t_i), v(t_i), a(t_i), a_{\text{lat}}(t_i), G(t_i), Q(t_i)]. \tag{4.13}$$

Let $\boldsymbol{u}(t_i)$ be a certain discrete state within $\tilde{\boldsymbol{u}}(t_k)$ at a certain discrete time t_i. In a vehicle that can also be controlled by the driver, it consists of the acceleration pedal position $u_{\text{a}}(t_i)$, the brake pedal position $u_{\text{b}}(t_i)$, the gear change $\Delta G(t_i)$, and the steering wheel angle $u_{\text{s}}(t_i)$:

$$\boldsymbol{u}(t_i) = [u_{\text{a}}(t_i), u_{\text{b}}(t_i), \Delta G(t_i), u_{\text{s}}(t_i)]. \tag{4.14}$$

Let $j(\tilde{\boldsymbol{x}}(t_k), \tilde{\boldsymbol{u}}(t_k))$ be the discrete transition cost function. Let $J(\tilde{\boldsymbol{x}}(t_k))$ be the discrete accumulated cost function. Let $j^*(\boldsymbol{x}(t_i), \boldsymbol{u}(t_i))$ be the optimal transition cost at the discrete time t_i. Let $J^*(\tilde{\boldsymbol{x}}(t_k))$ be the optimal accumulated cost at the discrete time t_k. Let $\boldsymbol{\Gamma}$ be the discrete set of all admissible discrete controls with respect to the employed discretization. For deterministic forward-backward dynamic programming (FBDP), the BE can be formulated in the recursive form:

$$J^*(\tilde{\boldsymbol{x}}(t_k)) = \min_{\boldsymbol{u}(t_k) \in \boldsymbol{\Gamma}} \left(j(\boldsymbol{x}(t_k), \boldsymbol{u}(t_k)) + \sum_{i=0}^{k-1} j^*(\boldsymbol{x}(t_i), \boldsymbol{u}(t_i)) \right). \tag{4.15}$$

More details about the BE are given in [Ber05] [Ber07].

4.5.2 Discrete problem reformulation

Although the original continuous optimization problem uses time t as argument, a formulation with respect to position s is actually better suited for the discrete DP optimization used in this thesis. The reasons are given in section 4.12. The discrete optimal decisions do not refer to discrete time but discrete positions. In the continuous formulation, describing the problem with respect to t is a necessity to ascertain that the differentiability with respect to time demanded by HJBE is always met. However, in the discrete case, it is possible to use a discrete trajectory tuple of discrete vectors instead of a continuously differentiable trajectory. The elements in the tuple must always have a strict temporal order that cannot be interchanged:

$$t_0 < t_1 < ... < t_i < ... < t_k. \tag{4.16}$$

Let s_i be the discrete position that corresponds to a discrete time t_i. As long as the vehicle is moving, both s_i and t_i increase. Special attention must be given to an idle vehicle that has stopped, e.g., at a traffic light. In this case, the position no longer increases, but the time still does. If the stopping position is s_i and the journey is temporarily halted, the corresponding t_i does not only describe the time of arrival $t_{i,\mathrm{toa}}$ at s_i but also the time of departure $t_{i,\mathrm{tod}}$ from s_i. Thus, t_i adopts two different values:

$$t_i = \begin{cases} t_{i,\mathrm{toa}} & \text{if } \; t = t_{i,\mathrm{toa}} \\ t_{i,\mathrm{tod}} & \text{if } \; t = t_{i,\mathrm{tod}} \end{cases} \tag{4.17}$$

depending on when the ego-vehicle stops and when it continues the journey. As t_i can adopt two different values for the same position s_i, the discrete time and the corresponding discrete position cannot be described by a function in the form of $t(s_i)$. But in the tuple, the pairs of $\{t_{i,\mathrm{toa}}, s_i\}$ and $\{t_{i,\mathrm{tod}}, s_i\}$ still have a clear order because $t_{i,\mathrm{toa}} < t_{i,\mathrm{tod}}$. If the vehicle is moving, t_i, $t_{i,\mathrm{toa}}$, and $t_{i,\mathrm{tod}}$ are the same.

Let $\tilde{\boldsymbol{x}}_k$ be the discrete state trajectory tuple from the start time t_0 to the discrete time t_k. Let $\boldsymbol{x}_i$ be the state vector within $\tilde{\boldsymbol{x}}_k$ at position s_i with $\boldsymbol{x}_0$ being the start state:

$$\tilde{\boldsymbol{x}}_k = (\boldsymbol{x}_0, \boldsymbol{x}_1, \boldsymbol{x}_2, ..., \boldsymbol{x}_i, ..., \boldsymbol{x}_k). \tag{4.18}$$

$\boldsymbol{x}_i$ consists of the time t_i, the lateral position d_i, the velocity v_i, the longitudinal acceleration a_i, the lateral acceleration $a_{\text{lat},i}$, the gear level G_i, and the battery charge Q_i in discrete form:

$$\boldsymbol{x}_i = [t_i, d_i, v_i, a_i, a_{\text{lat},i}, G_i, Q_i]. \tag{4.19}$$

Let $\tilde{\boldsymbol{u}}_k$ be the discrete control trajectory tuple from t_0 to t_k. Let $\boldsymbol{u}_i$ be the control vector within $\tilde{\boldsymbol{u}}_k$ at position s_i with $\boldsymbol{u}_0$ being the start control:

$$\tilde{\boldsymbol{u}}_k = (\boldsymbol{u}_0, \boldsymbol{u}_1, \boldsymbol{u}_2, ..., \boldsymbol{u}_i, ..., \boldsymbol{u}_k). \tag{4.20}$$

In a vehicle that can also be controlled by the driver, $\boldsymbol{u}_i$ consists of the acceleration pedal position $u_{\text{a},i}$, the brake pedal position $u_{\text{b},i}$, the change in gear level ΔG_i, and the steering wheel angle $u_{\text{s},i}$ in discrete form:

$$\boldsymbol{u}_i = [u_{\text{a},i}, u_{\text{b},i}, \Delta G_i, u_{\text{s},i}]. \tag{4.21}$$

Computing discrete optimal decisions at certain positions instead of points in time also leads to the consequence that the equidistant position interval Δs instead of the equidistant time interval Δt is used.

Let $\boldsymbol{\Gamma}_s$ be the discrete set of all admissible discrete controls with respect to the employed position discretization. The discrete optimization problem with position dependent decisions can be formulated in the recursive form:

$$J^*(\tilde{\boldsymbol{x}}_k) = \min_{\boldsymbol{u}_k \in \boldsymbol{\Gamma}_s} \left(j(\boldsymbol{x}_k, \boldsymbol{u}_k) + \sum_{i=0}^{k-1} j^*(\boldsymbol{x}_i, \boldsymbol{u}_i) \right). \tag{4.22}$$

As the optimal discrete state trajectory tuple $\tilde{\boldsymbol{x}}_k^*$ contains both discrete time and its corresponding discrete position, the optimal discrete state trajectory $\tilde{\boldsymbol{x}}^*(t_k)$ can be easily constructed from $\tilde{\boldsymbol{x}}_k^*$. If equidistant decisions with respect to time are a necessary requirement, a solution can be constructed through interpolation.

Another alteration to the original problem formulation refers to the optimization with respect to controls. One way to solve the discrete optimization problem is to directly use control variation in DP to find the optimal control trajectory. Given a certain state, it is possible to use a certain control and the system equations to compute the next state. As described in section 4.1, the primary goal of PEEMTO is to find the optimal state trajectory. The computation of the optimal control trajectory is optional. Instead of using control variations in the DP algorithm to find the optimal state trajectory, it is also possible to use different state transition variations to find the optimal discrete state trajectory directly as described in section 4.7. If demanded, the optimal control trajectory can be subsequently constructed using the vehicle model once the optimal state trajectory is available.
It is important to note that in reality, the controls are still necessary to realize the state transition. But the focus of this thesis is the computation of the optimal state trajectory. After the trajectory has been computed, it can be used to guide a subsequent controller. Thus, discrete optimization can also be described as cost minimization with respect to discrete states. Let $\boldsymbol{\Theta}_s$ be the discrete set of all admissible discrete states with respect to the employed position discretization. The recursive formulation can be described as:

$$J^*(\tilde{\boldsymbol{x}}_k) = \min_{\boldsymbol{x}_k \in \boldsymbol{\Theta}_s} \left(j(\boldsymbol{x}_k, \boldsymbol{u}_k) + \sum_{i=0}^{k-1} j^*(\boldsymbol{x}_i, \boldsymbol{u}_i) \right). \tag{4.23}$$

If the optimal control trajectory $\tilde{\boldsymbol{u}}_k^*$ is additionally computed using the optimal state trajectory $\tilde{\boldsymbol{x}}_k^*$ and the vehicle model, it is also the solution to equation (4.22). If the discrete time-dependent optimal trajectories $\tilde{\boldsymbol{x}}(t_k)$ and $\tilde{\boldsymbol{u}}(t_k)$ are retrieved from $\tilde{\boldsymbol{x}}_k^*$ and $\tilde{\boldsymbol{u}}_k^*$, they are also the solution to the original BE given in equation (4.15), albeit without equidistant time discretization. The discrete solution of the BE is the optimal discrete approximation of the corresponding HJBE problem. But due to finite discretization precision, the continuous solution can never be truly obtained in practice. More details regarding the DP algorithm are provided in sections 4.6 to 4.12.

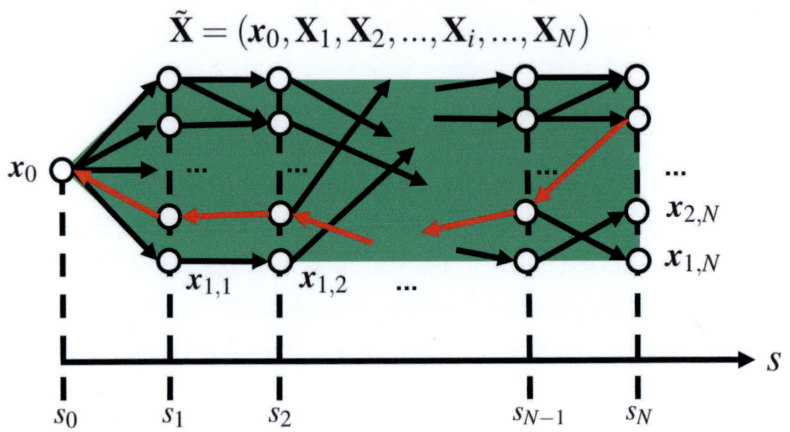

Figure 4.2: Structure of regular state graph used in PEEMTO. The green colored background of the state graph represents the abstract symbolic illustration of the state graph. States are represented by circles. Black arrows represent state transitions. Red arrows represent DP backtracing.

4.6 State graph structure

The structure of the regular state graph $\tilde{\mathbf{X}}$ used in PEEMTO is shown in Figure 4.2. The state graph consists of the start state of the ego-vehicle $\boldsymbol{x}_0$ and a certain number of decision stages $\mathbf{X}_i$. Each $\mathbf{X}_i$ refers to a discrete position s_i. The graph is directed and acyclic, i.e., the state transitions from one stage to the next are irreversible. Thus, reverse driving is omitted from the optimization. Let s_0 be the current position of the ego-vehicle. Let s_N be the last position within $\tilde{\mathbf{X}}$. The state graph can be described as:

$$\tilde{\mathbf{X}} = (\boldsymbol{x}_0, \mathbf{X}_1, \mathbf{X}_2, ..., \mathbf{X}_i, ..., \mathbf{X}_N). \tag{4.24}$$

Each decision stage $\mathbf{X}_i$ is associated with a certain number of discrete states $\boldsymbol{x}_{b,i}$ at position s_i. Let b the state enumeration index for states at a stage $\mathbf{X}_i$. A decision stage can be described by:

$$\mathbf{X}_i = \{\boldsymbol{x}_{1,i}, \boldsymbol{x}_{2,i}, ..., \boldsymbol{x}_{b,i}, ...\}. \tag{4.25}$$

A discrete state $\boldsymbol{x}_{b,i}$ is composed of its specific discrete state values, which are travel duration $t_{b,i}$, lateral position $d_{b,i}$, velocity $v_{b,i}$, longitudinal acceleration $a_{b,i}$, lateral acceleration $a_{\text{lat},b,i}$, gear level $G_{b,i}$, and battery charge $Q_{b,i}$. They all refer to the discrete position s_i:

$$\boldsymbol{x}_{b,i} = [t_{b,i}, d_{b,i}, v_{b,i}, a_{b,i}, a_{\text{lat},b,i}, G_{b,i}, Q_{b,i}]. \tag{4.26}$$

Each state transition from one stage to the next (e.g., the state transition from $x_{1,1}$ to $x_{1,2}$) is associated with a state transition cost. The cost formulation is described in section 4.3.

The graph has one single start state $\boldsymbol{x}_0$, which is the current state of the ego-vehicle. This also means that the first decision stage $\mathbf{X}_0$ only consists of $\boldsymbol{x}_0$. The graph has an open end, i.e., the last stage is just another intermediate stage with more than one end state. If only one end state is chosen, it usually has to be predefined using some form of heuristic. In PEEMTO, an open end is mandatory for the selection of the optimal end state. Further explanations are given in section 4.12. After each optimization, DP yields the optimal state trajectory tuple $\tilde{\boldsymbol{x}}_N^*$ composed of the optimal state $\boldsymbol{x}_i^*$ at each decision stage $\mathbf{X}_i$ from the start state $\boldsymbol{x}_0$ to the optimal end state $\boldsymbol{x}_N^*$:

$$\tilde{\boldsymbol{x}}_N^* = (\boldsymbol{x}_0, \boldsymbol{x}_1^*, \boldsymbol{x}_2^*, ..., \boldsymbol{x}_i^*, ..., \boldsymbol{x}_N^*). \tag{4.27}$$

In most real-world applications, the state graph only represents a subset of the original problem as computing the solution of the entire problem is computationally too complex. Thus, $\tilde{\boldsymbol{x}}^*$ is only optimal within $\tilde{\mathbf{X}}$. The range of $\tilde{\mathbf{X}}$, which stretches from s_0 to s_N, is the horizon $\Delta s_{\tilde{\mathbf{X}}}$. When $\tilde{\boldsymbol{x}}_N^*$ has been computed, PEEMTO declares the element $\boldsymbol{x}_1^*$ as the optimal next state and guides the vehicle towards it. Once the vehicle has reached s_1, a new state graph is constructed, and the new vehicle state is chosen as the new start state $\boldsymbol{x}_0$. Thus, the state graph has essentially moved the distance $\Delta s = s_1 - s_0$. Note that s_0, s_1, ..., s_N do not refer to the same positions in the world forever. As soon as a new state graph is constructed, they refer to new positions in the world. Indeed, the enumeration actually refers to the index of the decision stage.

In reality, the vehicle may not be able to precisely realize the optimal next state. The real-world deviation depends on the model precision, the possibly unknown disturbances, and the employed controller. In practice, the controller can only attempt to follow the computed trajectory to the best of its capability. As discussed in section 4.1, this thesis only investigates trajectory optimization and not the subsequent controller. Independent of the precise controller execution, PEEMTO does adapt to the new situation in the real world because it always starts the optimization with the currently available measurements. In the evaluations conducted in chapter 5, it is assumed that the ego-vehicle is able to realize the computed trajectory.

4.7 Forward-backward dynamic programming

DP can be used on discrete problems that do not contradict the PO. Generally, it must be possible to break down the original problem into simpler subproblems in a recursive manner, i.e., one part of the problem is initially solved and then the intermediate result is used to solve another part of the problem. It is often additionally assumed that a decision is only dependent on the previous decision. The problem described by the state graph in Figure 4.2 is a suitable example of the employment of DP. Once the state graph is defined, DP uses the BE to recursively compute optimal decisions until the entire optimization problem is solved.

The stagewise DP optimization involves two different steps. In the first step, all state transitions are evaluated for each stage. In the second step, the optimal trajectory is retrieved. In forward-backward dynamic programming (FBDP), DP starts at the start state and evaluates all state transitions for each stage while moving towards the last stage (forward process). Once the last stage is fully evaluated, an optimal end state is chosen. The optimal trajectory is retrieved, starting from the optimal end state and following optimal predecessor states towards the start state (backward process or backtracing).

During the forward process, DP evaluates all state transition costs $j(\boldsymbol{x}_{b,i-1}, \boldsymbol{x}_{c,i})$ from a stage $\mathbf{X}_{i-1}$ to the next stage $\mathbf{X}_i$ for all stages within the state graph $\tilde{\mathbf{X}}$. After a state transition cost is identified, PEEMTO evaluates if the transition violates any of the constraints as defined in section 4.4. Finally, it evaluates if the transition leads to collisions with other vehicles or traffic light violations, which are further explained in section 4.9 and section 4.11. Beginning from the decision stage $\mathbf{X}_1$ at s_1 onward, states start working with minimum accumulated costs of the states from the previous stage. The accumulated minimum cost $J^*(\boldsymbol{x}_{c,i})$ of a state $\boldsymbol{x}_{c,i}$ at stage $\mathbf{X}_i$ is the minimum sum of all possible transition costs $j(\boldsymbol{x}_{b,i-1}, \boldsymbol{x}_{c,i})$ and accumulated minimum costs $J^*(\boldsymbol{x}_{b,i-1})$ from all predecessor states $\boldsymbol{x}_{b,i-1}$ to the state $\boldsymbol{x}_{c,i}$:

$$J^*(\boldsymbol{x}_{c,i}) = \min_{\boldsymbol{x}_{b,i-1} \in \mathbf{X}_{i-1}} \Big(j(\boldsymbol{x}_{b,i-1}, \boldsymbol{x}_{c,i}) + J^*(\boldsymbol{x}_{b,i-1}) \Big). \tag{4.28}$$

After the states of a decision stage are fully evaluated, every state with the exception of the start state has one unique optimal predecessor state unless constraint violations forbid it. A state may have several or no successors.

By repeating the optimization described in equation (4.28) for all decision stages, the discrete optimization described in equation (4.23) of section 4.5.2 is solved.

During backtracing, the optimal state trajectory is constructed by following the identified tuple of optimal states from the optimal end state $\boldsymbol{x}_N^*$ on the last stage $\mathbf{X}_N$ to the start state $\boldsymbol{x}_0$.

In state graphs with one single end state, the optimal end is naturally the single existing end state. If the horizon end is open, the choice of the optimal end state may not be clear. The selection of the optimal end state at the end of the horizon is discussed in section 4.12. If the horizon reaches the end of the journey, it is likely that the vehicle has to stop. In this case, there is indeed only one single end state, namely the complete stop of the vehicle. There is also the possibility that the passenger takes over control at some point during the journey, i.e., the route is not as long as the entire journey. In this case, PEEMTO never encounters the end of the journey.

As discussed in section 4.1, the variation of controls like acceleration pedal position and brake pedal position is not considered in PEEMTO. Velocities and gear choice are of particular importance if energy-efficient driving is discussed. The discretization of velocity is able to precisely capture speed limits, which are always integer numbers. If controls like acceleration pedal position or brake pedal position were used instead of velocity variation, the optimization would not necessarily lead to velocities that match the speed limits. If, for example, the continuous optimal cruise velocity is the same as the speed limit, the discrete optimization may never choose the speed limit as the optimal result because the finite discretization precision may not include this possibility. This is the primary reason why the discrete optimization problem is reformulated in equation (4.23) to conduct the optimization using state variations.

4.8 Implicit discretization

If states $\boldsymbol{x}_{b,i}$ are fully expanded in the state graph $\tilde{\mathbf{X}}$, the optimization has to deal with numerous continuous state dimensions. This leads to high computational complexity.

An observation made during the DP computation is that some state components actually cannot deviate from the other state components independently. For example, while the gear level can deviate from the velocity within a large operation range, time progression is actually bound to the position and the velocity trajectory. The simplification used in this work is to remove several dependent state dimensions from the explicit search process. The only state components that are explicitly used in the discretization during the DP optimization are the longitudinal position, lateral position, velocity, and gear level. All other time components are computed along the possible trajectories of the remaining state components. This strategy shall be called *implicit discretization* in this thesis because some state components are not explicitly regarded during the search but rather implicitly chosen along the possible trajectories of the remaining state components. This leads to the implicit evaluation of the omitted state components during the search process.

To the best knowledge of the author, the proposed implicit discretization has not been used in other scientific publications with the exception of the implicit discretization of other vehicles [Zie+16]. The evaluation of other vehicles is discussed in section 4.9.

The implicit discretization does not exclude the employment of other forms of approximate dynamic programming and can be combined with other search space reduction strategies, e.g., [HT09] [Wah15]. In this thesis, only implicit discretization is used.

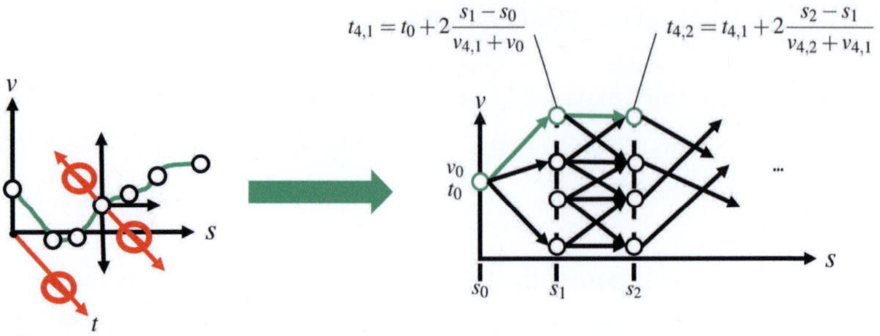

Figure 4.3: Implicit discretization of time. Explicit expansion of the time dimension is removed from the search space. Time progression is computed along possible velocity trajectories with respect to position.

4.8.1 Travel duration

The implicit discretization of time shall be used as an example to explain the general strategy. Figure 4.3 shows how the travel duration is computed along different trajectories of velocity with respect to position. The travel duration from $\boldsymbol{x}_0$ to any states $\boldsymbol{x}_{b,1}$ on the first decision stage can be computed using the distance $s_1 - s_0$, and the average velocity of v_0 and $v_{b,1}$. This leads to $t_{b,1}$ at $\boldsymbol{x}_{b,1}$ without any explicit discretization of time:

$$t_{b,1} = t_0 + 2\frac{s_1 - s_0}{v_{b,1} + v_0}. \tag{4.29}$$

The procedure is similar for transitions between regular decision stages. After all possible transitions from a state $\boldsymbol{x}_{c,i+1}$ to all states on the previous stage $\mathbf{X}_i$ have been evaluated, $\boldsymbol{x}_{c,i+1}$ knows its optimal predecessor at $\mathbf{X}_i$. For the purpose of explanation, let $\boldsymbol{x}_{b,i}$ be the optimal predecessor of $\boldsymbol{x}_{c,i+1}$ at s_i without loss of generality. The travel duration from $\boldsymbol{x}_{b,i}$ to $\boldsymbol{x}_{c,i+1}$ can be computed using their distance between s_i and s_{i+1} as well as the average velocity of $\boldsymbol{x}_{b,i}$ and $\boldsymbol{x}_{c,i+1}$. The discrete time $t_{c,i+1}$ of $\boldsymbol{x}_{c,i+1}$ is therefore the sum of $t_{b,i}$ and the incremental travel duration:

$$t_{c,i+1} = t_{b,i} + 2\frac{s_{i+1} - s_i}{v_{c,i+1} + v_{b,i}}. \tag{4.30}$$

4.8.2 Battery charge

The implicit discretization of the battery charge or SOC uses the vehicle model to compute the battery current and the resulting charge variation but otherwise follows the same procedure as the implicit discretization of travel duration. The computation of the battery charge variation is discussed in section 3.1.1. Let $Q_{b,i}$ be the battery charge of a state $\boldsymbol{x}_{b,i}$ at stage $\mathbf{X}_i$. Let $\Delta Q\left(\boldsymbol{x}_{b,i}, \boldsymbol{x}_{c,i+1}\right)$ be the change in battery charge from $\boldsymbol{x}_{b,i}$ to another state $\boldsymbol{x}_{c,i+1}$ on the next stage $\mathbf{X}_{i+1}$. The resulting battery charge of $\boldsymbol{x}_{c,i+1}$ is:

$$Q_{c,i+1} = Q_{b,i} + \Delta Q\left(\boldsymbol{x}_{b,i}, \boldsymbol{x}_{c,i+1}\right). \tag{4.31}$$

4.8.3 Longitudinal and lateral acceleration

The implicit discretization of the longitudinal acceleration uses the travel duration $t_{c,i+1} - t_{b,i}$ from a state $\boldsymbol{x}_{b,i}$ at stage $\mathbf{X}_i$ to a state $\boldsymbol{x}_{c,i+1}$ on the next stage $\mathbf{X}_{i+1}$ and the corresponding velocities:

$$a_{c,i+1} = \frac{v_{c,i+1} - v_{b,i}}{t_{c,i+1} - t_{b,i}}. \tag{4.32}$$

Different from the implicit discretization of the travel duration, it is not necessary to propagate the acceleration over multiple stages because the acceleration is directly computed from the velocities and the travel duration. The lateral acceleration $a_{\text{lat},c,i+1}$ is directly computed from the average velocity and the lateral vehicle model as discussed in section 3.1.2.

4.8.4 Longitudinal and lateral jerk

The longitudinal and lateral jerk are derived from the longitudinal and lateral acceleration. In fact, the jerk estimation is the primary reason why the two forms of acceleration are part of the state definition. The jerk is estimated from two subsequent discrete accelerations. Let $a_{c,i+1}$ be the longitudinal acceleration, and let $a_{\text{lat},c,i+1}$ be the lateral acceleration of a state $\boldsymbol{x}_{c,i+1}$ at stage $\mathbf{X}_{i+1}$. Let $a_{b,i}$ be the longitudinal acceleration, and let $a_{\text{lat},b,i}$ be the lateral acceleration of a state $\boldsymbol{x}_{b,i}$ at the previous stage $\mathbf{X}_i$. The longitudinal jerk $\zeta_{c,i+1}$ of $\boldsymbol{x}_{c,i+1}$ is:

$$\zeta_{c,i+1} = \frac{a_{c,i+1} - a_{b,i}}{t_{c,i+1} - t_{b,i}}. \tag{4.33}$$

The lateral jerk $\zeta_{\text{lat},c,i+1}$ of $\boldsymbol{x}_{c,i+1}$ is:

$$\zeta_{\text{lat},c,i+1} = \frac{a_{\text{lat},c,i+1} - a_{\text{lat},b,i}}{t_{c,i+1} - t_{b,i}}. \tag{4.34}$$

4.8.5 Gear shift progress

As previously discussed, the gear level expands its own state dimension within the state graph. But as mentioned in section 3.1.1 and section 4.4, it is assumed that a gear shift requires one second to complete in the case of the REM-2030 transmission. As the optimization may have a higher update rate than 1 Hz, the new optimization may have already started before the gear shift is completed. To solve the problem, the point in time of the last gear shift within a trajectory is saved and propagated to succeeding decision stages. A new gear shift can only be performed if the previous gear shift has been fully realized.

4.8.6 Brake pad utilization

Brake pad utilization is not part of the state vector but still needed in the optimization. Similar to acceleration, the necessity for brake pad utilization can be directly computed. In this case, the vehicle model is needed. Using the brake torque demand associated with a state transition, it is possible to evaluate if the torque demand exceeds the engine's capability. If this is the case, the brake pads are necessary. If the maximum brake torque of the engine is exceeded, the engine will still absorb the maximum amount. The remaining brake torque demand has to be met by the brake pads. As discussed in section 3.1.1, there is a maximum brake force depending on the maximum brake slip. If the maximum brake force of the brake pads is insufficient, the state transition is not feasible.

4.8.7 Coasting

In the case of the REM-2030 EV, it is possible to open the clutch and separate the engine from the transmission. Alternatively, it is also possible to simply target operation points in the engine efficiency map that do not lead to any torque, i.e., there is no power flow and no additional resistance. As in the case of brake pad utilization, the state transitions lead to different engine torque demands that also include low and no torque. Therefore, coasting is already implicitly evaluated without creating any additional steps.

4.9 Other vehicles

The other vehicles all have their own states within the state graph $\tilde{\mathbf{X}}$ for every state of the ego-vehicle as illustrated in Figure 4.4. Let h be the vehicle index of another vehicle that can be detected by the sensors of the ego-vehicle. The state $\boldsymbol{x}_{h,b,i}$ of another vehicle always refers to a certain ego-vehicle state $\boldsymbol{x}_{b,i}$ at a certain decision stage $\mathbf{X}_i$. Note that the state $\boldsymbol{x}_{h,b,i}$ is usually different for every ego-vehicle state, even for the same vehicle h.

At the beginning of the optimization, the ego-vehicle is in the start state $\boldsymbol{x}_0$. The start states of the other vehicles $\boldsymbol{x}_{h,0}$ are the states as observed by the sensors of the ego-vehicle. In this thesis, the range of an ACC long-range radar of 250 m shall be used [Win+15] [Bos16]. Thus, only vehicles within a 250 m radius of the ego-vehicle are considered in the optimization. The state

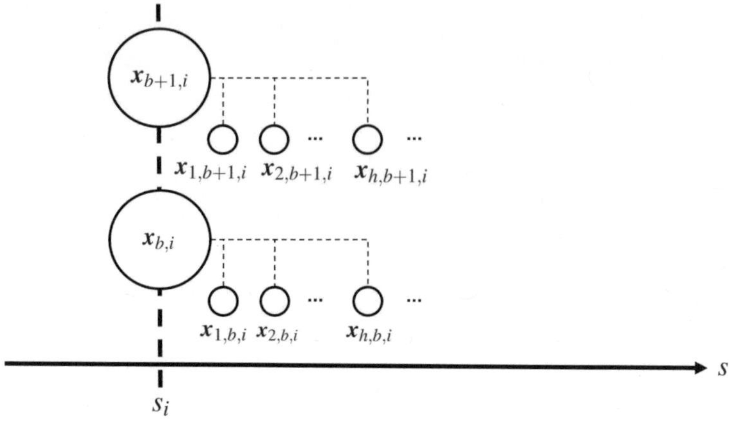

Figure 4.4: The detected other vehicles have their own states. The states of the other vehicles $\boldsymbol{x}_{h,b,i}$ in the state graph always refer to a certain ego-vehicle state $\boldsymbol{x}_{b,i}$. The state of a vehicle h can be different for different ego-vehicle states.

of another vehicle $\boldsymbol{x}_{h,b,i}$ consists of the vehicle's point in time $t_{h,b,i}$, lateral position $d_{h,b,i}$, and velocity $v_{h,b,i}$:

$$\boldsymbol{x}_{h,b,i} = \left[t_{h,b,i}, d_{h,b,i}, v_{h,b,i}\right]. \tag{4.35}$$

In theory, each vehicle can expand its own state space and have its own motion trajectory. But this would quickly lead to an infeasible computational complexity. Therefore, implicit discretization is used for the other vehicles during the optimization, which has some similarities to the approach used in [Zie+16]. Further details are given in section 4.9.3.

The evaluation of other vehicles in the optimization is divided into three steps: Identification of relevant neighbors, collision avoidance during state transition evaluation, and progression of other vehicles within the state graph. Further explanations are given in section 4.9.1 to section 4.9.3.

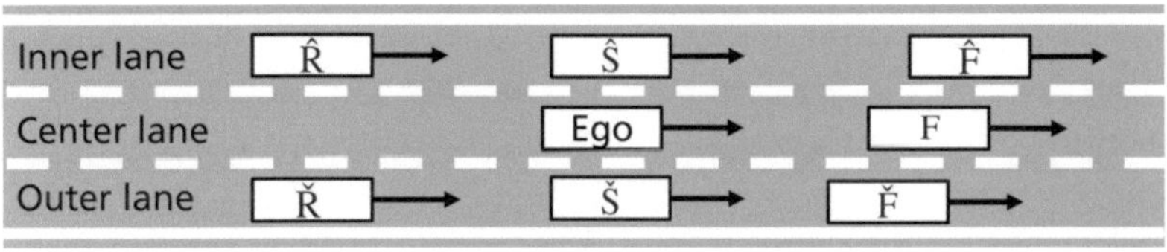

Figure 4.5: Relevant neighbors of the ego-vehicle. The neighbor type symbols F̂, F, F̌, Ŝ, Š, R̂, Ř denote the type of neighbor.

In this thesis, the optimization treats the other vehicles as deterministic constraints. Safety-related probabilistic costs can be difficult to formulate in monetary form as the monetary cost of human injury and human life can be difficult to define from an ethical point of view. Existing probabilistic approaches of other authors are mentioned in chapter 2. The extension of PEEMTO to incorporate probabilistic monetary costs to deal with collision avoidance is possible but requires significantly more debate.

4.9.1 Identification of closest neighbors

Not all detected vehicles are equally important to the ego-vehicle. In fact, PEEMTO only considers seven of the closest neighbors in all lanes surrounding the ego-vehicle to evaluate collision avoidance. Naturally, the number of neighbors may also be smaller than seven if there are very few cars on the road. An illustration of the closest seven neighbors is given in Figure 4.5. Without loss of generality, they shall be denoted by the neighbor type symbols F̂, F, F̌, Ŝ, Š, R̂, Ř without loss of generality. A vehicle right behind the ego-vehicle in the same lane is not deemed as relevant.

The neighbor type symbol denotes the role of the neighbor. For example, neighbor F is the front neighbor of the ego-vehicle in the same lane. The vehicles Ŝ and Š are vehicles adjacent to the ego-vehicle, left and right respectively. Apart from the neighbor type symbol, the neighbors still have their regular vehicle index h. Thus, if neighbor F̂ has, e.g., the vehicle index

$h = 13$ and refers to the ego-vehicle state $\boldsymbol{x}_{b,i}$, the state $\boldsymbol{x}_{\hat{\mathrm{F}},b,i}$ of neighbor F̂ is the same as the state $\boldsymbol{x}_{13,b,i}$.

Depending on the situation, certain neighbors may not exist. Sometimes, the role of a neighbor may be somewhat ambiguous. For example, a vehicle that is in the process of changing lanes may be occupying both the inner lane and the center lane. In this case, it takes on the role of both F̂ and F. As these topics are implementation details, the explanation shall not be expanded any further.

If the state transition does not involve a lane change, only vehicle F is relevant to the ego-vehicle. If a lane change to the left is evaluated, only the vehicles F̂, F, Ŝ, and R̂ are relevant. The lane change to the left can only be considered if vehicle Ŝ does not exist. If a lane change to the right is evaluated, only the vehicles F, F̌, Š, and Ř are relevant. The lane change to the right can only be considered if vehicle Š does not exist. For each state transition, PEEMTO must identify the relevant neighbors. The identification of closest neighbors takes place before new state transitions to the next stage are evaluated.

The velocities of the closest neighbors also have an impact on the position discretization. As described in Table A.11 in the appendix, PEEMTO uses different position discretizations depending on the speed limit. If the average velocity of the closest neighbors is below the speed limit, the average velocity replaces the speed limit and guides the discretization instead.

4.9.2 Collision avoidance during state transition evaluations

In order to evaluate possible collisions, PEEMTO uses the states $\boldsymbol{x}_{h,b,i}$ of the other vehicles that are saved at the most recently evaluated stage $\mathbf{X}_i$ through implicit discretization as described in section 4.9.3. If the optimization has just started, the currently observed states $\boldsymbol{x}_{h,0}$ of the other vehicles are used.

The evaluation of the numerous state transitions between decision stages is the most time-consuming part of the optimization. As the SDM described in section 3.4.2 consists of many computation steps, it is beneficial to avoid using the SDM during state transition evaluations in order to reduce computational complexity. The next states of the other vehicles in $\mathbf{X}_{i+1}$ are not computed, i.e., the other vehicles at stage $\mathbf{X}_i$ are not moved to stage $\mathbf{X}_{i+1}$ during the collision evaluation. Thus, essentially, a snapshot of the other vehicles are taken. However, PEEMTO does move the ego-vehicle to the next state in $\mathbf{X}_{i+1}$. An example illustration of collision avoidance for a lane change to the left is given in Figure 4.6.

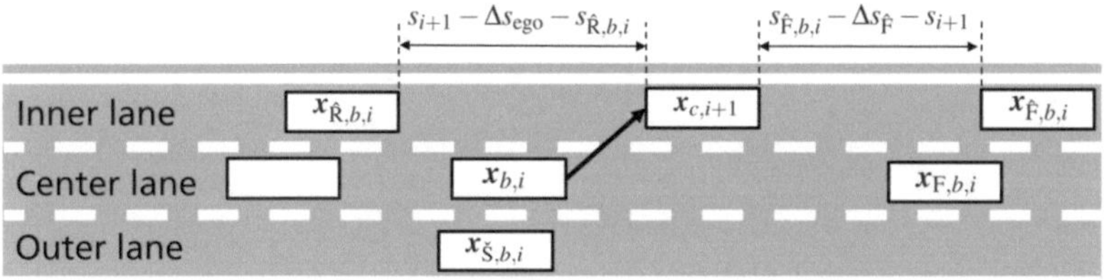

Figure 4.6: Example of collision evaluation for a certain ego-vehicle state transition from $\boldsymbol{x}_{b,i}$ to $\boldsymbol{x}_{c,i+1}$, involving a potential lane change of the ego-vehicle from the center lane to the inner lane. The position snapshot of the neighbors referring to the ego-vehicle state $\boldsymbol{x}_{b,i}$ is shown. The snapshot of the other vehicles refers to $\boldsymbol{x}_{b,i}$. The other vehicles are not moved during the state transition evaluation. Therefore, no driver model is used. PEEMTO evaluates the spatial gaps of the new state $\boldsymbol{x}_{c,i+1}$ in relation to the states of the neighbors.

In order to evaluate the gaps between the ego-vehicle and the neighbors, the time gap thresholds $\Delta t_{\text{gap,min}}$ and $\Delta t_{\text{gap,max}}$ described in section 4.4 shall be used. In a state transition from $\boldsymbol{x}_{b,i}$ to $\boldsymbol{x}_{c,i+1}$, the next position of the ego-vehicle's front is $s_{c,i+1}$, the next lateral position is $d_{c,i+1}$, and the next velocity is $v_{c,i+1}$. Let Δs_{ego} be the vehicle length of the ego-vehicle. The rear position of the ego-vehicle after the lane change is, therefore, $s_{c,i+1} - \Delta s_{\text{ego}}$. Let $s_{\check{\mathrm{F}},b,i}$ be the front position of vehicle Ḟ with reference to the ego-vehicle state $\boldsymbol{x}_{b,i}$. Let $\Delta s_{\check{\mathrm{F}}}$ be the vehicle length of vehicle F̌. The rear position of vehicle F̌ is therefore $s_{\check{\mathrm{F}},b,i} - \Delta s_{\check{\mathrm{F}}}$. The notations of the other neighbors follow the same pattern. As described in section 4.4, $\Delta t_{\text{gap,min}}$ of one second should be used for urban scenarios up to a speed limit of 70 $\frac{\text{km}}{\text{h}}$ and $\Delta t_{\text{gap,max}}$ of two seconds should be used otherwise. The collision evaluation largely follows these rules. But as the other vehicles, including the neighbors, do not move during the collision evaluation, while the ego-vehicle does move, a slight adaptation is used within PEEMTO. $\Delta t_{\text{gap,min}}$ shall always be used for the gap computation with respect to the front neighbors F̌, F, F̌, and $\Delta t_{\text{gap,max}}$ shall always be used for the gap computation with respect to the rear neighbors R̂, Ř. Thus, for a lane change to the left, the collision avoidance constraints

$$s_{\hat{\mathrm{F}},b,i} - \Delta s_{\hat{\mathrm{F}}} - s_{i+1} \geq v_{c,i+1} \Delta t_{\text{gap,min}} \tag{4.36}$$

$$s_{\mathrm{F},b,i} - \Delta s_{\mathrm{F}} - s_{i+1} \geq v_{c,i+1} \Delta t_{\text{gap,min}} \tag{4.37}$$

$$s_{i+1} - \Delta s_{\text{ego}} - s_{\hat{\mathrm{R}},b,i} \geq v_{\hat{\mathrm{R}},b,i} \Delta t_{\text{gap,max}} \tag{4.38}$$

are used. For a lane change to the right, the collision avoidance constraints

$$s_{\check{\mathrm{F}},b,i} - \Delta s_{\check{\mathrm{F}}} - s_{i+1} \geq v_{c,i+1} \Delta t_{\text{gap,min}} \tag{4.39}$$

$$s_{\mathrm{F},b,i} - \Delta s_{\mathrm{F}} - s_{i+1} \geq v_{c,i+1} \Delta t_{\text{gap,min}} \tag{4.40}$$

$$s_{i+1} - \Delta s_{\text{ego}} - s_{\check{\mathrm{R}},b,i} \geq v_{\check{\mathrm{R}},b,i} \Delta t_{\text{gap,max}} \tag{4.41}$$

are used.

After all ego-vehicle state transitions from a stage $\mathbf{X}_i$ to the next stage $\mathbf{X}_{i+1}$ have been evaluated, the minimum accumulated costs of all feasible ego-vehicle states at $\mathbf{X}_{i+1}$ are found. Only collision-free transitions are chosen.

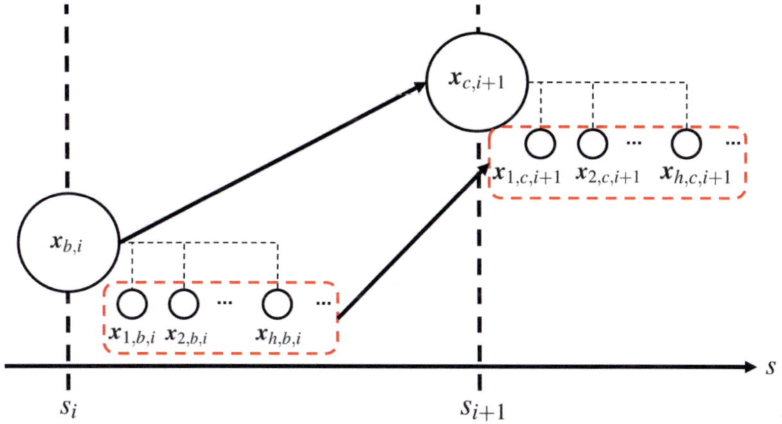

Figure 4.7: After all ego-vehicle state transitions between the stages $\mathbf{X}_i$ and $\mathbf{X}_{i+1}$ at s_i and s_{i+1} are evaluated, the transitions of the other vehicles are identified. For a state $\boldsymbol{x}_{b,i}$, whose optimal successor state is $\boldsymbol{x}_{c,i+1}$, the states $\boldsymbol{x}_{h,b,i}$ of the other vehicles referring to $\boldsymbol{x}_{b,i}$ change to their new states $\boldsymbol{x}_{h,c,i+1}$ referring to $\boldsymbol{x}_{c,i+1}$. The transitions of the other vehicles are realized through the SDM.

4.9.3 Progression of other vehicles in the state graph

Once all state transitions of a stage $\mathbf{X}_i$ are evaluated, the most time-consuming part is completed. The next step is to move the other vehicles from $\mathbf{X}_i$ to the next stage $\mathbf{X}_{i+1}$. As previously mentioned, the other vehicles cannot be allowed to expand their own state space because such a step would drastically increase the search space. Therefore, implicit discretization is used to move the other vehicles. An example illustration is provided in Figure 4.7.

After the evaluation of the state transitions, the ego-vehicle states $\boldsymbol{x}_{c,i+1}$ at $\mathbf{X}_{i+1}$ know their optimal ego-vehicle predecessor states $\boldsymbol{x}_{b,i}$ at $\mathbf{X}_i$. The other vehicles associated with the optimal predecessor states are now moved to the corresponding states at $\mathbf{X}_{i+1}$ using the SDM described in section 3.4.2 with the default parameters given in Table A.5 in the appendix.

When the other vehicles are moved, they treat the ego-vehicle as yet another vehicle. As the states of the other vehicles are always associated with an ego-vehicle state, the other vehicles and the ego-vehicle all have the same travel duration but otherwise may have completely different state components.

4.10 Lane changes and keep-right directive

During a lane change, the vehicle has a lateral movement component and traverses a slightly longer distance for the same change in longitudinal direction. Furthermore, if the road is not straight, i.e., has some curvature, the outer lane leads to a slightly longer distance than the inner lane. It seems reasonable to use the slight changes in driven distance due to the previously stated reasons to formulate lane change penalties. This would, e.g., encourage the optimization to choose shorter lanes when facing road curvature, which is also common practice for Olympic runners.

However, the keep-right directive described in section 4.4 demands that the vehicle should try to choose the outer lane during cruising, even if the vehicle is in a left turn curve. Therefore, the previously described aspects are not further considered in the optimization, i.e., lane changes do not lead to a shorter or longer driven distance from the perspective of the optimization. If two state transitions lead to the same amount of cost and one of the two transitions leads to a lane change to the right, the optimization shall prefer the lane change to the right. In practice, this definition leads to the consequence that the optimization prefers relatively late overtaking maneuvers, i.e., the optimization prefers to first approach the front vehicle in the same lane before changing to the left adjacent lane in order to begin the overtaking procedure. Furthermore, PEEMTO is unlikely to overtake more than one vehicle at a time. If the lateral discretization divides the width of the lane into separate states, the lane change shall not be interrupted, unless there is a safety concern.

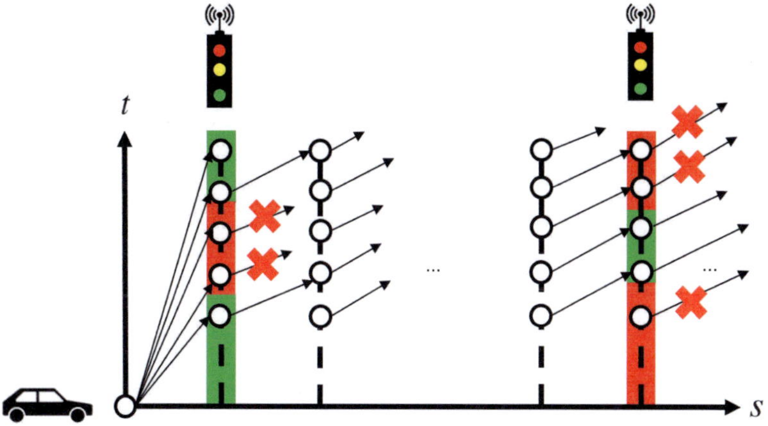

Figure 4.8: Optimization with respect to traffic light phases in the state graph. The yellow phases of the traffic lights are incorporated into the closest green phases. Through implicit discretization, the time of arrival at the traffic light can be computed. States that refer to a red phase are only feasible if the velocity component of the state is zero, i.e., the ego-vehicle stops. The ego-vehicle cannot continue while it is within a red phase.

In practice, drivers do not necessarily follow the keep-right directive. As previously discussed, using shorter lanes in strong curvatures can be energy-efficient. In general, traffic regulations can be at odds with other optimization criteria. An interesting topic for future work is the question of if and how certain regulations can be occasionally ignored to improve the optimization. This question is not only an engineering problem but also has legal aspects. Within the scope of this work, the keep-right directive is enforced, unless safety constraints forbid it.

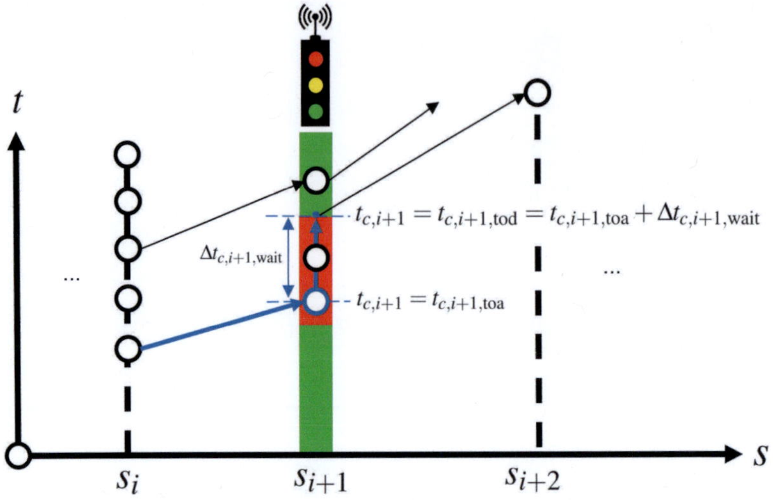

Figure 4.9: If the state transition leads into a red phase, the vehicle has to wait at the red traffic light until it turns green. In this case, a distinction between time of arrival and time of departure must be made.

4.11 Traffic lights

PEEMTO treats traffic light phases as deterministic constraints. In PEEMTO, a yellow traffic light phase is by definition part of the closest green phase. Thus, PEEMTO only distinguishes between red and green phases. Of course, there can also be more conservative definitions, e.g., merging a yellow phase with the closest red phase or splitting a yellow phase between the closest red and green phase. As traffic lights are dynamic obstacles, PEEMTO only responds to traffic lights within the regular horizon $\tilde{\mathbf{X}}$. The reaction of other vehicles to the traffic light within the optimization follows the SDM.

The optimization only notices a traffic light when the state transition evaluation has reached the decision stage that is closest to the traffic light. The positions of traffic lights can either match the position discretization, or they are situated between decision stages. If there is a traffic light between two stages s_i and s_{i+1}, the optimization simply assumes that the traffic light is situated at s_i. In practice, the ego-vehicle either stops directly at the traffic light or a few meters in front of it depending on the real-world traffic light position and the employed position discretization.

Figure 4.8 and Figure 4.9 illustrate how PEEMTO evaluates the possibilites to pass traffic lights. Let there be a traffic light associated to the position s_{i+1}. Let the stage $\mathbf{X}_i$ be already fully evaluated. Thus, the travel duration $t_{b,i}$ at each state $\boldsymbol{x}_{b,i}$ is already computed through implicit discretization. PEEMTO now evaluates the state transitions between $\mathbf{X}_i$ and $\mathbf{X}_{i+1}$. The transition from a state $\boldsymbol{x}_{b,i}$ to a state $\boldsymbol{x}_{c,i+1}$ is initially evaluated without incorporating the traffic light. Using $t_{b,i}$, the time $t_{c,i+1}$ of $\boldsymbol{x}_{c,i+1}$ is computed through implicit discretization. With the computed $t_{c,i+1}$, it is possible to evaluate if the ego-vehicle will meet a red phase. If that is not the case, there is no additional penalty for the state transition.

If the state transition does meet a red phase, the evaluation has to be adapted. In this case, the state $\boldsymbol{x}_{c,i+1}$ can only be feasible if the velocity is zero, i.e., the state refers to a complete stop of the ego-vehicle. An example illustration is shown in Figure 4.9. Due to the red light, the ego-vehicle must initially remain at s_{i+1} and wait for the traffic light to turn green. As discussed in section 4.5.2, if the ego-vehicle has to wait, the time of arrival and the time of departure are no longer the same point in time. In this case, the additional time the ego-vehicle has to wait at the red traffic light must be added. Let $t_{c,i+1,\text{toa}}$ be the time of arrival, and let $t_{c,i+1,\text{tod}}$ be the time of departure in the example. Let $\Delta t_{c,i+1,\text{wait}}$ be the time duration from $t_{c,i+1,\text{toa}}$ until the end of the red phase, which is also the time of departure. In general, a time component $t_{c,i+1}$ adopts the time of arrival $t_{c,i+1,\text{toa}}$ if the ego-vehicle does not need to wait. It adopts the time of departure

$$t_{c,i+1,\text{tod}} = t_{c,i+1,\text{toa}} + \Delta t_{c,i+1,\text{wait}} \tag{4.42}$$

if the ego-vehicle has to wait. Thus, the longer travel duration will naturally have a direct impact on the travel duration cost.

The traffic light evaluation for a state transition is only performed if there is no other vehicle between the ego-vehicle and the traffic light for that specific state transition. If there are other vehicles between the ego-vehicle and the red traffic light, the ego-vehicle adapts to the waiting front vehicle in front of it. The SDM driver model used in the optimization predicts how a vehicle decelerates in front of a red traffic light or behind another decelerating vehicle. But it does not predict how the vehicle continues the journey once the traffic light turns green. In fact, the assumption is that the vehicle does not move. If there are other idle vehicles ahead of the ego-vehicle and if PEEMTO cannot overtake them, PEEMTO will lead the ego-vehicle to a full stop behind another vehicle and waits until the other vehicles start to move.

In order to avoid the red phases of a traffic light or at least mitigate the disadvantages of red phases, there are roughly three main strategies if the phases are known in advance:

- Do not decelerate if the traffic light is about to change to the green phase.
- Drive more quickly to catch the green phase before the traffic light changes to red.
- If the red phase of the traffic light is unavoidable, move slowly towards it. The assumption is that arriving at a red traffic light early does not lead to any advantages.

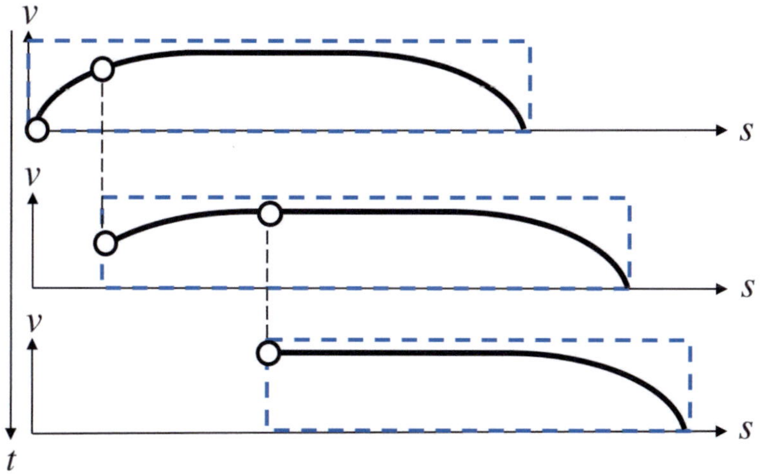

Figure 4.10: Illustration of trajectory optimization without terminal cost. The finite horizon is illustrated as a blue box with dashed edges. The computed velocity trajectory resides within the horizon. The horizon moves along with the ego-vehicle. Without a terminal cost, the velocity will usually drop to some extent at the end of the horizon because deceleration often leads to less energy consumption.

Within the constraints of PEEMTO, the second idea can be difficult to follow because PEEMTO is not allowed to plan velocities that are faster than the speed limit unless there is an emergency. If the optimal velocity is already the speed limit, it is likely that PEEMTO is already choosing the speed limit. The other two ideas are more likely choices within the PEEMTO algorithm although PEEMTO does not explicitly realize rules as in the case of truly rule-based systems. Instead, favorable decisions are contained within favorable trajectories.

4.12 Long-range auxiliary horizon extension

The optimization is rarely able to incorporate the entire route because it could be stretched out over a long distance and therefore lead to high computational complexity. For a finite horizon, the computational complexity can be kept in check. But the optimal end state $\boldsymbol{x}_N^*$ at the end of the horizon is usually unknown because the route usually does not end at the final stage of the horizon.

A finite horizon that does incorporate the end of the route needs some kind of optimization estimation beyond the horizon. Otherwise, the undefined behavior at the end of the horizon can lead to problems in practice. An example is the deceleration at the end of the horizon, which is illustrated in Figure 4.10. On even straight roads, the optimization will usually compute a trajectory that favors lower velocities towards the end of the horizon although the journey is far from over. This is due to the fact that the optimization within a finite horizon only considers what happens within the finite horizon. From the perspective of the optimization, the route ends with the horizon although in reality the route may be far from over. As the optimization only refers to the finite horizon and because deceleration usually leads to less energy consumption or even energy recuperation, some amount of deceleration at the end of the finite horizon is often part of the computed trajectory. As the optimization only uses the first element in the computed trajectory, the deterioration of the result at the end of the horizon may not always be visible. But it can have a negative impact if the next optimal decision heavily depends on the entire optimal trajectory. Due to this problem, there needs to be some form of prediction beyond the finite horizon.

This section discusses two strategies to estimate the optimal behavior beyond the horizon. The first method shall be called the stationary horizon extension (SHE). The second method is the novel long-range auxiliary horizon extension (LRAHE) proposed in this thesis.

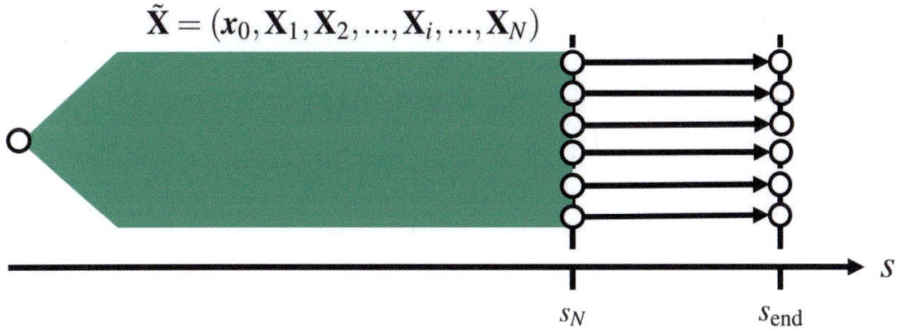

Figure 4.11: Stationary horizon extension (SHE). The abstract symbolic representation in Figure 4.2 for the regular state graph $\tilde{\mathbf{X}}$ is used for the illustration.

4.12.1 Stationary extension

The stationary horizon extension (SHE) is an existing approach, encountered in many works, for example [Ter09] [Hel10]. Several simplifications are used. First, the remaining road until the end of the route is assumed to be even and straight. Furthermore, dynamic obstacles like traffic lights and other vehicles are ignored. Finally, it is often assumed that there is an optimal time-invariant stationary state consisting of constant cruise velocity and gear choice that can be maintained. In [Ter09] for example, weighted absolute deviation from the assumed optimal stationary state is used as the terminal cost. Alternatively, it is also possible to directly add the assumed optimal stationary end state to the end of the horizon.

As this thesis uses monetary costs without reliance on manually adjusted weights, the approach of [Ter09] is adapted in order to make direct comparisons with LRAHE possible. But the original idea of guiding the optimal trajectory towards an optimal stationary state shall be maintained in the SHE. Instead of using state deviation penalties, a rough stationary cost estimate from the end of the horizon s_N to the end of the route s_{end} is used.
A symbolic illustration is shown in Figure 4.11. Let $\mathbf{X}_N$ be the last decision stage of the horizon. Let $\boldsymbol{x}_{b,N}$ be any state within $\mathbf{X}_N$. Let $\boldsymbol{x}_{b,\text{end}}$ be a state

at the end of the route or the end of the journey with the same velocity and gear level as $\boldsymbol{x}_{b,N}$. The goal of the SHE is to estimate the optimal end state $\boldsymbol{x}_N^*$ on the last stage of the horizon. SHE estimates the remaining cost if the velocity and gear level of the states in $\mathbf{X}_N$ are maintained until the end of the route s_{end}. Thus, long-distance transition costs $j(\boldsymbol{x}_{b,N}, \boldsymbol{x}_{b,\text{end}})$ are estimated. The optimal end state is assumed to be the one that leads to the minimum overall cost at the end of the route:

$$\boldsymbol{x}_N^* \approx \arg \min_{\boldsymbol{x}_{b,N} \in \mathbf{X}_N} \Big(J^*(\boldsymbol{x}_{b,N}) + j(\boldsymbol{x}_{b,N}, \boldsymbol{x}_{b,\text{end}}) \Big). \tag{4.43}$$

4.12.2 Long-range extension

The basic idea of the long-range auxiliary horizon extension (LRAHE) is to create two separate state graphs. The regular horizon $\tilde{\mathbf{X}}$ has a relatively short horizon $\Delta s_{\tilde{\mathbf{X}}}$. It is always completely evaluated during every new optimization and incorporates all obstacles, including other vehicles and traffic lights. This ascertains that the optimal solution within $\tilde{\mathbf{X}}$ always adapts to changes in the environment and possible deviations from the motion trajectory planning. At the same time, a separate long-range auxiliary state graph $\breve{\breve{\mathbf{X}}}$ is constructed. Within $\breve{\breve{\mathbf{X}}}$, dynamic obstacles, lanes, lateral position, and travel duration are not considered. Thus, $\breve{\breve{\mathbf{X}}}$ uses states $\breve{\boldsymbol{x}}_{b,i}$ with a reduced state dimension:

$$\breve{\boldsymbol{x}}_{b,i} = [v_{b,i}, a_{b,i}, a_{\text{lat},b,i}, G_{b,i}, Q_{b,i}]. \tag{4.44}$$

Precomputation

Before the vehicle's journey is initiated, $\breve{\breve{\mathbf{X}}}$ is precomputed based on the chosen route, i.e., the entire forward DP computation of all state transitions within the initial $\breve{\breve{\mathbf{X}}}$ is performed before the vehicle starts moving. The horizon length $\Delta s_{\breve{\breve{\mathbf{X}}}}$ of $\breve{\breve{\mathbf{X}}}$ is ideally significantly longer than that of $\tilde{\mathbf{X}}$ and depends on how much time the user is willing to wait before starting the journey. In this thesis, PEEMTO uses an initial default auxiliary horizon length of 1 km length unless explicitly stated otherwise.

Truncation of the auxiliary state graph

During the journey, the DP forward computation is conducted for both $\tilde{\mathbf{X}}$ and $\breve{\tilde{\mathbf{X}}}$ separately. When the DP forward computation is concluded for both state graphs, the information contained within $\tilde{\mathbf{X}}$ and $\breve{\tilde{\mathbf{X}}}$ is merged at the last stage s_N of $\tilde{\mathbf{X}}$. The merging process is illustrated in Figures 4.12 to 4.14. Before the merging process, the initial stages of $\breve{\tilde{\mathbf{X}}}$ may refer to positions that are smaller than s_N. As $\tilde{\mathbf{X}}$ already contains the minimum accumulated costs from the vehicle's current position s_0 to s_N, only the stages of $\breve{\tilde{\mathbf{X}}}$ that lie beyond s_N are needed. Therefore, all stages of $\breve{\tilde{\mathbf{X}}}$ whose positions are equal or smaller than s_N are permanently discarded from memory.
For sake of simplicity, the index notation of the auxiliary horizon shall follow the index notation of the current regular horizon.

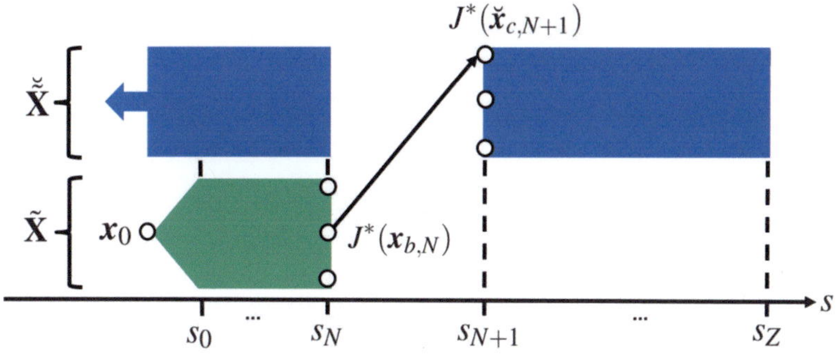

Figure 4.12: Merging process between the regular state graph $\tilde{\mathbf{X}}$ (green) and the auxiliary state graph $\breve{\tilde{\mathbf{X}}}$ (blue). Part of $\breve{\tilde{\mathbf{X}}}$, which is no longer relevant, is truncated before the merging process begins. During the merging process, all state transitions between $\mathbf{X}_N$ and $\breve{\mathbf{X}}_{N+1}$ are evaluated. For sake of simplicity, the index notation of $\breve{\tilde{\mathbf{X}}}$ shall follow the index notation of the current $\tilde{\mathbf{X}}$.

Merging of the regular and the auxiliary state graph

As the minimum accumulated costs at $\breve{\mathbf{X}}_{N+1}$ have been computed independently of $\tilde{\mathbf{X}}$, new state transitions between the states of $\mathbf{X}_N$ and the states of the first remaining stage $\breve{\mathbf{X}}_{N+1}$ of $\breve{\breve{\mathbf{X}}}$ must be established in order to merge the information of $\tilde{\mathbf{X}}$ and $\breve{\breve{\mathbf{X}}}$. Thus, all state transitions between $\mathbf{X}_i$ and $\breve{\mathbf{X}}_{i+1}$ are evaluated. This changes the minimum accumulated costs and the battery charge of all states within $\breve{\mathbf{X}}_{N+1}$. Following the example given in Figure 4.12 and without loss of generality, let there a state $\boldsymbol{x}_{b,N}$ of $\mathbf{X}_N$, and let there a state $\breve{\boldsymbol{x}}_{c,N+1}$ of $\breve{\mathbf{X}}_{N+1}$. Let $\boldsymbol{x}_{b,N}$ be the new optimal predecessor of $\breve{\boldsymbol{x}}_{c,N+1}$. In this case, the new minimum accumulated cost of $\breve{\boldsymbol{x}}_{c,N+1}$ is:

$$J^*(\breve{\boldsymbol{x}}_{c,N+1}) = J^*(\boldsymbol{x}_{b,N}) + j(\boldsymbol{x}_{b,N}, \breve{\boldsymbol{x}}_{c,N+1}). \tag{4.45}$$

The correction procedure is repeated for all states in $\breve{\mathbf{X}}_{N+1}$. After the merging process is completed, the optimal predecessor states of $\breve{\mathbf{X}}_{N+1}$ are composed of the states of $\mathbf{X}_N$.

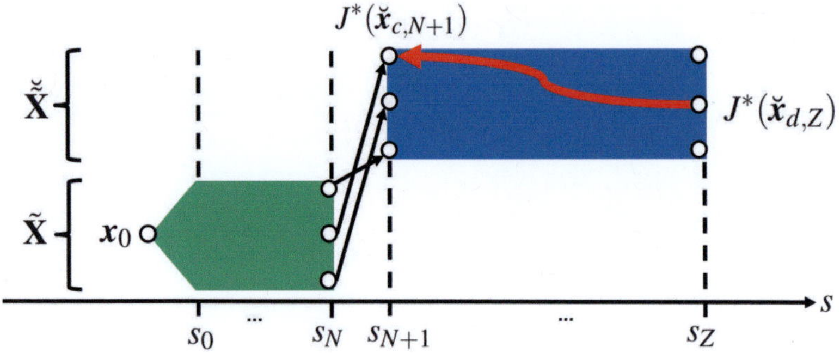

Figure 4.13: Correction at the last stage of the auxiliary state graph $\breve{\breve{\mathbf{X}}}$. The red arrow denotes DP backtracing. For sake of simplicity, the index notation of $\breve{\breve{\mathbf{X}}}$ shall follow the index notation of the current $\tilde{\mathbf{X}}$.

Correction at the last stage of the auxiliary state graph

The minimum accumulated costs of the last auxiliary stage $\breve{\mathbf{X}}_Z$ at the position s_Z are corrected depending on the merging result between $\mathbf{X}_N$ and $\breve{\mathbf{X}}_{N+1}$. The correction process of $\breve{\mathbf{X}}_Z$ is illustrated in Figure 4.13. Let there be a state $\breve{\boldsymbol{x}}_{d,Z}$ of $\breve{\mathbf{X}}_Z$. Let $J^*_{\text{old}}(\breve{\boldsymbol{x}}_{d,Z})$ be the minimum accumulated cost of $\breve{\boldsymbol{x}}_{d,Z}$ before the correction. Let $\breve{\boldsymbol{x}}_{c,N+1}$ be the optimal state at stage $\breve{\mathbf{X}}_{N+1}$ during DP backtracing with respect to $\breve{\boldsymbol{x}}_{d,Z}$. Let $J^*_{\text{old}}(\breve{\boldsymbol{x}}_{c,N+1})$ be the minimum accumulated cost of $\breve{\boldsymbol{x}}_{c,N+1}$ before the merging process of $\tilde{\mathbf{X}}$ and $\breve{\breve{\mathbf{X}}}$. Let $J^*(\breve{\boldsymbol{x}}_{c,N+1})$ be the minimum accumulated cost of $\breve{\boldsymbol{x}}_{c,N+1}$ after the merging process. In this case, the correction of $J^*(\breve{\boldsymbol{x}}_{d,Z})$ is:

$$J^*(\breve{\boldsymbol{x}}_{d,Z}) = J^*_{\text{old}}(\breve{\boldsymbol{x}}_{d,Z}) - J^*_{\text{old}}(\breve{\boldsymbol{x}}_{c,N+1}) + J^*(\breve{\boldsymbol{x}}_{c,N+1}). \qquad (4.46)$$

The correction procedure is repeated for all states in $\breve{\mathbf{X}}_Z$. The decision stages between $\breve{\mathbf{X}}_{N+1}$ and $\breve{\mathbf{X}}_Z$ are not re-evaluated. The relationship between optimal predecessors of these stages is not changed. Thus, the vast majority of historically accumulated costs is reused. Let $\Delta Q(\breve{\boldsymbol{x}}_{c,N+1}, \breve{\boldsymbol{x}}_{d,Z})$ be the battery charge difference for the entire optimal trajectory from $\breve{\boldsymbol{x}}_{c,N+1}$ to $\breve{\boldsymbol{x}}_{d,Z}$. The reutilization of historically accumulated costs also means that none of the charge differences $\Delta Q(\breve{\boldsymbol{x}}_{c,N+1}, \breve{\boldsymbol{x}}_{d,Z})$ between $\breve{\mathbf{X}}_{N+1}$ and $\breve{\mathbf{X}}_Z$ are changed. The battery charge of the states $\breve{\boldsymbol{x}}_{d,Z}$ in $\breve{\mathbf{X}}_Z$ are corrected based on the battery charge of the states $\breve{\boldsymbol{x}}_{c,N+1}$ in $\breve{\mathbf{X}}_{N+1}$:

$$Q_{d,Z} = Q_{c,N+1} + \Delta Q(\breve{\boldsymbol{x}}_{c,N+1}, \breve{\boldsymbol{x}}_{d,Z}). \qquad (4.47)$$

Growth of the auxiliary state graph

The next step is to grow the auxiliary state graph $\breve{\breve{\mathbf{X}}}$. If the initial auxiliary horizon was not further extended, the regular state graph $\tilde{\mathbf{X}}$ would eventually move past the auxiliary state graph. In this case, the entire auxiliary state graph would be entirely deleted. In order to grow, $\breve{\breve{\mathbf{X}}}$ needs to be extended by at least one stage if $\tilde{\mathbf{X}}$ also only moves ahead by one stage. If $\breve{\breve{\mathbf{X}}}$ should grow faster than $\tilde{\mathbf{X}}$, at least two additional stages must be added to the end of $\breve{\breve{\mathbf{X}}}$. The growth of $\breve{\breve{\mathbf{X}}}$ is illustrated in Figure 4.14. The DP forward evaluation process is only applied to the additional stages beyond the stage $\breve{\breve{\mathbf{X}}}_Z$, while the previously evaluated stages in $\breve{\breve{\mathbf{X}}}$ are not re-evaluated. Thus, again, the vast majority of historically accumulated costs is reused.

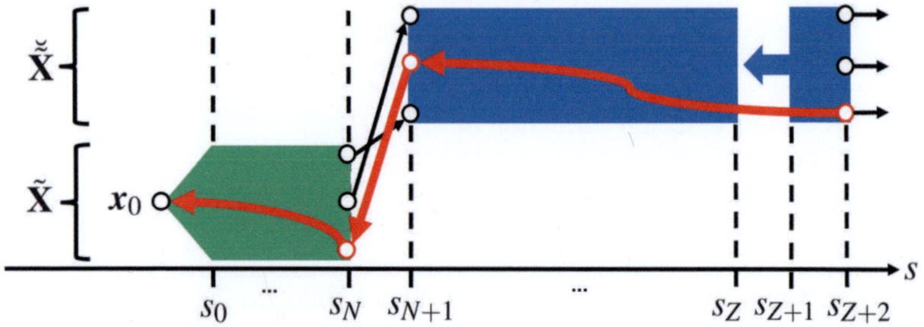

Figure 4.14: The auxiliary state graph $\breve{\breve{\mathbf{X}}}$ grows by two additional stages. The last stage of $\breve{\breve{\mathbf{X}}}$ is now $\breve{\breve{\mathbf{X}}}_{Z+2}$. The assumed optimal end state at s_{Z+2} is chosen using stationary horizon extension (SHE). The red arrows denote DP backtracing starting at the assumed optimal end state until the beginning of the regular state graph $\tilde{\mathbf{X}}$ is reached. For sake of simplicity, the index notation of $\breve{\breve{\mathbf{X}}}$ shall follow the index notation of the current $\tilde{\mathbf{X}}$.

Backtracing using the auxiliary state graph

Once the new stages are added to the end of $\breve{\breve{\mathbf{X}}}$ and are fully evaluated, the DP backtracing procedure can begin. The process is illustrated in Figure 4.14. The DP backtracing has to construct the optimal state trajectory beginning with the optimal end state at the last stage of $\breve{\breve{\mathbf{X}}}$. The algorithm then follows all optimal predecessors throughout $\breve{\breve{\mathbf{X}}}$ and $\tilde{\mathbf{X}}$ until the start state of $\tilde{\mathbf{X}}$ is reached. Thus, the first step of backtracing is to select the optimal end state at the last stage of $\breve{\breve{\mathbf{X}}}$. While the purpose of $\breve{\breve{\mathbf{X}}}$ is to estimate the optimal behavior beyond $\tilde{\mathbf{X}}$, there is no other auxiliary state graph to guide $\breve{\breve{\mathbf{X}}}$. Therefore, the SHE method is used to approximate the costs beyond $\breve{\breve{\mathbf{X}}}$. Note that the two state graphs are never truly merged into one single state graph. After the ego-vehicle has progressed to its new state, $\tilde{\mathbf{X}}$ is discarded and entirely re-built. In contrast, $\breve{\breve{\mathbf{X}}}$ continues to exist until $\tilde{\mathbf{X}}$ reaches the end of the route s_{end}.

If there is sufficient memory, the long-range cost assessment will eventually reach the end of the route's final destination, which might be hundreds or thousands of kilometers away from the ego-vehicle's start position. As only a few (for example two) additional stages with reduced state dimension have to be evaluated, the additional computation burden is relatively low, while the cost assessment using $\breve{\breve{\mathbf{X}}}$ stretches over a very long distance that is further extended with every new optimization. If $\breve{\breve{\mathbf{X}}}$ grows faster than $\tilde{\mathbf{X}}$, $\breve{\breve{\mathbf{X}}}$ will reach the end of the route long before the ego-vehicle. Another advantage is that the existing discretization within $\breve{\breve{\mathbf{X}}}$ can be as precise as in the regular horizon $\tilde{\mathbf{X}}$. If there is not enough memory, $\breve{\breve{\mathbf{X}}}$ will grow until the memory is exhausted. As all state transitions between $\mathbf{X}_N$ and $\breve{\mathbf{X}}_{N+1}$ are fully evaluated, the entire optimal trajectory from the beginning of $\tilde{\mathbf{X}}$ to the end of $\breve{\breve{\mathbf{X}}}$ is physically feasible.

The long-range horizon estimation is the main reason, why the optimization is referring to discrete position instead of discrete time. If equidistant points in time were used as reference, the position, instead of travel duration, would be calculated through implicit discretization. This has the consequence that the states of a decision stage would all have the same discrete time but different positions. This would make the merging process of $\tilde{\mathbf{X}}$ and $\breve{\breve{\mathbf{X}}}$ more difficult to compute. The reason starts with $\breve{\breve{\mathbf{X}}}$, which is primarily focused on time-invariant aspects like road slope, etc. Therefore, it is beneficial for $\breve{\breve{\mathbf{X}}}$ to use position-dependent decision stages. If $\tilde{\mathbf{X}}$ was referring to time and $\breve{\breve{\mathbf{X}}}$ was referring to position, it is is not apparent which stage of $\breve{\breve{\mathbf{X}}}$ should be connected with $\tilde{\mathbf{X}}$. In fact, possibly a large number of different stages in $\breve{\breve{\mathbf{X}}}$ would have to be evaluated to find all feasible succeeding states in $\breve{\breve{\mathbf{X}}}$ during the merging process.

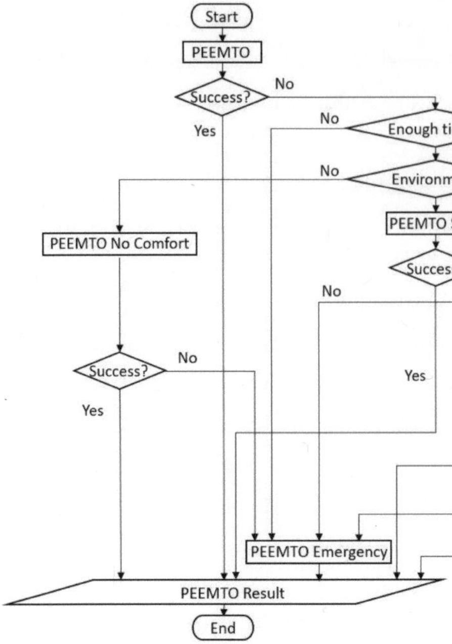

Figure 4.15: Flow diagram of PEEMTO dealing with cases, in which a solution cannot be successfully found. Depending on the reason of failure, the optimization is repeated with certain constraints adapted or removed. This can only happen if there is still enough computation time left. In the worst case scenario, emergency braking is suggested.

4.13 Constraint relaxation and emergency situations

It is theoretically possible that PEEMTO is sometimes not able to find a feasible solution. This can happen if, for example, another vehicle suddenly changes the lane and positions itself right in front of the ego-vehicle. If PEEMTO is not able to find a feasible solution trajectory, the following steps are made in the given order:

1. At the last feasible decision stage, PEEMTO verifies the reasons why the optimization stopped prematurely.

2. If the optimization stops because of other vehicles or traffic lights, the optimization shall choose to lead the ego-vehicle to a full stop at the last feasible decision stage, which contains this possibility. This scenario is actually not an emergency and simply refers to normal procedures of section 4.11.

3. If there are ways to avoid other vehicles and red traffic light phases, but the optimization still stops prematurely, PEEMTO restarts the optimization without comfort constraints.

4. If the optimization stops prematurely because of extremely difficult road characteristics, the optimization shall choose to lead the ego-vehicle to a full stop at the last feasible decision stage, which contains this possibility. This scenario is unlikely because most real-world roads are usually constructed with the physical limits of road vehicles in mind.

5. There is also the possibility that the optimization stops because of dynamic obstacles, but there are no trajectories that can lead the ego-vehicle to a full stop. If steps 3 and 4 do not resolve the problem, PEEMTO restarts the optimization without comfort constraints, speed limits, and lane change regulations.

6. If the previous step fails, PEEMTO readjusts the velocity-dependent safety gap constraints of section 4.9.2. For all state transition evaluations, PEEMTO now assumes that other vehicles will maintain their velocity. It then evaluates which state transitions lead to collisions. Thus, the safety gaps are reduced to a minimum.

7. If a collision seems avoidable, PEEMTO seeks out the trajectory with the lowest end velocity. This can be supported by changing the cost formulation to only penalize velocity.

8. If the ego-vehicle is about to crash into an obstacle and there is no time for optimization, PEEMTO simply sets the target velocity to zero. In this case, the ego-vehicle will initiate emergency braking without doing anything else.

A graphical illustration is given in Figure 4.15.

Optimal behavior in unavoidable collisions is not only an engineering problem but also an ethical question. For example, if the ego-vehicle cannot avoid a collision but can choose the obstacle to collide into, the question is how the choice should be made. The question can become complicated if the obstacle is another traffic participant. This thesis is primarily focused on energy-efficient driving. More elaborate collision avoidance strategies are not further investigated in this thesis but can be part of future work.

4.14 Computational complexity

The computational complexity of FBDP depends on the number of states of each decision stage and the number of decision stages. All state transitions between stages have to be evaluated. This leads to a quadratic complexity with respect to the number of states at each stage. By precomputing the time-invariant state transition cost and saving the results for later use, the vehicle model computations are no longer needed during the optimization. This reduces the computation duration of state transition evaluation at the expense of higher memory demand. But in any case, the cost of different state transitions still need to be compared. Let n_x be the number of states of an intermediate decision stage, excluding the first stage, which only consists of the solitary start state. Let N be the number of intermediate stages. The computational complexity of regular stages in FBDP with an open end is $\mathcal{O}(Nn_{\mathbf{x}}^2)$ if all intermediate decision stages have the same number of states.

The state graph used by PEEMTO has different state components. The explicit discretization of all state components for a single stage leads to different numbers of discrete values for time n_t, lateral position n_d, velocity n_v, acceleration n_a, lateral acceleration $n_{a_{\text{lat}}}$, gear level n_G, and battery charge n_Q. Excluding the states of the other vehicles, the complexity is $\mathcal{O}\left(N(n_t n_d n_v n_a n_{a_{\text{lat}}} n_G n_Q)^2\right)$.

Through implicit discretization, the computation complexity is reduced to $\mathcal{O}\left(N(n_d n_v n_G)^2\right)$. The consideration of other vehicles and traffic lights adds several logical operations during the state transition evaluation. But due to implicit discretization, the search space dimension is not further increased.

The long-range auxiliary horizon extension adds some complexity to the algorithm. In general, the number $\breve{N}$ of additional stages to be evaluated is significantly smaller than N. The default horizon extension merges $\tilde{\mathbf{X}}$ with $\breve{\breve{\mathbf{X}}}$. Furthermore, two additional stages are added to the end of $\breve{\breve{\mathbf{X}}}$. This leads to $\breve{N} = 3$ of additional stages that need to be evaluated. Note that $\breve{N}$ does not denote the entire length of $\breve{\breve{\mathbf{X}}}$. Furthermore, note that the states of the auxiliary state graph have a reduced state dimension, e.g., there is no lateral position. Thus, the combined complexity of PEEMTO is $\mathcal{O}\left((Nn_d^2 + \breve{N})(n_v n_G)^2\right)$.

By confining the state transitions to lanes that are adjacent to each other the complexity can be reduced one last time. Let n_{lane} be the number of lanes of the route. By omitting whole groups of non-feasible transitions, the complexity can be further reduced to $\mathcal{O}\left(\left(N(3n_{\text{lane}} - 2)\left(\frac{n_d}{n_{\text{lane}}}\right)^2 + \breve{N}\right)(n_v n_G)^2\right)$. If every discrete lateral position only refers to one lane (i.e., $n_d = n_{\text{lane}}$), the complexity is $\mathcal{O}\left(\left(N(3n_{\text{lane}} - 2) + \breve{N}\right)(n_v n_G)^2\right)$.

The long-range auxiliary horizon extension adds $n_v n_G$ additional states to the memory demand for every stage. If the state transition costs are precomputed, additional memory is necessary. Let n_φ be the number of discrete road slope angle values. Let n_κ be the number of discrete road curvature values. The memory needed to save the state transition costs is $(n_\varphi n_\kappa n_v n_G)^2$.

4.15 Optimality

As previously stated in section 4.2, the DP algorithm yields the globally optimal discrete solution of the BE with respect to the employed discretization. As the BE is the discrete formulation of the continuous HJBE, the discrete solution is the optimal approximation of the continuous solution to the HJBE with respect to the employed discretization. Note that although the DP algorithm yields the globally optimal discrete solution, it is always an approximation of the continuous solution due to the finite discretization precision.

As PEEMTO is a DP algorithm, it yields the globally optimal solution with respect to the employed explicit discretization, the implicit discretization, and the constraints within the given search space. But due to the reduced state dimension as a result of implicit discretization, the search space itself can be heavily confined. This, in turn, can confine the possible solution space. Therefore, it is possible that the result of PEEMTO can be suboptimal compared to the result of a state graph in which all state dimensions are explicitly expanded.

The finite horizon is another challenge. Existing predictive optimization methods can only roughly estimate the optimal behavior at the end of the horizon. The LRAHE provides a better estimate but does not entirely solve the problem either. As previously discussed in section 4.12, the LRAHE reuses historically accumulated costs. Thus, the state transitions within $\breve{\mathbf{X}}$

are not all re-evaluated. Furthermore, dynamic obstacles are not considered within $\breve{\breve{\mathbf{X}}}$. Therefore, it is generally possible that a regular horizon with the same length yields a more precise solution than the auxiliary horizon can offer. But in the end, the goal of LRAHE is to provide a better estimate of the optimal end state at the end of the regular horizon, instead of the precise computation of the entire optimal solution to the end of the route. Indeed, the precise computation of the entire optimal solution to the end of the route is often impossible in practice because the behavior of other traffic participants cannot be reliably predicted into the distant future.

Just like many other forms of approximate dynamic programming, it is not possible to analytically ascertain the reduction of optimization precision or compute a non-trivial worst-case limit. In general, reduction of search space dimension and reduction in discretization precision should only be used if the computational complexity is otherwise too high. For the optimization problems discussed in this thesis, search space reduction is a necessity.

5 Results

This chapter evaluates PEEMTO optimization results in different simulated scenarios. The evaluation starts with isolated and simple examples to help the reader understand the decisions of PEEMTO before complex scenarios are discussed. The simulation includes scenarios that refer to real-world routes with truly existing speed limits, road topography, road curvature, lanes, and traffic lights.

As described in chapter 2, there are numerous approaches to energy-efficient driving of varying complexity. Many authors compare their approach to human drivers or existing cruise control systems [Ter09] [Hel10] [Sch14] [Koh+14] [Wah15].

This thesis uses two other contenders to compare to PEEMTO. Due to similar prerequisites, one of the contenders is a model predictive optimization called the *predictive energy efficiency optimization* with the acronym PEEO. It represents existing energy-efficient driving optimization strategies. It is similar to PEEMTO but does not change lanes and only uses the SHE. The second contender is a simulated driver who controls the ego-vehicle and shall be called the *ego-vehicle driver* in this thesis. Different from the optimization, which uses the SDM, the ego-vehicle driver uses the extended driver model (EDM). The same applies to the simulation environment that controls all other vehicles except the ego-vehicle. More details about PEEO, the ego-vehicle driver, the EDM, and the simulation environment can be found in the appendix.

In the evaluated scenarios, the contenders PEEMTO, PEEO, and the ego-vehicle driver use the default parameters as described in the appendix, unless explicitly stated otherwise. The driver parameters of the other traffic participants are usually randomly chosen. The end of the journey shall be 100 km away from the start of the journey in all scenarios. The SHE shall always refer to the end of the journey. The route has a shorter length than the journey in all scenarios, and the length is different depending on the scenario.

The quantitative comparison of different results is usually expressed in positive percental values. The description usually refers to how much more cost one contender creates compared to another contender. For example, if PEEMTO leads to cost savings compared to PEEO, the description is usually about how much more cost PEEO creates than PEEMTO. Different from the scenarios discussed in most sections, the random scenarios in section 5.8 always describe the cost comparisons in terms of PEEMTO's cost savings. Thus, if PEEMTO leads to higher costs, the cost saving is a negative percental value. The reader shall also be reminded that the numeric percental values may not be the same for different expressions of the same relation due to the nature of percentage computation. For example, if PEEO leads to 100 % higher costs than PEEMTO, the alternative expression is that PEEMTO leads to 50 % lower costs than PEEO instead of 100 %.

Note that the different processes in the illustrations of this chapter represent the discrete results as computed by the discrete optimization and the discrete simulation environment.

5.1 Resistance forces

An overview of the resistance forces are shown in Figure 5.1 for the REM-2030 vehicle. The slope resistance distinguishes low slope ($\varphi = 1°$), high slope ($\varphi = 5°$), and very high slope ($\varphi = 10°$). The acceleration resistance considers low acceleration and high acceleration. According to [DDK00], calm drivers use an average acceleration of at least 0.45 $\frac{\mathrm{m}}{\mathrm{s}^2}$. This value shall be used as an example of low acceleration. High acceleration shall be 2.78 $\frac{\mathrm{m}}{\mathrm{s}^2}$, which is the average acceleration needed to accelerate from 0 $\frac{\mathrm{km}}{\mathrm{h}}$ to 100 $\frac{\mathrm{km}}{\mathrm{h}}$ in 10 s. The low curve resistance refers to a large curve radius of 1000 m, while the high curve resistance refers to a small curve radius of 30 m.

As illustrated in Figure 5.1, the low curve resistance is almost negligible below 150 $\frac{\mathrm{km}}{\mathrm{h}}$. But the high curve resistance rises very quickly with vehicle velocity. As high velocity on road sections with strong curvature is unrealistic in practice, the high curve resistance is only shown up to a vehicle velocity of 60 $\frac{\mathrm{km}}{\mathrm{h}}$.

Below 300 $\frac{\mathrm{km}}{\mathrm{h}}$, high acceleration and very high slopes are the strongest resistances acting on the vehicle. They are only illustrated up to 150 $\frac{\mathrm{km}}{\mathrm{h}}$ because their appearance for higher velocities is unrealistic in the real world.

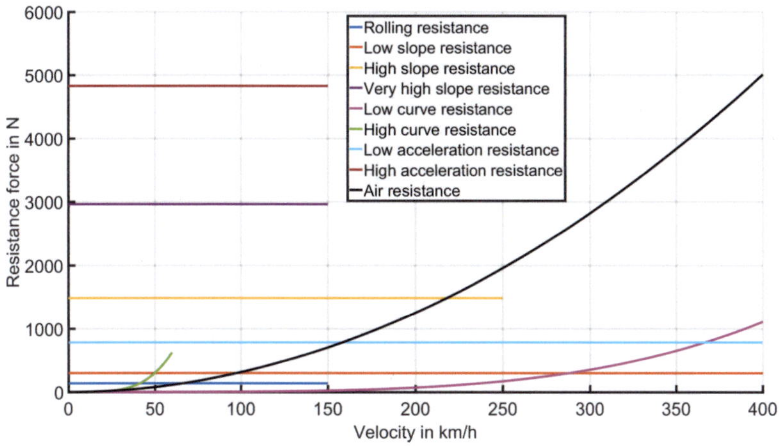

Figure 5.1: Resistance forces with respect to vehicle velocity.

The rolling resistance is relatively small compared to the other resistance forces. But as discussed in section 3.1.1, the vehicle model does not consider the drastic increase of the rolling resistance for very high velocities. Therefore, the rolling resistance is only shown for velocities up to 150 $\frac{\mathrm{km}}{\mathrm{h}}$.

The air resistance is comparatively small for low velocities. At a vehicle velocity of 50 $\frac{\mathrm{km}}{\mathrm{h}}$, even the rolling resistance is stronger. The situation drastically changes as the velocity increases. Beyond 150 $\frac{\mathrm{km}}{\mathrm{h}}$, the air resistance is larger than the low acceleration resistance. In practice, the combination of high velocity and high acceleration, or the combination of high velocity and strong inclination is unrealistic due to limited engine power. Therefore, it can be assumed that the air resistance becomes the dominant resistance force beyond 150 $\frac{\mathrm{km}}{\mathrm{h}}$. If the vehicle is merely cruising on an even, straight road, the air resistance becomes the dominant force beyond 70 $\frac{\mathrm{km}}{\mathrm{h}}$ in the case of the REM-2030 vehicle.

5.2 Constant cruise velocity and gear choice

This section investigates the optimal choice of constant cruise velocity and gear choice on an even plane without speed limits, curvatures, and dynamic obstacles.

5.2.1 Different cruise velocities

The energy consumption cost and the travel duration cost can have an inverse impact on each other. Figure 5.2 shows the energy consumption cost and travel duration cost with respect to different constant cruise velocities, at gear level two, on even, straight roads, for a distance of 1 km. The travel duration cost refers to the minimum gross labor cost (GLC) of 8.5 $\frac{€}{\mathrm{h}}$. The travel duration cost is excessively higher for very low velocities but quickly decreases as the travel duration is reduced for higher velocities. The energy

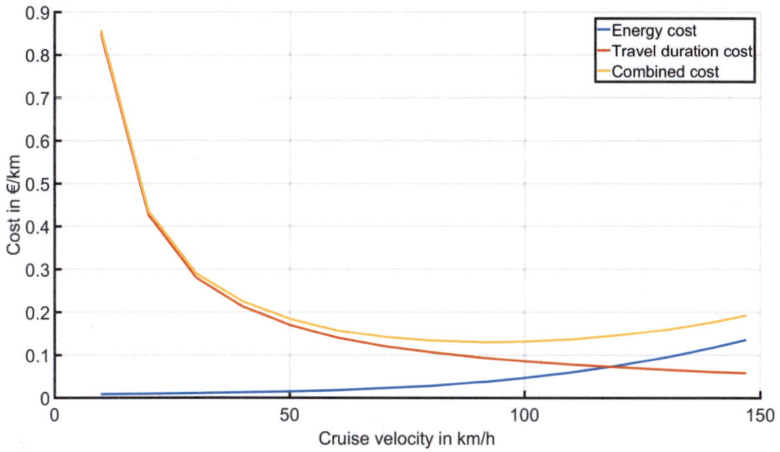

Figure 5.2: Cost at different cruise velocities. Energy consumption cost, travel duration cost, and combined cost with respect to different constant vehicle cruise velocities, at gear level two, on even, straight roads, over a distance of 1 km. The travel duration cost refers to the minimum gross labor cost of 8.5 $\frac{€}{h}$.

consumption cost increases in a parabolic fashion with respect to vehicle velocity because of the air resistance. At approximately 118 $\frac{km}{h}$, the energy consumption cost becomes larger than the travel duration cost. The combined cost reaches its minimum at 92 $\frac{km}{h}$.

As discussed in section 4.3.2, the optimization has to use some amount of minimum travel duration cost even if travel duration cost is not explicitly defined. The general assumption in section 4.3.2 is that the vehicle should at least accelerate to the speed limit in urban scenario and follow traffic regulations. Figure 5.3 shows the results of a GLC of 0.7 $\frac{€}{h}$. Compared to the previous example, the energy consumption cost outmatches the travel duration cost at smaller cruise velocities. In this case, 50 $\frac{km}{h}$ is the velocity at which the energy consumption cost becomes higher than the travel duration cost. The minimum of the combined cost is also at 50 $\frac{km}{h}$.

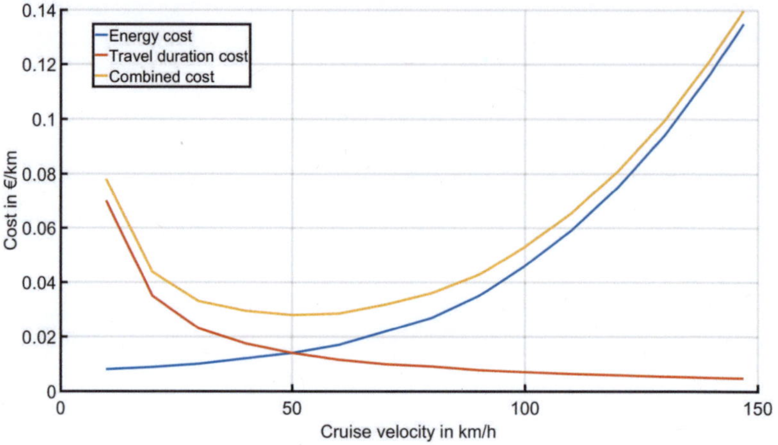

Figure 5.3: Cost at different cruise velocities. Energy consumption cost, travel duration cost, and combined cost with respect to different constant vehicle cruise velocities, at gear level two, on even, straight roads, over a distance of 1 km. The travel duration cost refers to a gross labor cost of 0.7 $\frac{€}{h}$.

5.2.2 Different labor costs

Figure 5.4 provides an overview of the optimal cruise velocity for different gross labor costs on even, straight roads. The optimal gear choice is always level two, even for low velocities. This can be different for scenarios with velocity variation. The minimum GLC of 8.5 $\frac{€}{h}$ leads to an optimal cruise velocity of 92 $\frac{km}{h}$. The average GLC of 16.97 $\frac{€}{h}$ leads to 109 $\frac{km}{h}$. The average GLC of the upper 10 % income class is 31 $\frac{€}{h}$ and leads to 128 $\frac{km}{h}$.

As discussed in section 4.3.2, if the travel duration is unimportant, PEEMTO still has to choose a labor cost in order to reach the minimum cruise velocity. As discussed in section 4.3.2, the minimum cruise velocity is assumed to be the speed limit up to a speed limit of 80 $\frac{km}{h}$. In that regard, Figure 5.4 can also be used to find the minimum GLC needed to adopt a certain minimum cruise velocity. For example, a GLC of 0.7 $\frac{€}{h}$ refers to an optimal cruise

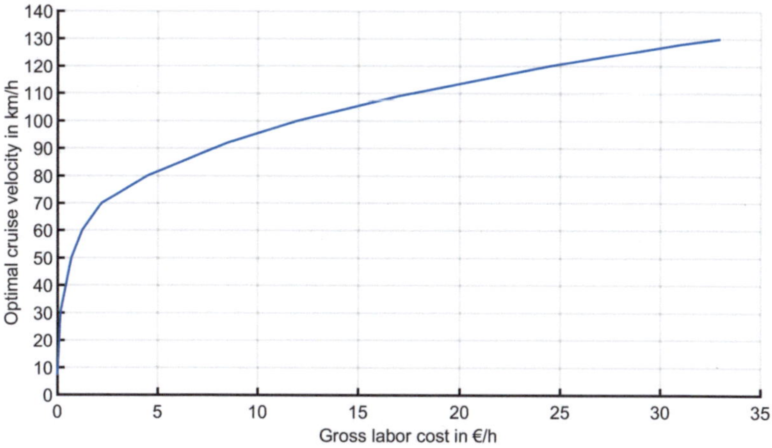

Figure 5.4: Optimal cruise velocities on even, straight roads, at gear level two, for different gross labor costs.

velocity of 50 $\frac{\text{km}}{\text{h}}$ while an optimal cruise velocity of 80 $\frac{\text{km}}{\text{h}}$ requires a GLC of 4.5 $\frac{€}{\text{h}}$.

5.2.3 Different vehicle mass

The vehicle mass can vary with passengers and cargo. Figure 5.5 shows the optimal cruise velocities for minimum GLC and different vehicle mass. The first entry of 1658 kg refers to the empty weight of the REM-2030 electric vehicle, while the second entry of 1738 kg assumes there is a passenger of 80 kg inside the vehicle. As shown in Figure 5.5, a vehicle mass increase leads to a decrease in the optimal cruise velocity. Due to higher rolling resistance, the energy consumption and engine torque demand will increase if there is no compensation from other sources. Due to the relatively high weight in combination with a maximum EE power of 80 kW, the REM-2030 EV cannot exceed 147 $\frac{\text{km}}{\text{h}}$ on even, straight roads.

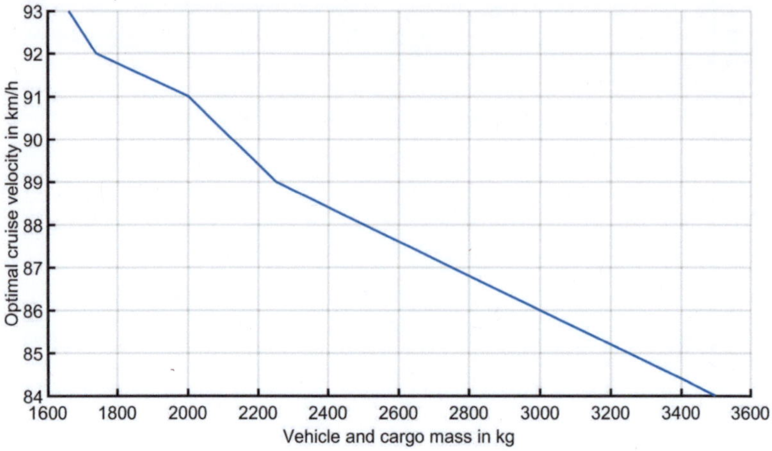

Figure 5.5: Optimal cruise velocity with respect to vehicle mass on even, straight roads. The travel duration cost refers to the minimum gross labor cost.

5.3 Velocity variation

This section evaluates the acceleration and deceleration optimization of PEEMTO on even, straight roads. The contenders are the ego-vehicle driver, PEEO, and PEEMTO.

5.3.1 Acceleration

In this example, the acceleration behavior of PEEMTO to a higher velocity is demonstrated. The vehicle accelerates from a complete stop to a higher velocity with the speed limit set to 50 $\frac{\text{km}}{\text{h}}$.

No comfort constraint

Figures 5.6 to 5.10 show the results without comfort constraints. Figure 5.6 shows the results of velocity, gear level, and brake pad utilization with respect to equidistant positions as originally computed by PEEO and PEEMTO.

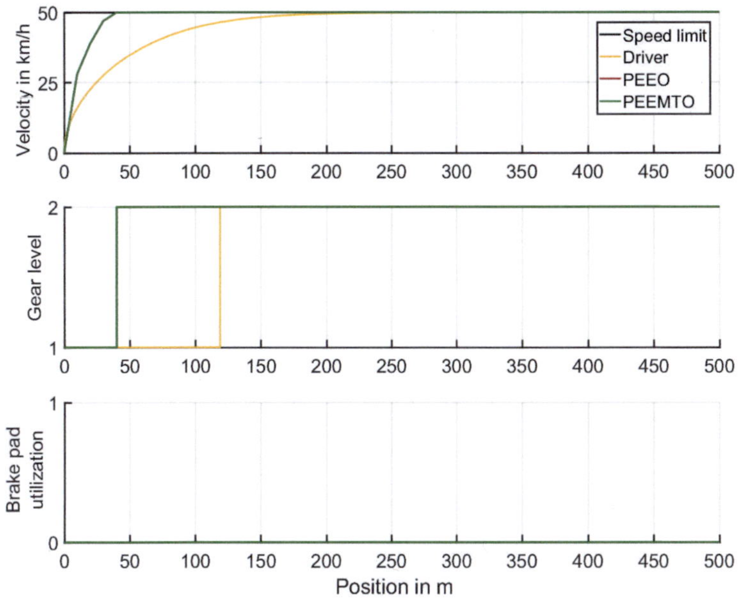

Figure 5.6: Acceleration without comfort constraints. Results of the ego-vehicle driver, PEEO, and PEEMTO with respect to position. The speed limit is set to 50 $\frac{\text{km}}{\text{h}}$. Similar results may overlap each other in the illustration.

Figures 5.7 to 5.9 show the corresponding results with respect to discrete time, which may not have an equidistant duration between decisions.

The illustrated gear level refers to the integer target gear level that the ego-vehicle should adopt. As illustrated in the Figures, the target gear level changes instantly. As discussed in section 3.1.1, the real-world gear shift process cannot instantly change and needs some time to complete. Thus, the target gear level should only be understood as the signal to initiate the gear shift. The brake pad utilization refers to the necessity to use the brake pads at the wheels when the engine in generator mode cannot provide the demanded brake torque. The brake pad necessity is denoted by 1 if brake pad application is necessary, while 0 means the brake pads are not needed.

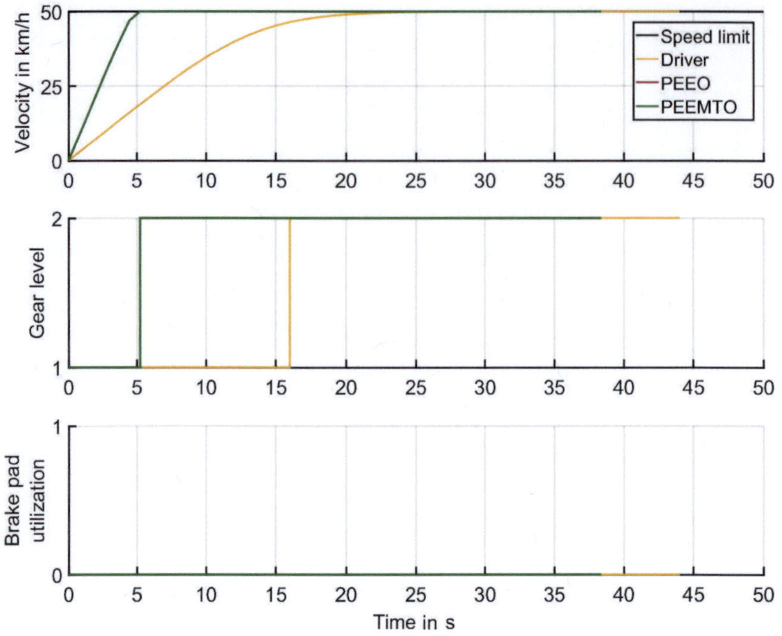

Figure 5.7: Acceleration without comfort constraints. Results of the ego-vehicle driver, PEEO, and PEEMTO with respect to time. The speed limit is set to 50 $\frac{\text{km}}{\text{h}}$. The results of PEEO and PEEMTO are identical and therefore overlap each other.

Similar to the target gear level, it can instantly change in the illustrations. Thus, it should also be understood as the signal to initiate the brake pads.

PEEO and PEEMTO yield the same results, which overlap each other in the illustrations. As shown in Figure 5.7, the ego-vehicle driver, PEEO, and PEEMTO all eventually choose the speed limit as the optimal cruise velocity. While the urban speed limit is by definition the desired velocity of the ego-vehicle driver, PEEO and PEEMTO also choose the speed limit because the optimal cruise velocity for even, straight roads is 92 $\frac{\text{km}}{\text{h}}$.

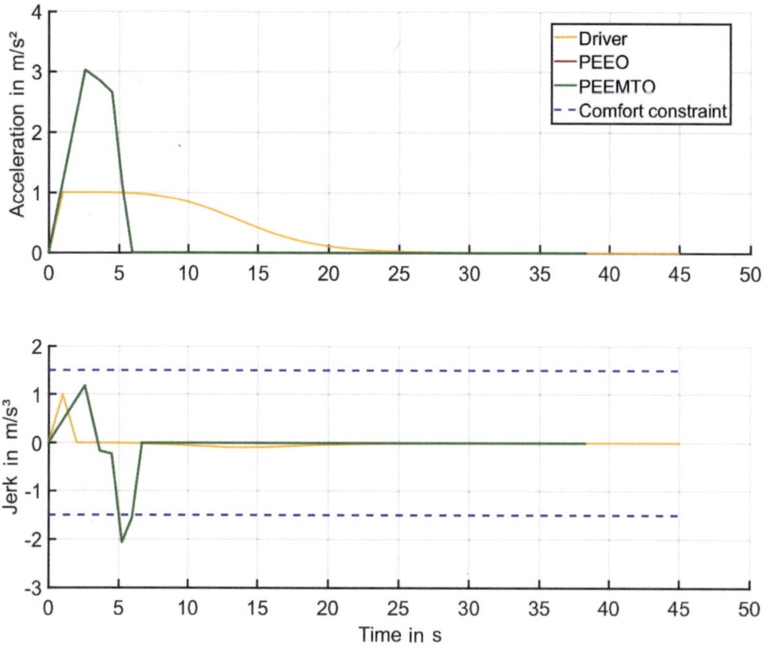

Figure 5.8: Acceleration without comfort constraints. Results of the ego-vehicle driver, PEEO, and PEEMTO. Comfort constraints refer to jerks of 1.5 $\frac{m}{s^3}$ and -1.5 $\frac{m}{s^3}$. The results of PEEO and PEEMTO are identical and therefore overlap each other.

As illustrated in Figure 5.8, PEEMTO uses high acceleration to reach the speed limit quickly. In comparison, the ego-vehicle driver has a significantly lower acceleration and needs more time to approach the speed limit. The temporary strong acceleration of PEEMTO is due to the strong influence of the travel duration cost. As discussed in section 5.2.1, the travel duration cost can be significantly higher than the energy consumption cost for speed limits in urban scenarios.

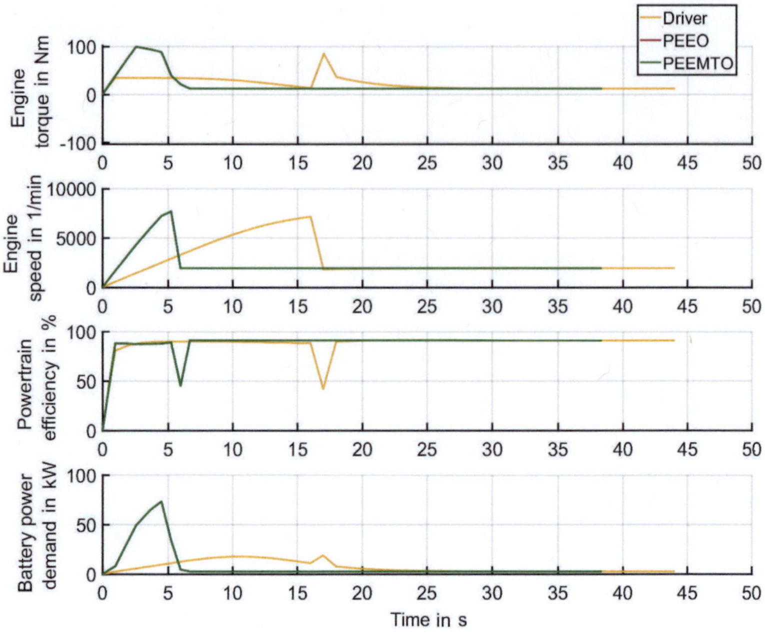

Figure 5.9: Acceleration without comfort constraints. Results of the ego-vehicle driver, PEEO, and PEEMTO. The results of PEEO and PEEMTO are identical and therefore overlap each other.

The jerk of PEEMTO does not exceed the comfort constraint of 1.5 $\frac{\mathrm{m}}{\mathrm{s}^3}$ during the acceleration. But as the vehicle velocity reaches the speed limit, the jerk temporarily drops below -1.5 $\frac{\mathrm{m}}{\mathrm{s}^3}$ because there is little transition from acceleration to cruising.

The engine torque, engine speed, and the resulting powertrain efficiency are shown in Figure 5.9. At some point, PEEMTO uses almost the maximum engine torque of 103 Nm to accelerate, which corresponds to the strong acceleration seen in Figure 5.8. Figure 5.9 shows the efficiency of the entire powertrain, which is composed of transmission efficiency, clutch efficiency, power electronics efficiency, engine efficiency, and battery efficiency. For

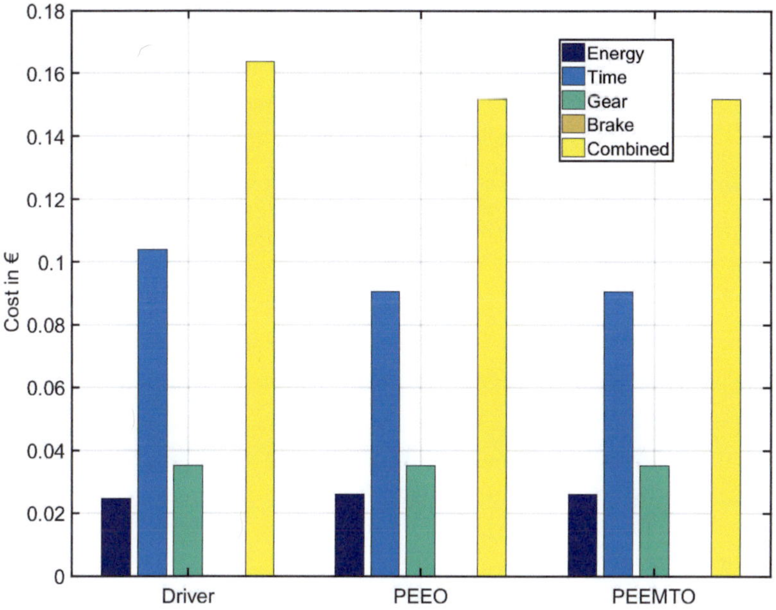

Figure 5.10: Acceleration without comfort constraints. Resulting costs of the different contenders at the end of the experiment without comfort consideration.

more details on the different types of efficiency, the reader can turn to section 3.1.1. The powertrain efficiency is zero if the engine torque or the engine speed is zero and increases when the vehicle starts to move. The efficiency slightly drops when the engine torque is close to its maximum. The slight drop occurs because high engine torque at low engine speed tends to reduce engine efficiency as shown in Figure 3.2. Furthermore, high engine torque leads to high battery current, which slightly reduces the battery efficiency. A strong drop in powertrain efficiency occurs during the gear shift while the engine speed is adjusted.

The ego-vehicle eventually reaches the speed limit and no longer accelerates. The engine torque drops and remains constant. Cruising at the speed limit leads to the highest engine and powertrain efficiency in this scenario, which are 97.5 % and 90.8 % respectively. This is different compared to ICEs which usually have their peak efficiency at high engine torque.

Figure 5.9 also shows the instantaneous power demanded from the battery. As discussed in section 3.1.1, the power demand is composed of engine torque, engine speed, and powertrain efficiency. In order to reduce energy consumption, one can reduce the engine torque, reduce the engine speed, or increase the powertrain efficiency. Due to the short acceleration phase, high power demand of PEEMTO is heavily concentrated within a small time frame. In comparison, the power demand of the ego-vehicle driver is spread out. Once the ego-vehicle reaches the speed limit it only needs to maintain the velocity. Thus, the power demand is greatly reduced.

Note that the efficiency and other elements in Figure 5.9 may have a small delay compared to the target gear level progression in Figure 5.7. As explained earlier, the target gear level illustration can instantly change and should only be understood as the signal to initiate the gear shift. The real gear shift process and reaction in the powertrain take some time to unfold.

Figure 5.10 shows the different cost components of the different contenders in €. The cost of PEEO and PEEMTO are the same. Due to the simplicity of the route, the auxiliary horizon does not lead to any improvements. The travel duration cost is the largest cost component. The energy consumption has the smallest impact. All contenders have the same gear shift cost. In this example, PEEMTO has a 4.7 % higher energy consumption than the ego-vehicle driver due to strong acceleration at the beginning. The ego-vehicle driver has a 14.3 % longer travel duration than PEEMTO. Due to the longer travel duration and the higher impact of the travel duration cost, the ego-vehicle driver has a combined cost that is 9.5 % higher than that of PEEMTO.

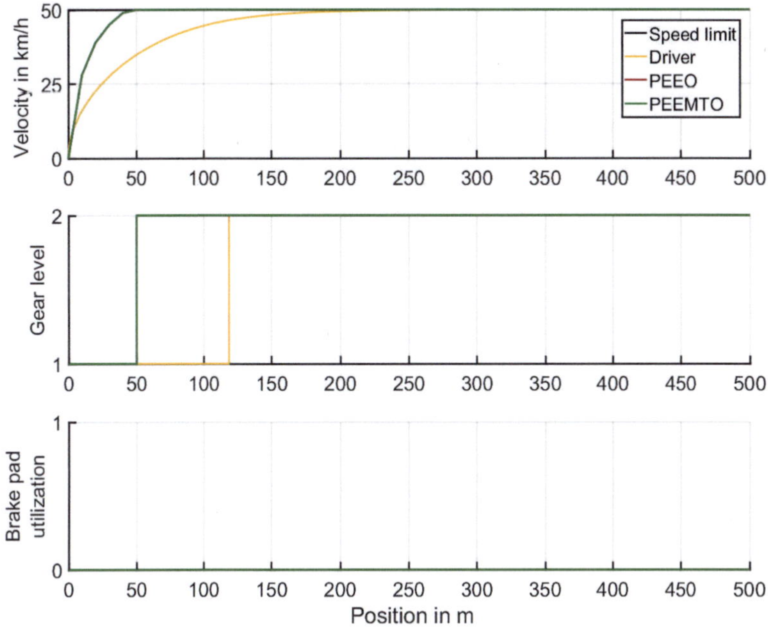

Figure 5.11: Acceleration with comfort constraints. Results of the ego-vehicle driver, PEEO and PEEMTO with respect to position. The speed limit is set to 50 $\frac{\text{km}}{\text{h}}$. Similar results may overlap each other in the illustration.

Comfort constraints

Figures 5.11 to 5.13 show the results with comfort constraints. PEEO and PEEMTO still yield the same result. Compared to the previous example, PEEMTO reaches the speed limit slightly later. There is slightly more transition from acceleration to cruising. This enables PEEMTO to fulfill the comfort constraints and keep the jerk below 1.5 $\frac{\text{m}}{\text{s}^3}$ and above -1.5 $\frac{\text{m}}{\text{s}^3}$ as shown in Figure 5.13. In this example, PEEMTO has a 4.4 % higher energy consumption than the ego-vehicle driver. The ego-vehicle driver has a 17.3 % longer travel duration. The combined cost of the ego-vehicle driver is still 9.5 % higher than that of PEEMTO.

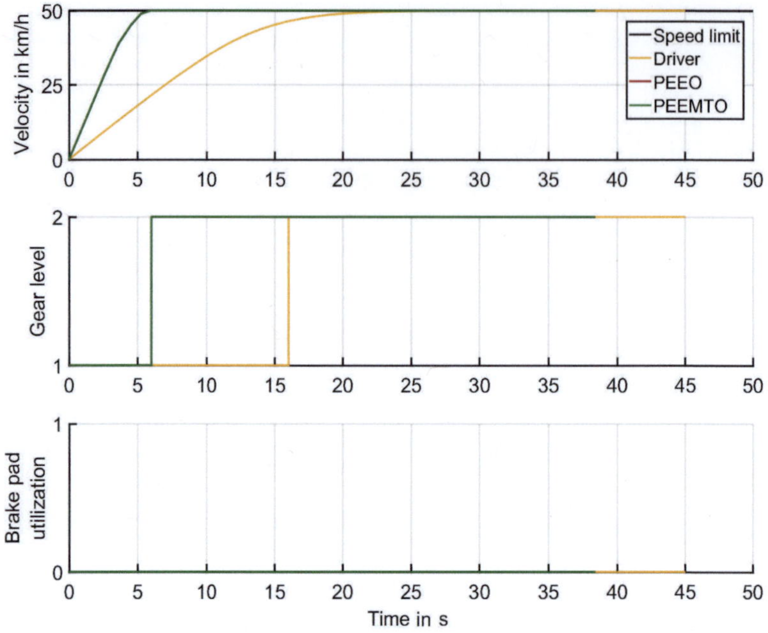

Figure 5.12: Acceleration with comfort constraints. Results of the ego-vehicle driver, PEEO and PEEMTO with respect to time. The speed limit is set to 50 $\frac{\text{km}}{\text{h}}$. The results of PEEO and PEEMTO are identical and therefore overlap each other.

No travel duration cost

In the previous two examples, the optimization with minimum GLC actually leads to higher energy consumption compared to the ego-vehicle driver, although the combined cost is smaller. An interesting question is what happens if the travel duration is not important. Figure 5.14 shows the velocity of PEEMTO if the travel duration cost is completely removed. Due to the relatively homogeneous engine efficiency map of the REM-2030 EE, PEEMTO only accelerates to 7 $\frac{\text{km}}{\text{h}}$, which is likely too low in the sense of traffic regulations. The choice of the low cruise velocity leads to a more than

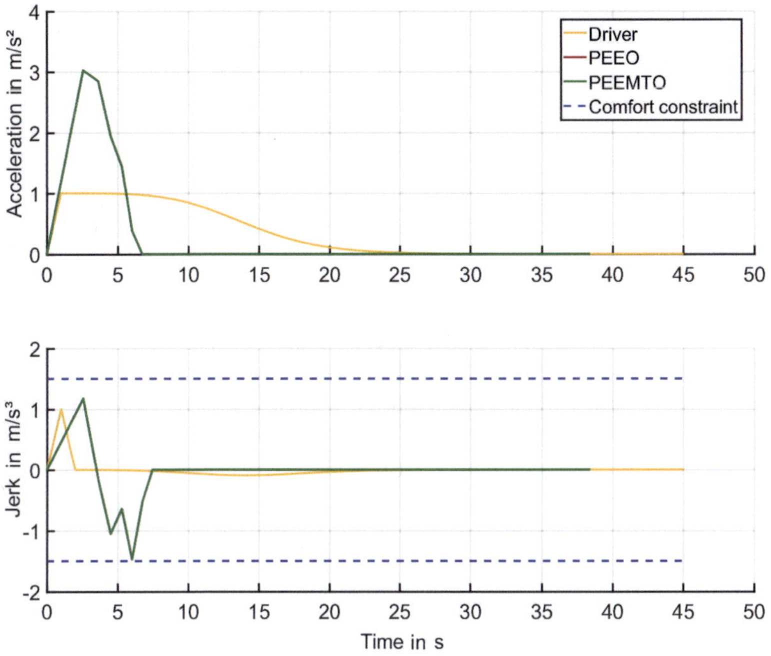

Figure 5.13: Acceleration with comfort constraints. Results of the ego-vehicle driver, PEEO and PEEMTO. Comfort constraints refer to jerks of 1.5 $\frac{\mathrm{m}}{\mathrm{s}^3}$ and -1.5 $\frac{\mathrm{m}}{\mathrm{s}^3}$. The results of PEEO and PEEMTO are identical and therefore overlap each other.

five times lower energy consumption and a more than seven times longer travel duration compared to the ego-vehicle driver.

Minimum travel duration cost

The issue of minimum cruise velocities has been discussed in section 4.3.2 and section 4.4.4. For urban scenarios, the minimum cruise velocity is assumed to be the same as the speed limit. In order to target a cruise velocity of 50 $\frac{\mathrm{km}}{\mathrm{h}}$, PEEMTO needs a minimum travel duration weight of 0.7 $\frac{€}{\mathrm{h}}$. If the travel duration weight was further reduced, PEEMTO would no longer choose the speed limit of 50 $\frac{\mathrm{km}}{\mathrm{h}}$ as the optimal cruise velocity.

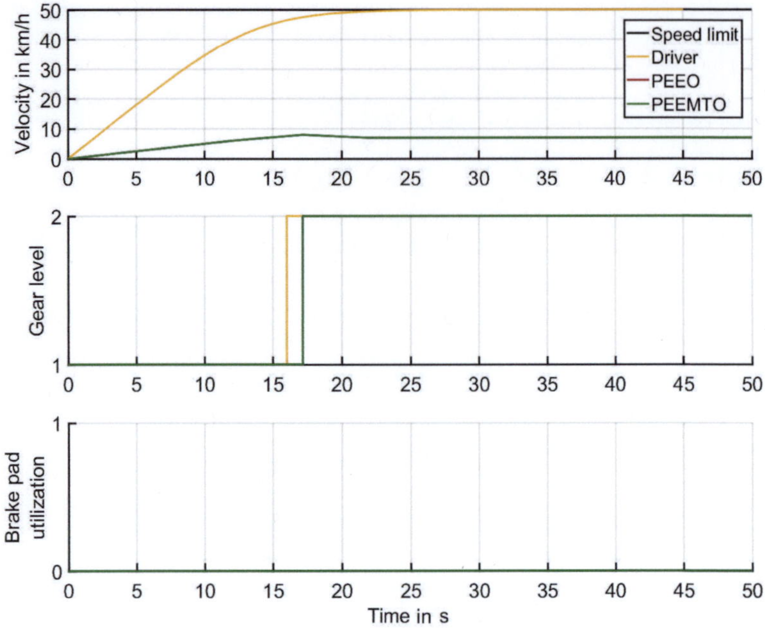

Figure 5.14: Optimization without any travel duration cost. Results of the ego-vehicle driver, PEEO, and PEEMTO. The speed limit is set to 50 $\frac{\text{km}}{\text{h}}$. The results of PEEO and PEEMTO are identical and therefore overlap each other.

The results are shown in Figures 5.15 to 5.18. The results of PEEO and PEEMTO are still the same. As illustrated in Figures 5.15 and 5.16, the acceleration of PEEMTO is smaller, and it needs more time to reach the speed limit. But the acceleration is still higher than in the case of the ego-vehicle driver.

Figure 5.18 shows the cost components without travel duration. The ego-vehicle driver has 2.2 % higher energy consumption than PEEMTO. The combined cost of the ego-vehicle driver is only 0.9 % higher than that of PEEMTO because the gear shift cost has a larger impact than the energy consumption. The reduction of energy consumption by PEEMTO is due to

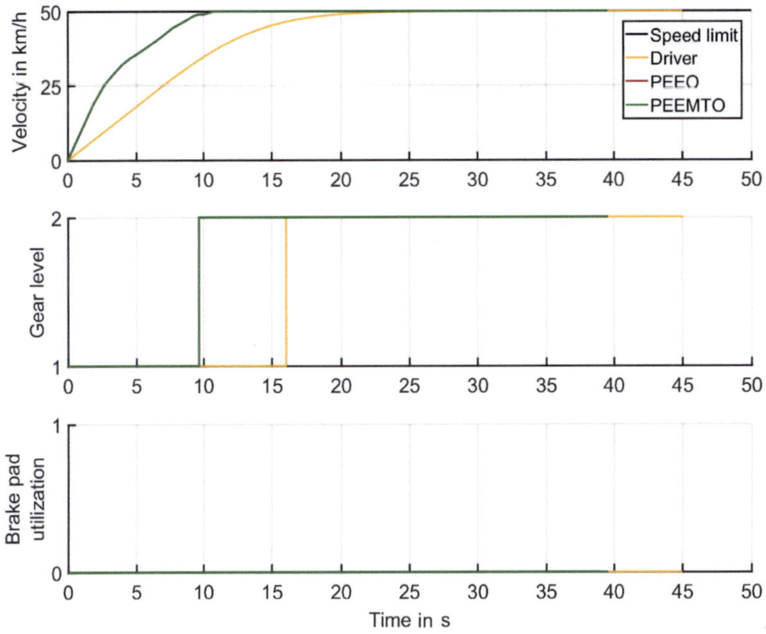

Figure 5.15: Optimization without explicit formulation of travel duration cost. Results of velocity, gear level, and brake pad utilization with respect to time for the ego-vehicle driver, PEEO, and PEEMTO. The speed limit is set to 50 $\frac{\text{km}}{\text{h}}$. The results of PEEO and PEEMTO are identical and therefore overlap each other.

slightly higher powertrain efficiency on a few occasions in combination with slightly better choice of engine torque and engine speed. Another reason is the optimal gear shift synchronization. As the gear shift occurs, PEEMTO maintains the velocity for a short moment instead of accelerating (see Figure 5.15). Thus, the drop in powertrain efficiency occurs when the power demand is low. In the case of the ego-vehicle driver, the gear shift and the drop in powertrain efficiency occurs as the ego-vehicle driver is still accelerating.

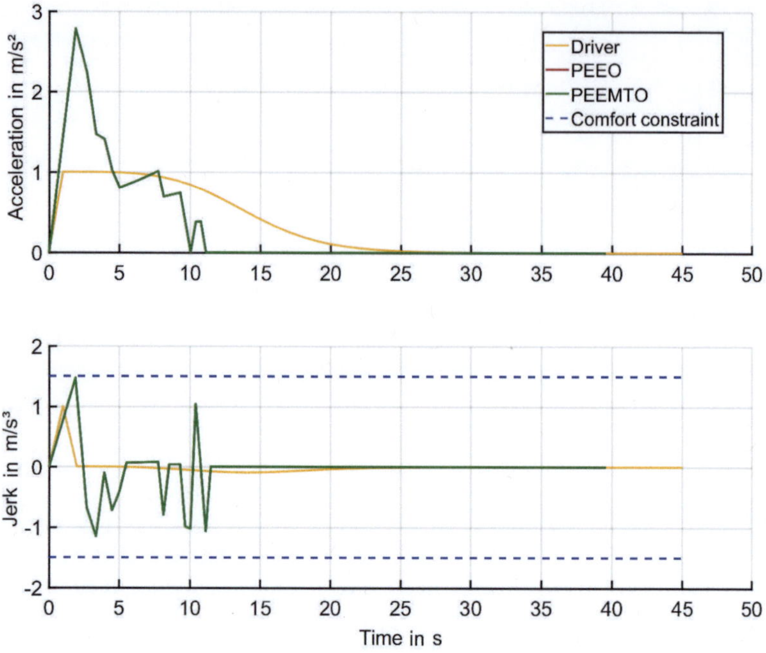

Figure 5.16: Optimization without explicit formulation of travel duration cost. Results of longitudinal acceleration and longitudinal jerk with respect to time for the ego-vehicle driver, PEEO, and PEEMTO. The results of PEEO and PEEMTO are identical and therefore overlap each other.

Furthermore, PEEMTO reaches the optimal cruise velocity earlier than the ego-vehicle driver. Once the vehicle reaches the optimal cruise velocity, it no longer needs to accelerate. Additionally, the powertrain efficiency is highest during cruising for the given scenario.

Different from ICEs, which have their peak efficiency only within a small operation area, EEs have high efficiency for the vast majority of operations points. This leads to the consequence that the optimal result can be harder to interpret, and the improvement to energy efficiency may be less obvious than in the case of ICEs [Ter09] [Hel10].

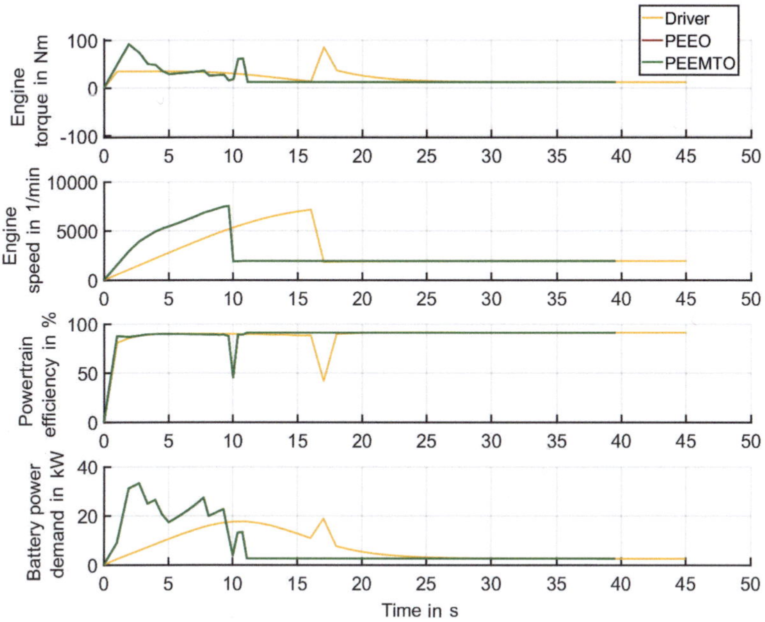

Figure 5.17: Optimization without explicit formulation of travel duration cost. Results of engine torque, engine speed, powertrain efficiency and battery power demand with respect to time for the ego-vehicle driver, PEEO, and PEEMTO. The results of PEEO and PEEMTO are identical and therefore overlap each other.

5.3.2 Deceleration

In this scenario, the deceleration behavior of PEEMTO is demonstrated. The vehicle starts at 50 $\frac{\text{km}}{\text{h}}$ and gear level two. The route ends after 500 m. The speed limit is set to 50 $\frac{\text{km}}{\text{h}}$. The road is even and straight. All contenders must come to a full stop at the end of the route.

No comfort constraints

Figures 5.19 to 5.23 show the results without any comfort consideration. PEEO and PEEMTO yield the same result. Compared to the acceleration scenario, the deceleration is generally stronger for all contenders including

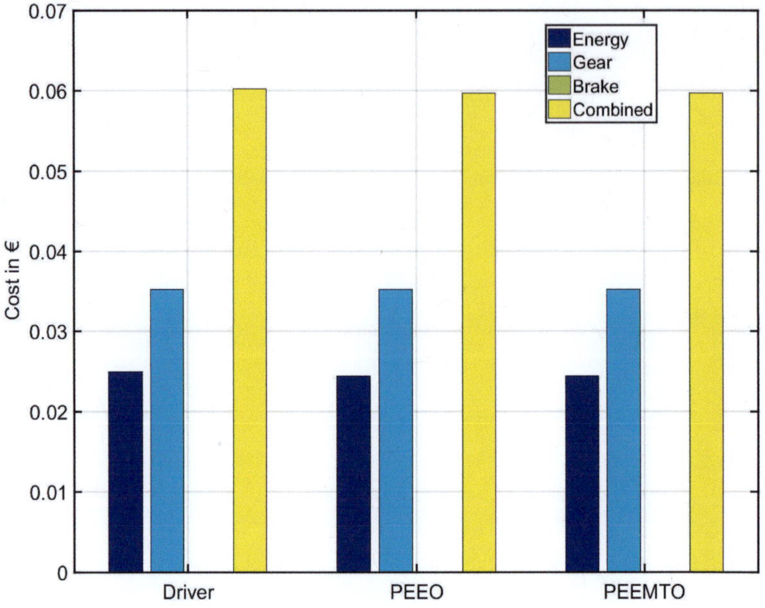

Figure 5.18: Optimization without explicit formulation of travel duration cost. Resulting costs of the different contenders at the end of the experiment.

the ego-vehicle driver. As illustrated in Figure 5.21, PEEMTO once again violates the jerk constraint of $-1.5\frac{\mathrm{m}}{\mathrm{s}^3}$ if comfort is not considered.

The engine torque turns negative during the deceleration process as illustrated in Figure 5.22. For negative engine torque, the EE becomes a generator and recuperates energy. As illustrated in Figure 5.20, none of the contenders need to use the brake pads and only decelerate through recuperation. Note that the avoidance of brake pad utilization often requires the reduction of the gear level in order to reduce generator torque. While high generator torque leads to stronger recuperation, an EE has a minimum engine torque or rather maximum generator torque, which is approximately -103 Nm between $0\,\frac{1}{\mathrm{min}}$ and $7{,}500\,\frac{1}{\mathrm{min}}$ in the case of the REM-2030 engine. In case of higher

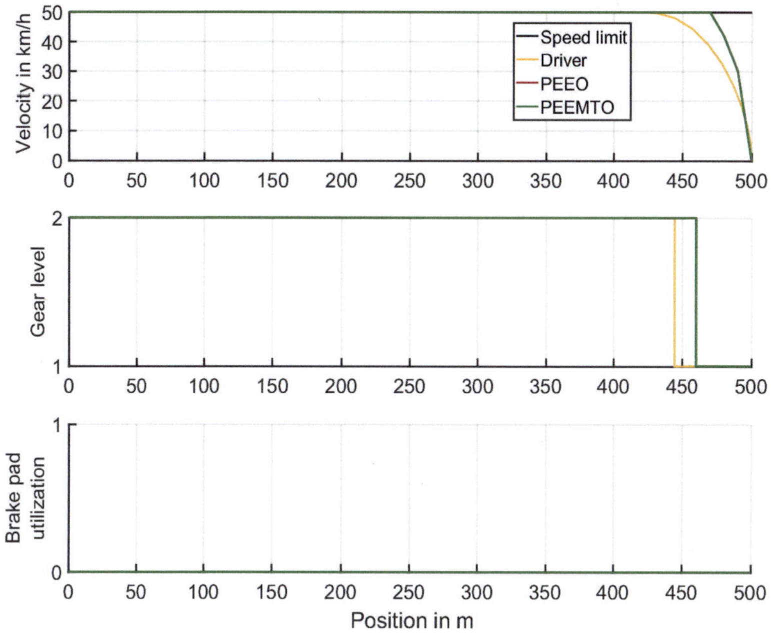

Figure 5.19: Deceleration without comfort constraints. Optimization results of velocity, gear level, and brake pad utilization with respect to position for the ego-vehicle driver, PEEO, and PEEMTO. The speed limit is set to 50 $\frac{\text{km}}{\text{h}}$. The results of PEEO and PEEMTO are identical and therefore overlap each other.

brake torque demand, the torque would have to be supplied by the brake pads. As illustrated in Figure 5.22, the engine torque of PEEMTO comes very close to the minimum engine torque of approximately -103 Nm. The deceleration would not be possible at gear level two because the brake torque demand would increase by four times. It is important to note that the energy dissipated by the brake pads cannot be recuperated by the EE.

Figure 5.23 shows the resulting costs. The ego-vehicle driver has the highest cost due to the longest travel duration, which is 7.8 % longer than that of PEEMTO. The contenders have the same gear shift cost. In this example,

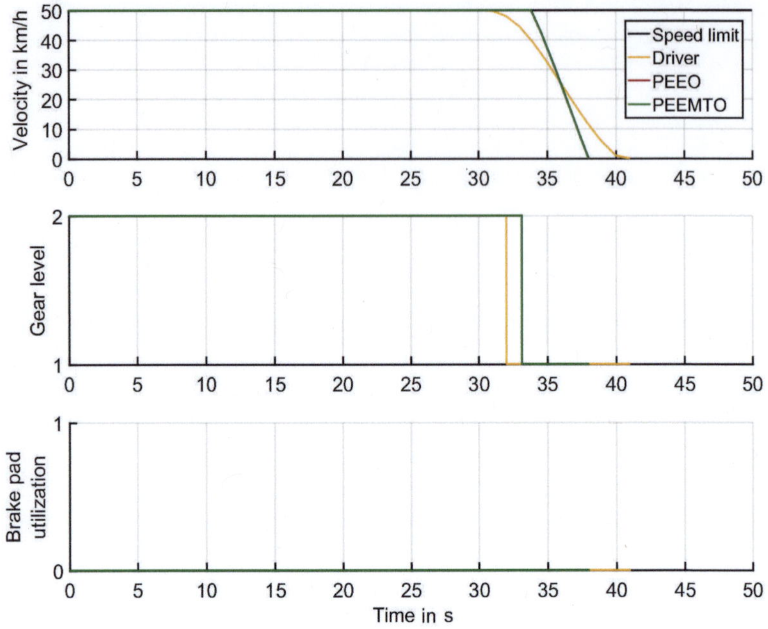

Figure 5.20: Deceleration without comfort constraints. Optimization results of velocity, gear level, and brake pad utilization with respect to time for the ego-vehicle driver, PEEO, and PEEMTO. The speed limit is set to 50 $\frac{\text{km}}{\text{h}}$. The results of PEEO and PEEMTO are identical and therefore overlap each other.

all contenders have a negative net energy consumption, i.e., more energy is recuperated than consumed. The net energy recuperation of the ego-vehicle driver, i.e., the remaining recuperated energy at the end of the scenario, is 20.9 % higher than that of PEEMTO. But the absolute difference is hardly noticeable. As the absolute cost of energy consumption is very small in this example, small absolute gains in energy recuperation can lead to relatively large percental gains. The combined cost of the ego-vehicle driver is 5.3 % higher than that of PEEMTO.

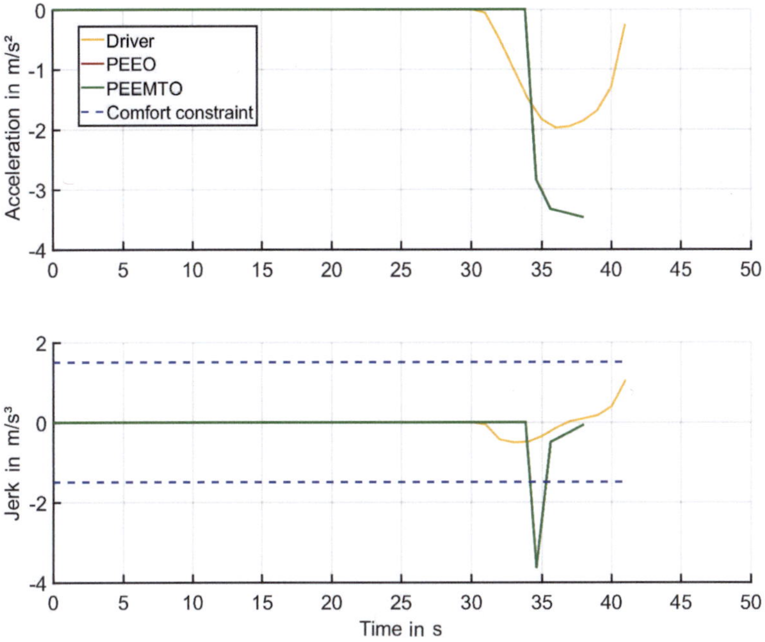

Figure 5.21: Deceleration without comfort constraints. Longitudinal acceleration and jerk with respect to time for the ego-vehicle driver, PEEO, and PEEMTO. The results of PEEO and PEEMTO are identical and therefore overlap each other.

Comfort constraints

Figures 5.24 to 5.26 show the results with comfort constraints. PEEMTO and PEEO still yield the same result. As illustrated in Figure 5.25, PEEMTO starts the deceleration approximately at the same time as the ego-vehicle driver with a stronger deceleration towards the end. As illustrated in Figure 5.26, the jerk can be kept well within the comfort constraints. In this example, the ego-vehicle driver has a 27.9 % larger net energy recuperation than PEEMTO. The ego-vehicle driver has a 6.3 % longer travel duration. The combined cost of the ego-vehicle driver is 4.1 % larger than that of PEEMTO.

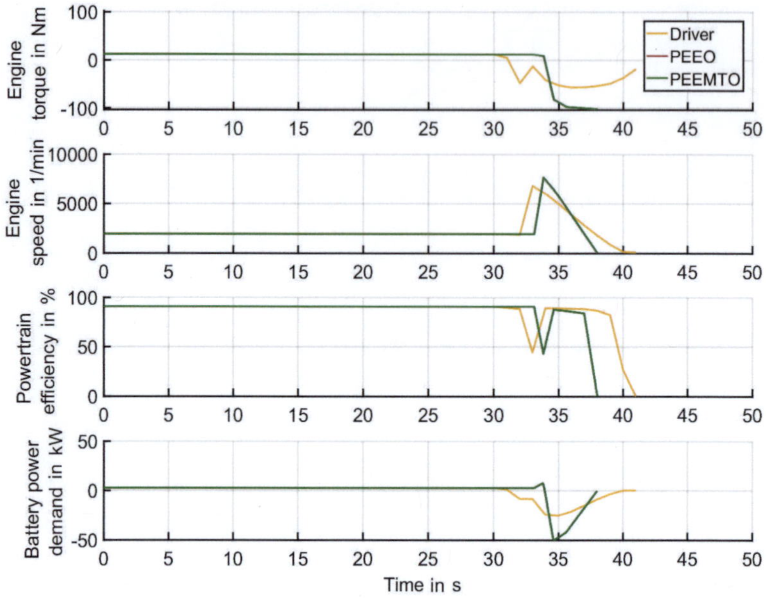

Figure 5.22: Deceleration without comfort constraints. Optimization results of engine torque, engine speed, powertrain efficiency, and battery power demand with respect to time for the ego-vehicle driver, PEEO, and PEEMTO. The results of PEEO and PEEMTO are identical and therefore overlap each other.

Minimum travel duration cost

Figures 5.27 to 5.29 show the results with comfort constraints if travel duration is unimportant. As illustrated in Figure 5.27, PEEMTO starts to decelerate significantly earlier than the ego-vehicle driver. The early deceleration leads to a final travel duration of PEEMTO that is 2.5 % longer than that of the ego-vehicle driver. As illustrated in Figure 5.28, the energy recuperation process of PEEMTO begins significantly earlier than in the case of the ego-vehicle driver. The early deceleration leads to smaller external resistance forces over a longer duration. Figure 5.29 shows the resulting costs without travel duration. The net energy recuperation of PEEMTO is 47 % higher than that of the ego-vehicle driver. The gear shift costs are the

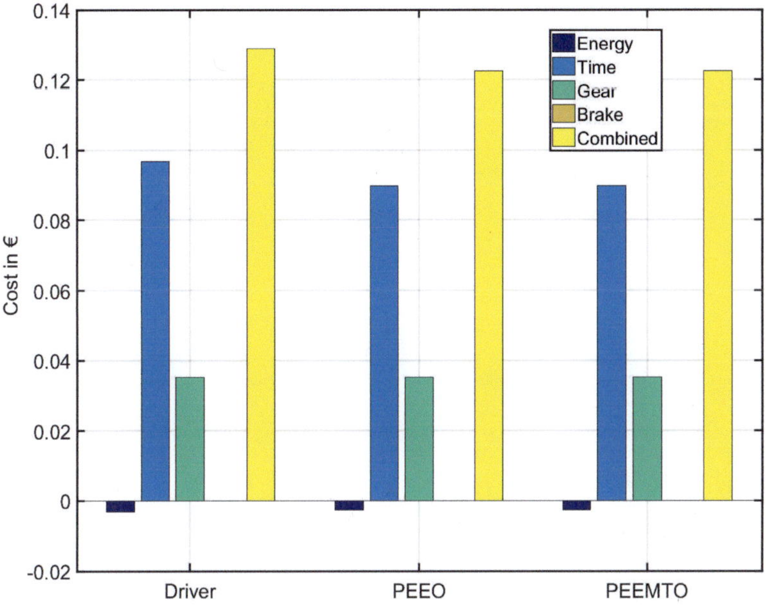

Figure 5.23: Deceleration without comfort constraints. Resulting costs of the different contenders at the end of the experiment.

same. In this example, the ego-vehicle driver has a 5 % higher combined cost than PEEMTO.

In general, energy efficiency as defined by the monetary cost formulation in section 4.3 does not necessarily lead to less energy consumption under all circumstances. This is due to the fact that the goal of the optimization is to reduce the combined cost. As illustrated in Figure 5.2 and the scenarios, the travel duration cost for minimum GLC can be significantly higher than the corresponding energy consumption in urban scenarios. If no travel duration cost is explicitly formulated, the optimization can sometimes reduce both energy consumption and travel duration, although the resulting combined cost would likely to be higher if the travel duration cost was formulated.

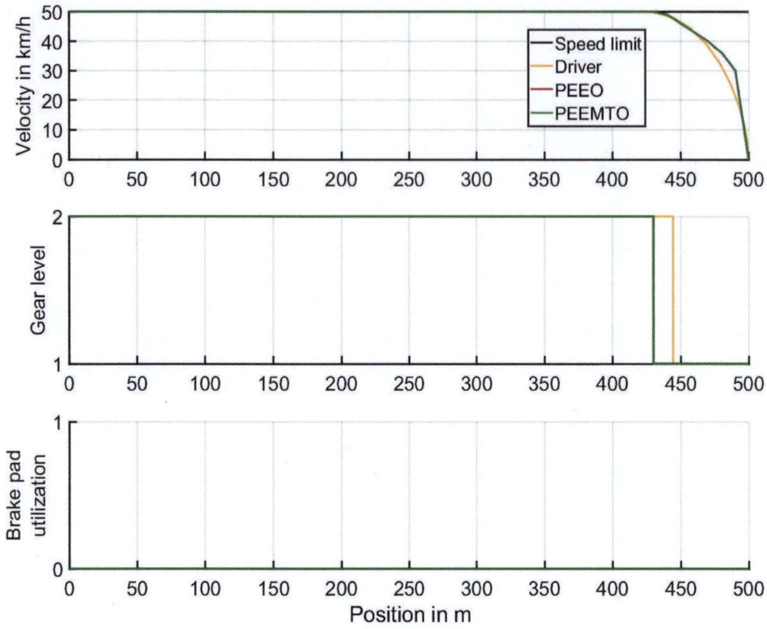

Figure 5.24: Deceleration with comfort constraints. Optimization results of velocity, gear level, and brake pad utilization with respect to position for the ego-vehicle driver, PEEO, and PEEMTO. The speed limit is set to 50 $\frac{\text{km}}{\text{h}}$. The results of PEEO and PEEMTO are identical and therefore overlap each other.

5.3.3 Recuperation

The EE is able to recuperate part of the energy. The example scenario in Figure 5.30 shows how much energy is recuperated by PEEMTO on an even and straight road with the speed limit set to 50 $\frac{\text{km}}{\text{h}}$. The vehicle is initially at the optimal cruise velocity and using the second gear level. In the first scenario, the ego-vehicle is allowed to maintain its velocity. The second scenario commands that the vehicle has to temporarily come to a complete stop at some point along the route. After it has stopped, it is allowed to continue. Figure 5.30 only shows the segment where the vehicle starts to

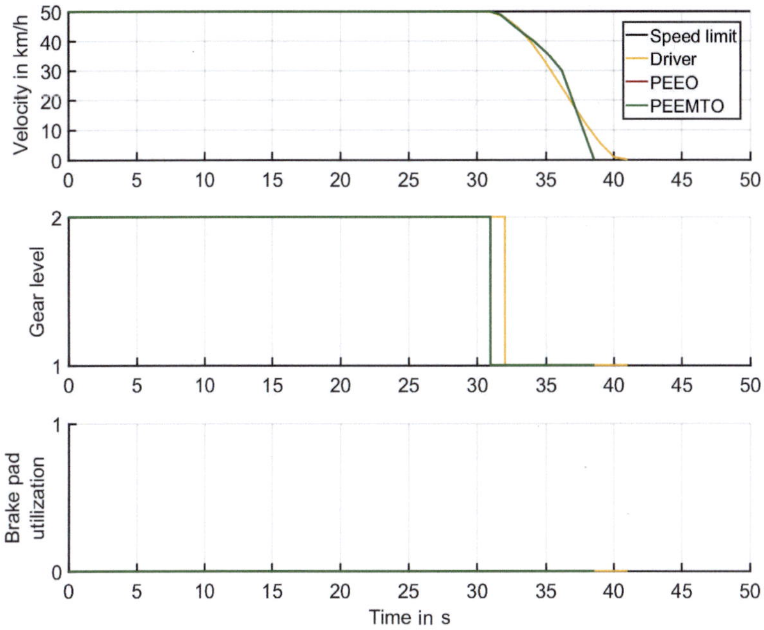

Figure 5.25: Deceleration with comfort constraints. Optimization results of velocity, gear level, and brake pad utilization with respect to time for the ego-vehicle driver, PEEO, and PEEMTO. The speed limit is set to 50 $\frac{\text{km}}{\text{h}}$. The results of PEEO and PEEMTO are identical and therefore overlap each other.

slow down before reverting back to the speed limit. The beginning of the velocity variation is set to 0 m.

As shown in Figure 5.30, the vehicle is able to recuperate more than 0.01 € worth of energy when it comes to a stop. But as it accelerates back to the speed limit, it eventually consumes more energy than it recuperates. In this example, the energy consumption is 0.0044 €. As discussed in section 5.3.1 and section 5.3.2, PEEMTO with the default choice of λ_t has a strong acceleration. Nevertheless, due to the inefficiency of the powertrain, complete recuperation is impossible.

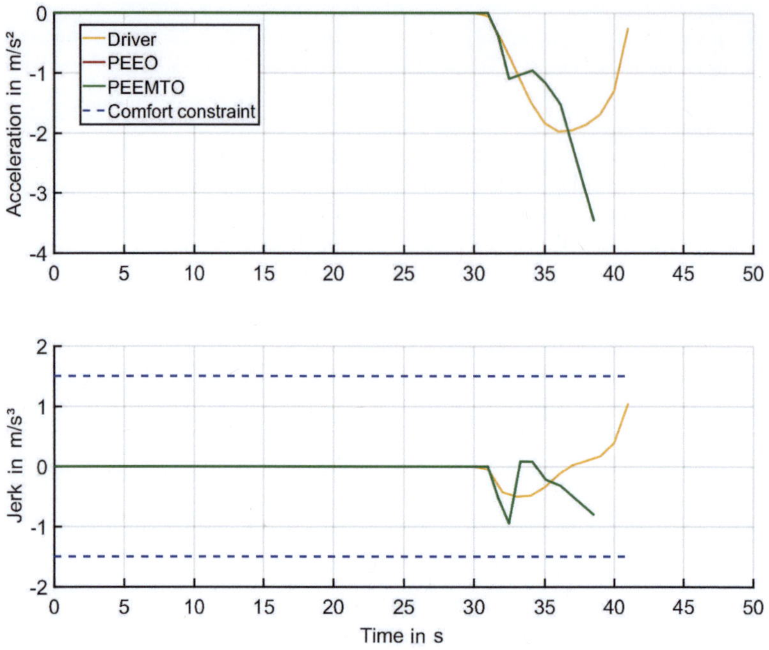

Figure 5.26: Deceleration with comfort constraints. Optimization results of longitudinal acceleration and longitudinal jerk with respect to time for the ego-vehicle driver, PEEO, and PEEMTO. The results of PEEO and PEEMTO are identical and therefore overlap each other.

Figure 5.30 also shows how much energy is saved if the vehicle does not stop but simply continues at the optimal cruise velocity. In this case, the energy consumption after the same travel distance is 57 % smaller compared to a temporary stop. As mentioned in section 5.3.1, traveling at the urban speed limit leads to high powertrain efficiency. Naturally, a temporary stop also leads to a longer travel duration and two gear shifts. The overall cost is 35 % smaller if the vehicle maintains the optimal cruise velocity.

The external resistance increases with velocity primarily due to the air resistance. Thus, a temporary decrease in velocity may seem beneficial for

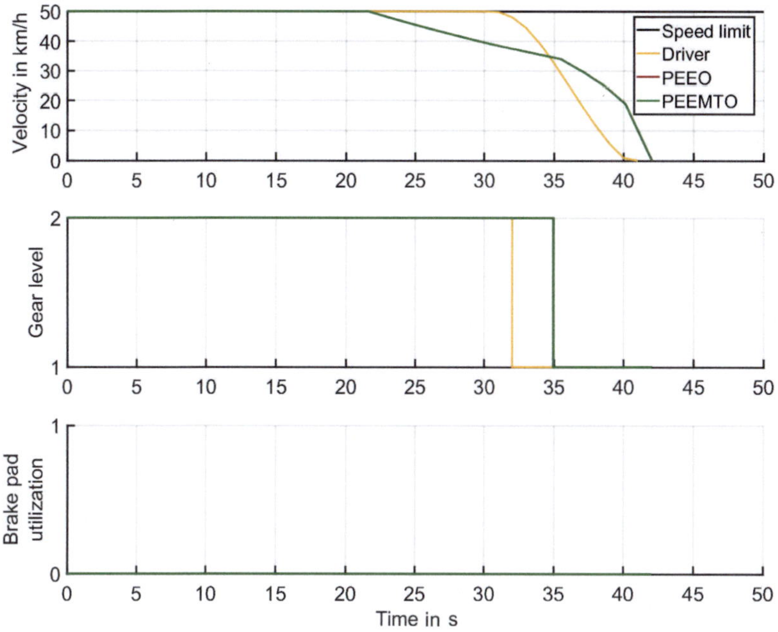

Figure 5.27: Deceleration without explicit formulation of minimum travel duration cost. Optimization results of velocity, gear level, and brake pad utilization with respect to time for the ego-vehicle driver, PEEO, and PEEMTO. The speed limit is set to 50 $\frac{\text{km}}{\text{h}}$. The results of PEEO and PEEMTO are identical and therefore overlap each other.

energy consumption. But as shown in Figure 5.1, the acceleration resistance is stronger than the external resistance forces from the environment for urban speed limits. Furthermore, as shown in the illustrations of section 5.3.1 and section 5.3.2, the powertrain efficiency is lowest when the vehicle starts to move or comes to a full stop. It significantly drops during gear shifts. On the other hand, the powertrain efficiency is often high for constant velocity. Thus, strong velocity variation can lead to higher energy consumption over the same driven distance. But note that the final outcome is always scenario dependent.

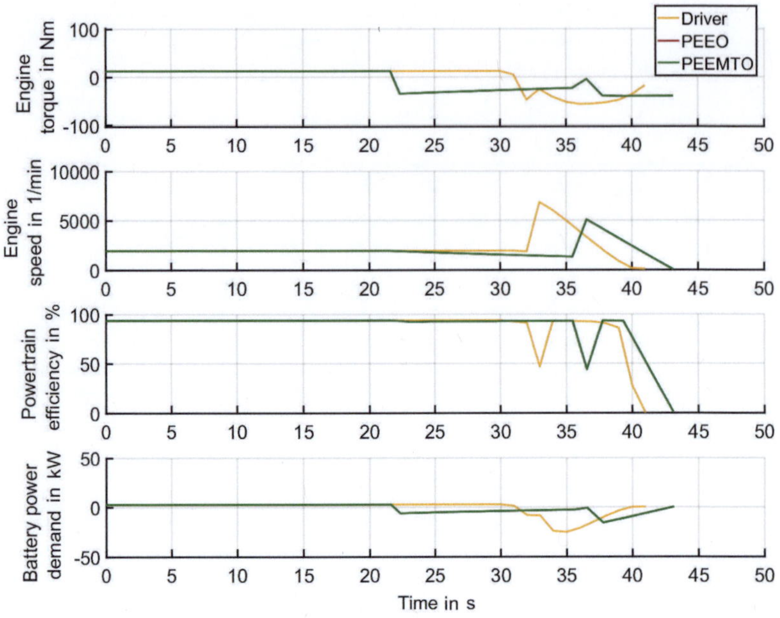

Figure 5.28: Deceleration without explicit formulation of minimum travel duration cost. Optimization results of engine torque, engine speed, powertrain efficiency, and battery power demand with respect to time for the ego-vehicle driver, PEEO and PEEMTO. The speed limit is set to 50 $\frac{km}{h}$. The results of PEEO and PEEMTO are identical and therefore overlap each other.

5.3.4 Velocity and state of charge

As discussed in section 3.1.1, the battery idle voltage changes with the battery state of charge (SOC). A low state of charge leads to a lower battery idle voltage. If the power demand from the battery remains the same, the battery has to compensate a lower battery voltage with a higher battery current according to the vehicle model in section 3.1.1. A higher battery current also leads to a higher loss in the internal resistance of the battery.

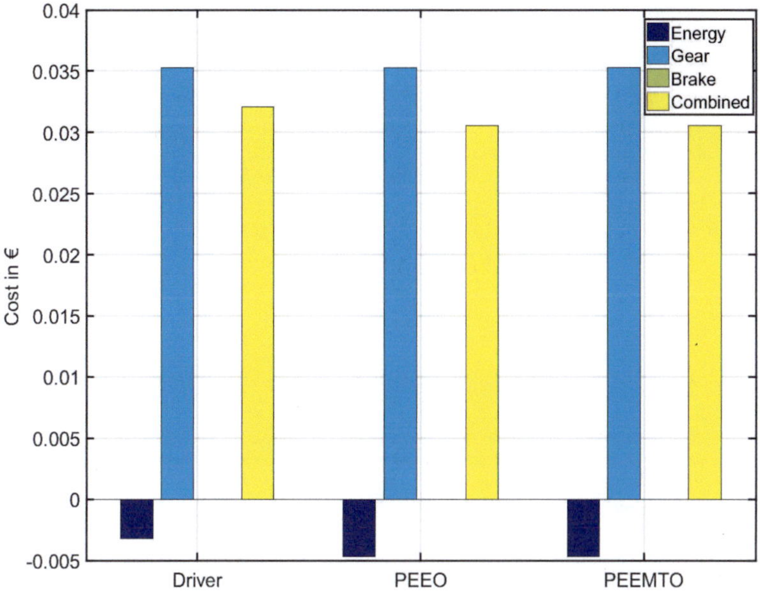

Figure 5.29: Deceleration without explicit formulation of minimum travel duration cost. Resulting costs of the different contenders at the end of the experiment.

Figure 5.31 shows scenarios, in which PEEMTO guides the ego-vehicle to the optimal cruise velocity for even, straight roads of 92 $\frac{\text{km}}{\text{h}}$. The battery cell current approaches the maximum battery cell discharge current of 20 A during the acceleration. Note that the nominal current of the battery cell is only 4 A. In general, it depends on the battery specifics if and how the battery can be used beyond the nominal values. If necessary, additional constraints can be set to limit the duration of battery currents beyond the nominal values. In the experiments, the battery usually only approaches its limits during strong acceleration and strong deceleration. As illustrated in Figure 5.31, the trajectory deviations for different SOC is only minor. The optimal cruise velocity remains the same and the ego-vehicle reaches the optimal cruise velocity only slightly faster at the maximum SOC of 95 %

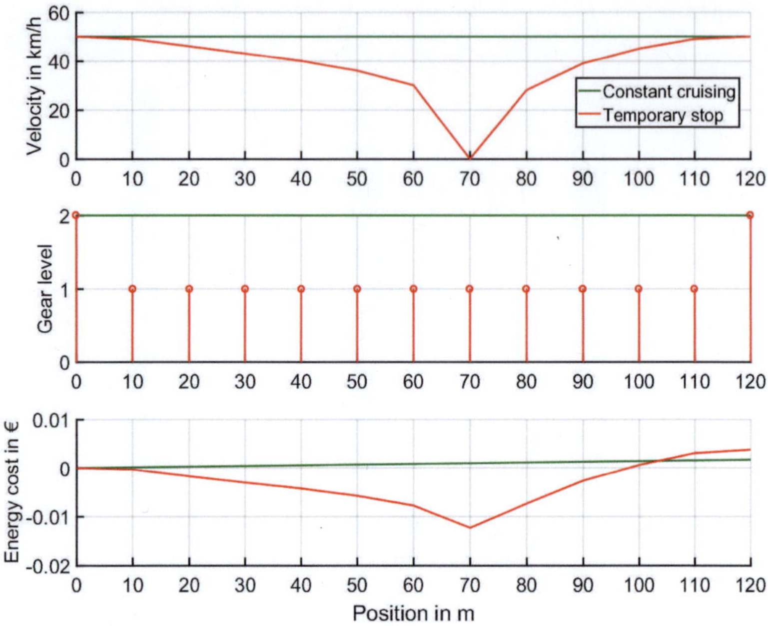

Figure 5.30: PEEMTO start and stop recuperation compared to constant cruising at optimal cruise velocity on an even and straight road. The speed limit set to 50 $\frac{\text{km}}{\text{h}}$.

compared to the minimum SOC of 25 %. As discussed in section 3.1.1, the idle battery voltage can only change between 3.55 V and 4 V within the SOC range of 25 % and 95 % in the case of the REM-2030 battery.

5.4 Road slopes

In this example, an artificially generated hill is evaluated. Curvatures and speed limits are left out to focus on the influence of the road slope. PEEMTO uses the LRAHE, while PEEO only uses SHE. The ego-vehicle driver is not evaluated in this example because the driver model is not able to realistically deal with strong road slopes and curvatures. In fact, some attempts were actually made. But the ego-vehicle driver always produced results that were

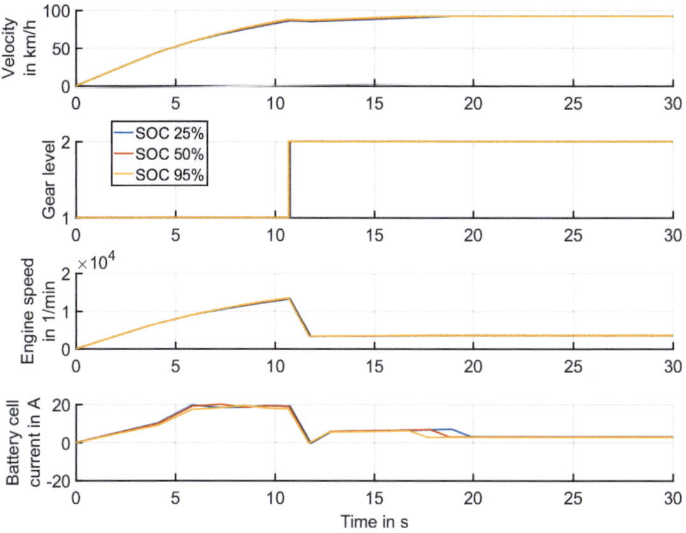

Figure 5.31: Acceleration of PEEMTO towards the optimal cruise velocity on even, straight roads at different states of charge (SOC). Similar results may overlap each other in the illustration.

at some point no longer physically feasible. This example and the examples in section 5.5 also represent scenarios that can be highly problematic for existing autonomous driving systems because they usually do not evaluate if the planned trajectory is physically feasible as discussed in section 2.3 and section 2.6.

The hill is illustrated in Figure 5.32. The hill starts on flat terrain. The road slope gradually increases until it reaches almost 6° at approximately 3500 m before gradually decreasing. The top of the hill is a flat plateau that gradually changes to a descent. The decline reaches almost -6° at approximately 9500 m before gradually changing back into flat terrain. The optimization evaluation ends after 13 km. The vehicle is initially not moving.

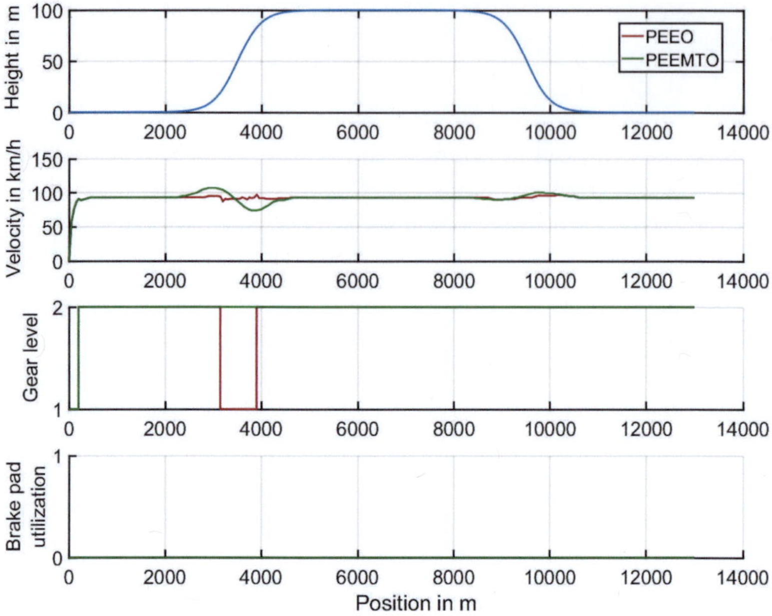

Figure 5.32: Height of road with respect to position. Optimization results of velocity, gear level, and brake pad utilization with respect to position for PEEO and PEEMTO. There is no speed limit and no road curvature. Similar results may overlap each other in the illustration.

Figures 5.32 to 5.35 show the results with comfort constraints. As illustrated in Figure 5.32, both PEEO and PEEMTO accelerate to velocities close to the optimal cruise velocity for even, straight roads of 92 $\frac{\text{km}}{\text{h}}$. At approximately 300 m, a gear shift to the second gear level is performed. As shown in Figure 5.34, the engine torque is almost zero during the gear shift, which means that the ego-vehicle is almost coasting. Indeed, as illustrated in 5.32, the velocity slightly drops after the first gear shift. PEEMTO soon adopts the optimal cruise velocity as the ego-vehicle approaches the hill.

When the ascent gradually begins, PEEMTO accelerates beyond 92 $\frac{\text{km}}{\text{h}}$ to gather kinetic energy before the slope becomes too steep. It starts to lose

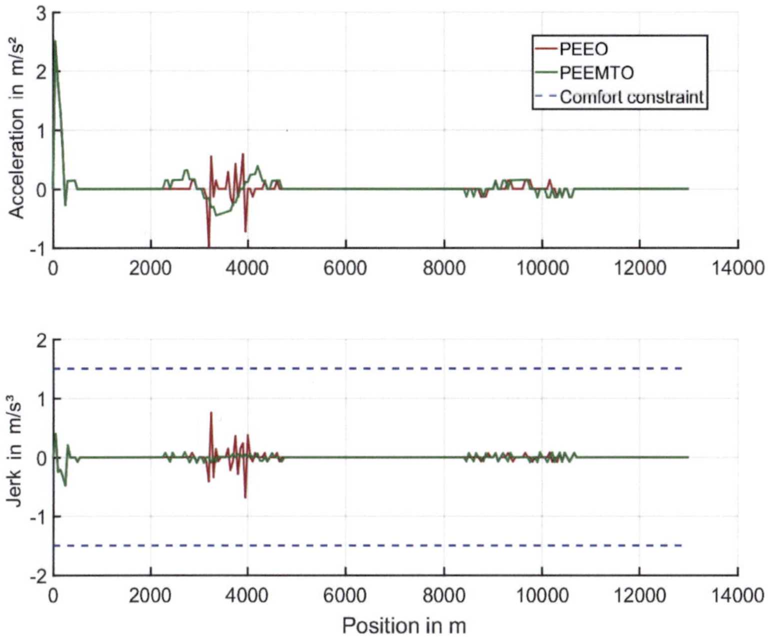

Figure 5.33: Optimization results of longitudinal acceleration and longitudinal jerk with respect to time for PEEO and PEEMTO. Similar results may overlap each other in the illustration.

speed at approximately 3000 m. Generally, changing to a lower gear level during a steep ascent can become necessary as the engine torque demand can quickly reach its maximum at a high gear level. Lowering the gear level decreases the torque demand while increasing the engine speed. In the case of the REM-2030 transmission, the engine torque demand is four times smaller at gear level one compared to gear level two. In this scenario, PEEMTO does not need to change to a lower gear as it has already gathered velocity when the slope was significantly smaller. The velocity of PEEMTO continues to drop until a minimum is reached, then gradually increases near the end of the ascent.

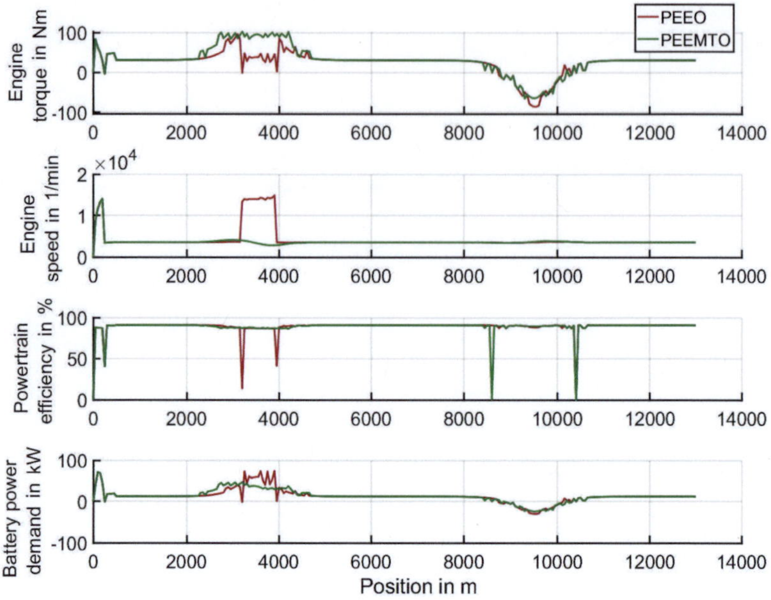

Figure 5.34: Optimization results of engine torque, engine speed, powertrain efficiency, and battery power demand with respect to time for PEEO and PEEMTO. Similar results may overlap each other in the illustration.

On the flat plateau, PEEMTO accelerates back to 92 $\frac{\text{km}}{\text{h}}$. During the descent, the optimization has to find a compromise between two options. It can use the potential energy to increase velocity or it transforms the potential energy into electric energy through recuperation. Increasing the velocity decreases travel duration. But accelerating to a very high velocity means that the air resistance consumes much of the potential energy and a stronger recuperation may actually be a better solution. As shown in Figure 5.34, the engine torque is partly negative during the descent. This means that the engine recuperates part of the energy while the rest is used to accelerate the vehicle. As the engine torque turns negative and then positive again, the engine temporarily uses coasting on two occasions, i.e., the engine torque and the engine effi-

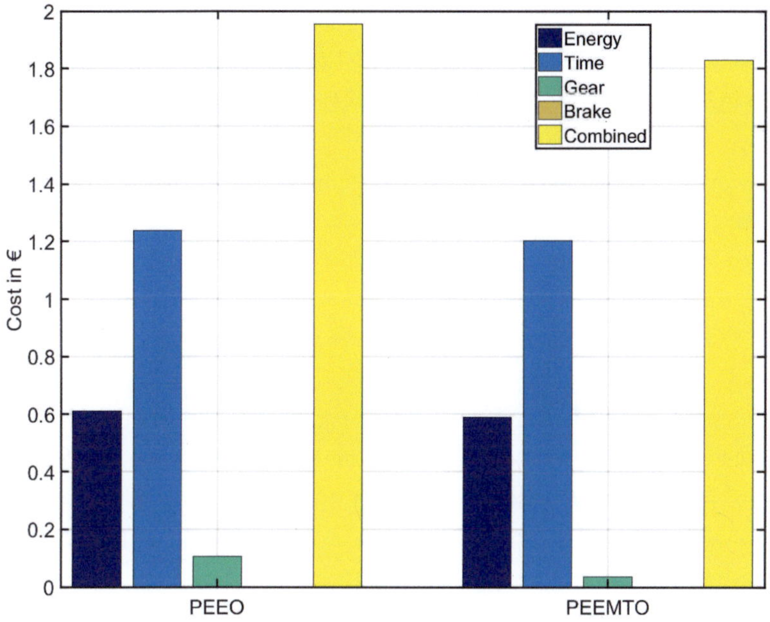

Figure 5.35: Resulting costs of PEEO and PEEMTO at the end of the experiment.

ciency is zero without any power transfer. PEEMTO eventually reaches the flat terrain and decelerates to the optimal cruise velocity.

PEEO also initially accelerates to 92 $\frac{\text{km}}{\text{h}}$. But due to the relatively short default horizon length of 250 m and the height variation over long distances, it does not show the same anticipatory behavior of PEEMTO. As illustrated in Figure 5.32, it does not gather sufficient velocity ahead of the steepest point and has to change to the first gear level. When the ego-vehicle approaches the plateau, PEEO changes back to the second gear level. As illustrated in Figure 5.32, PEEO is comparatively indecisive regarding the velocity trajectory during the ascension. As illustrated in Figure 5.34, this leads to a higher power demand and therefore higher energy consumption during the ascension in comparison to PEEMTO. During the descent, PEEO chooses a lower velocity than PEEMTO. This leads to slightly more energy recuperation as shown in Figure 5.34, but longer travel duration.

Figure 5.35 shows the resulting cost components. PEEO shifts gears three times more often than PEEMTO. Due to the inefficient hill ascension, PEEO has a 4.3 % higher energy consumption than PEEMTO. Furthermore, it also has a 3.2 % longer travel duration due to the lower velocity during the descent. PEEO has a 6.3 % higher combined cost than PEEMTO.

The reaction of PEEMTO towards slopes can be similar to existing research conducted on vehicles with ICEs. For example, gathering kinetic energy and avoiding gear shifts ahead of strong ascensions is also observed for vehicles with ICEs [Ter09]. The previously discussed behavior of PEEMTO, e.g., acceleration before steep ascensions and acceleration during the descent, may not always be apparent in every scenario involving hills and mountains. Sometimes other influences are more prominent. The scenarios, given in section 5.5, are examples, in which strong curvature has a much larger impact. In general, the precise energy-efficient behavior heavily depends on the given scenario.

5.5 Mountain roads

This scenario combines road topography, curvature, and speed limits. The real-world route is located close to the village Bergwald. The village is situated on a mountain southeast of the city of Karlsruhe. The chosen route is shown in Figure 5.36. It starts at the bottom of the mountain, ascents to the village via a curvy road, traverses through the village in the outer ring, and descends the mountain on the original road. The roads inside and outside the village only have one lane for each direction. The speed limit is mostly set to 100 $\frac{\text{km}}{\text{h}}$ despite some areas with strong curvature and slope. The speed limit in the village is capped at 30 $\frac{\text{km}}{\text{h}}$. Along the chosen route, there are several opportunities for other vehicles to enter the route from other roads that are not part of the chosen route. There are no traffic lights along the route that can control the intersecting traffic. As this thesis does not evaluate scenarios in which the right of way is of importance, vehicles that may enter the route from other roads are not simulated. The position discretization of 10 m is used for the entire route to adapt to fast changing slopes and curvatures. The vehicle starts at the bottom of the mountain and is initially idle.

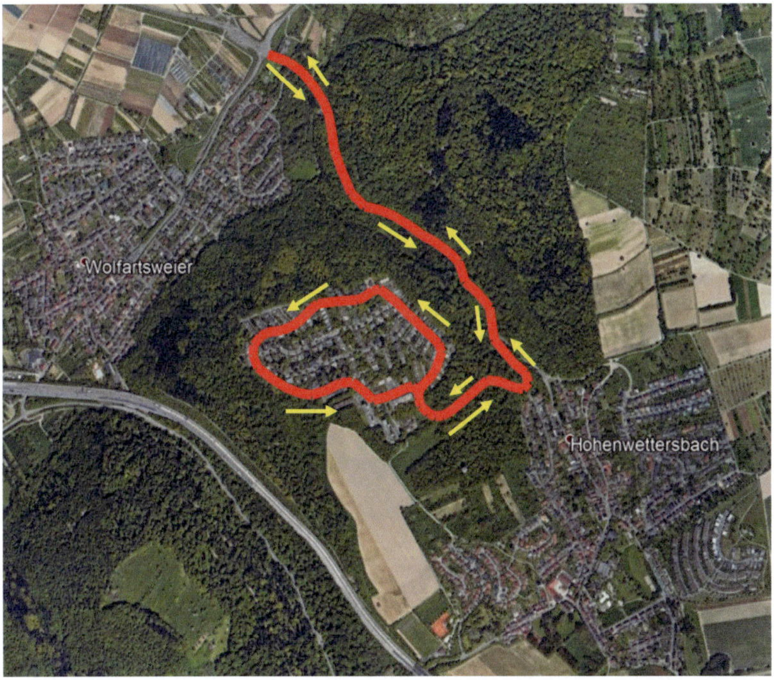

Figure 5.36: Bergwald route. The route (marked in red) starts at the bottom of the mountain, ascents to the village via a curvy road, traverses through the village Bergwald in the outer ring, and descends the mountain on the original road. Yellow arrows show the direction of travel. The image has been obtained from Google Earth.

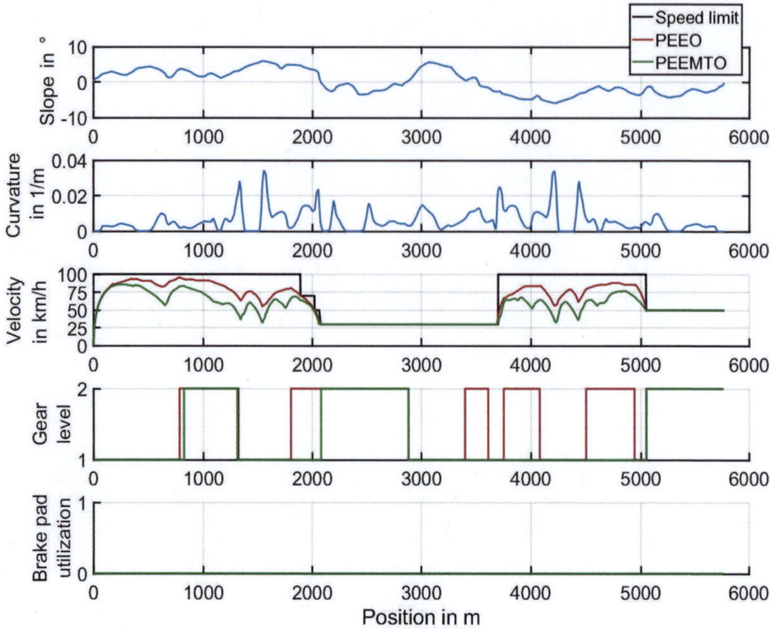

Figure 5.37: Scenario with short auxiliary horizon start length. Optimization results of velocity, gear level and brake pad utilization with respect to position for PEEO and PEEMTO. Similar results may overlap each other in the illustration.

5.5.1 Short auxiliary horizon start length

Figures 5.37 to 5.40 show the results with comfort constraints and a relatively short start auxiliary horizon length of 500 m. Compared to the previous scenario in section 5.4, the optimization is more heavily influenced by curves than the road slope.

The vehicle generally has to begin the deceleration well ahead of strong curvatures. PEEMTO never accelerates to the optimal cruise velocity of 92 $\frac{\text{km}}{\text{h}}$ for even, straight roads, although it is physically possible on certain sections of the road. In the village of Bergwald, the speed limit of 30 $\frac{\text{km}}{\text{h}}$ is

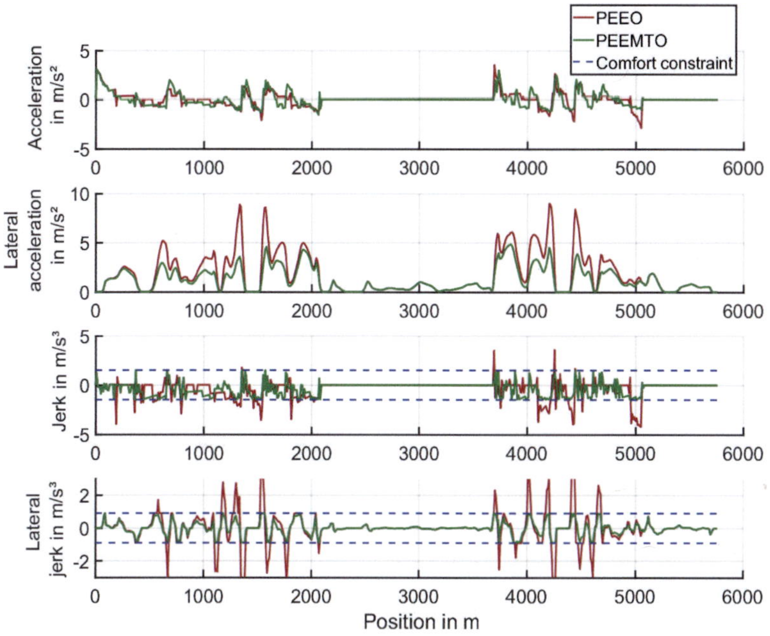

Figure 5.38: Short auxiliary horizon start length. Optimization results of longitudinal acceleration, lateral acceleration, longitudinal jerk, and lateral jerk with respect to position for PEEO and PEEMTO. Similar results may overlap each other in the illustration.

preferred by both PEEO and PEEMTO. The velocity of PEEO is generally higher due to the relatively short default horizon length of 250 m and the terminal cost that motivates the optimization to accelerate to 92 $\frac{\text{km}}{\text{h}}$ at the end of the horizon. The consequence of PEEO's relatively high velocity is shown in Figure 5.38. Both longitudinal and lateral jerk of PEEO violate the comfort constraints on multiple occasions. As PEEO accelerates to a relatively high velocity, it is sometimes surprised by strong curvature as the information enters the horizon. Thus, PEEO has to suddenly decelerate on several occasions. As the necessary deceleration can be quite strong, PEEO is not always able to find a feasible solution without violating the

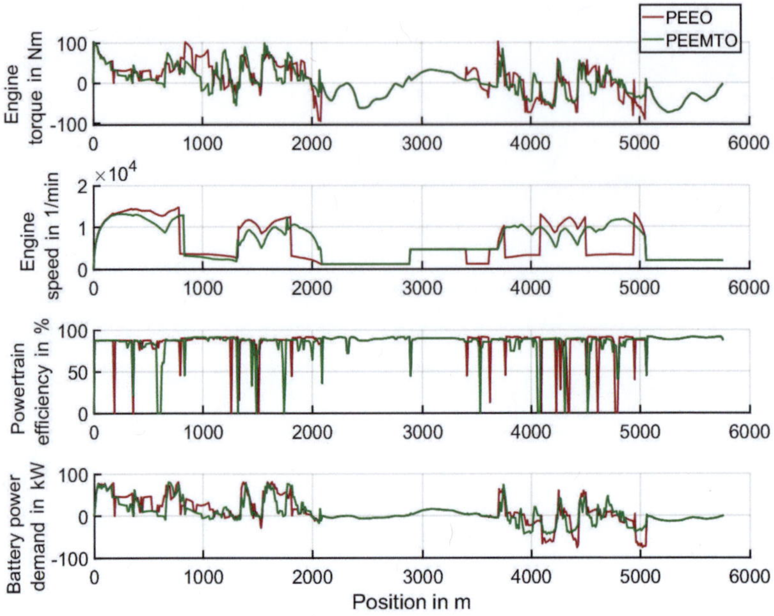

Figure 5.39: Scenario with short auxiliary horizon start length. Optimization results of engine torque, engine speed, powertrain efficiency, and battery power demand with respect to position for PEEO and PEEMTO. At gear level one, the engine speed is relatively high and resembles the velocity. At gear level two, the engine speed is significantly scaled down and the resemblance is less obvious. Similar results may overlap each other in the illustration.

comfort constraints. As described in section 4.13, in this case, the optimization is restarted without comfort constraints. In comparison, PEEMTO is able to compute feasible trajectories without any constraint violations, although the resulting jerk reaches the constraint limits on multiple occasions.

Figure 5.40 shows the different cost components. PEEO consumes 22.5 % more energy than PEEMTO. PEEMTO has a 10 % longer travel duration. PEEO changes the gear level 11 times while PEEMTO changes the gear level 5 times. PEEO has an 11 % higher combined cost than PEEMTO. Despite

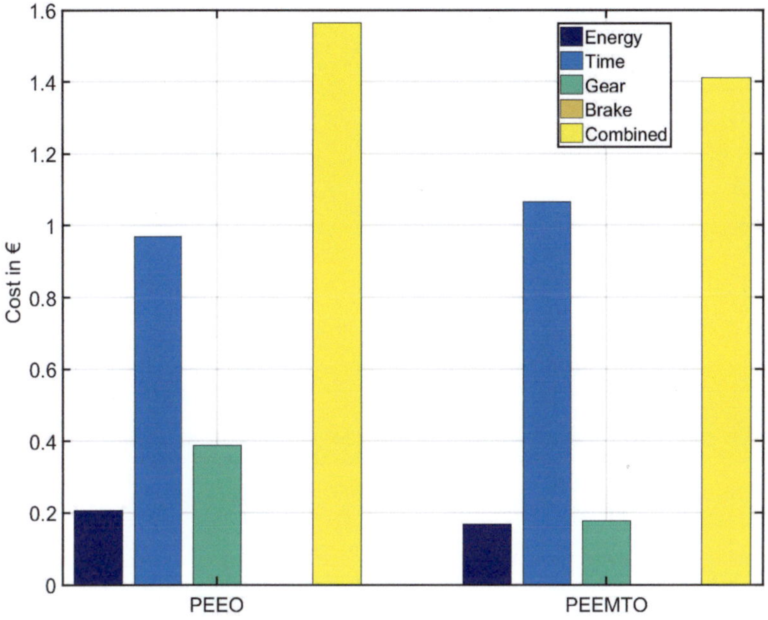

Figure 5.40: Short auxiliary horizon start length. Resulting costs of PEEO and PEEMTO at the end of the experiment.

speed limits, strong curvatures, and road slope changes, neither PEEO nor PEEMTO have to use the brake pads.

5.5.2 Long auxiliary horizon start length

Figure 5.41 shows the optimization results if the default start auxiliary horizon length of 1000 m is used for PEEMTO. The result is the same if the optimization is precomputed for the entire route.

As illustrated in Figure 5.41, the primary difference to the previous example lies with the gear shifts. PEEMTO decides to avoid gear shifts completely until the vehicle has left the mountain. This is due to the changes in road

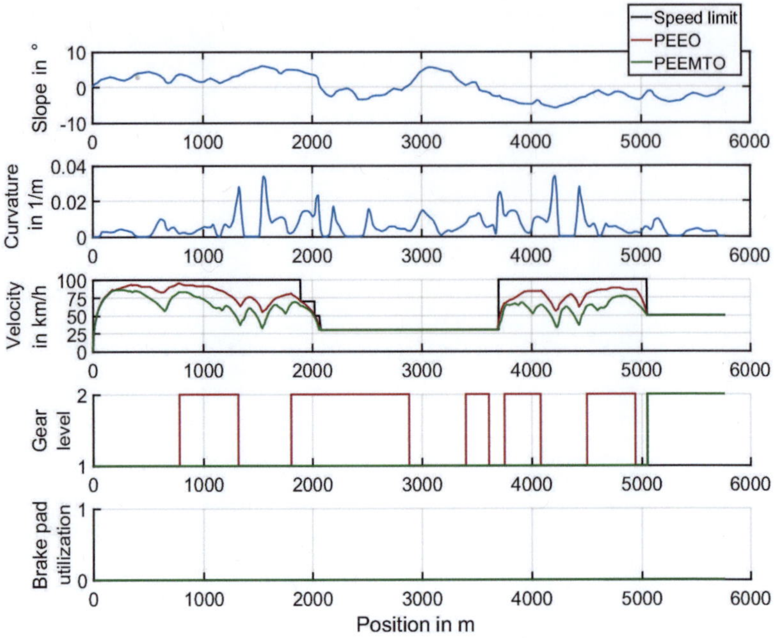

Figure 5.41: Scenario with long auxiliary horizon start length. Optimization results of velocity, gear level, and brake pad utilization with respect to position for PEEO and PEEMTO. Similar results may overlap each other in the illustration.

slope and road curvature that sometimes require high torque for sufficient acceleration and deceleration. With a longer start auxiliary horizon length, PEEMTO is able to predict that gear level one will become necessary on multiple occasions along the route. Therefore, shifting up to the second gear level is not worth the effort.

Compared to the new PEEMTO result, PEEO has a 20.3 % higher energy consumption and 11 times more gear shifts. PEEMTO has 9.8 % longer travel duration. PEEO has a 23 % higher combined cost than PEEMTO due to significantly more gear shifts.

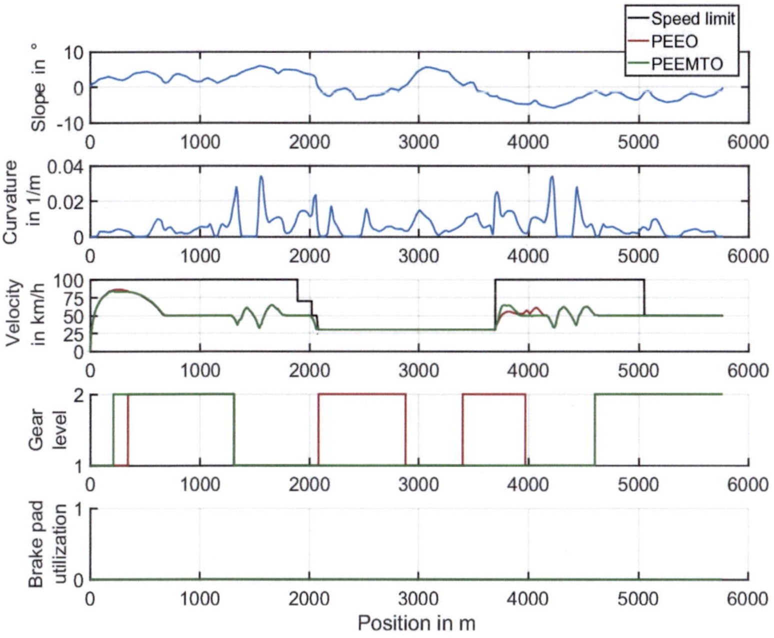

Figure 5.42: Scenario with slow front vehicle. Optimization results of velocity, gear level, and brake pad utilization with respect to position for PEEO and PEEMTO. Similar results may overlap each other in the illustration.

5.5.3 Impact of other vehicles on the auxiliary horizon

In the previous examples, no other vehicles were considered. An interesting question is what happens if there is another vehicle ahead of the ego-vehicle.

Slow front vehicle

Let there be another vehicle that prefers a velocity of 50 $\frac{\mathrm{km}}{\mathrm{h}}$. The driver parameters of the other vehicle are only randomly chosen once and used for both PEEMTO and PEEO. The start position shall be 200 m ahead of the ego-vehicle and the start velocity shall be 50 $\frac{\mathrm{km}}{\mathrm{h}}$. As mentioned in section 3.4.2, the driver model does not react to slopes and curvatures. In this example, the front vehicle shall simply maintain a velocity of 50 $\frac{\text{km}}{\text{h}}$ unless the speed limit drops to a lower value.

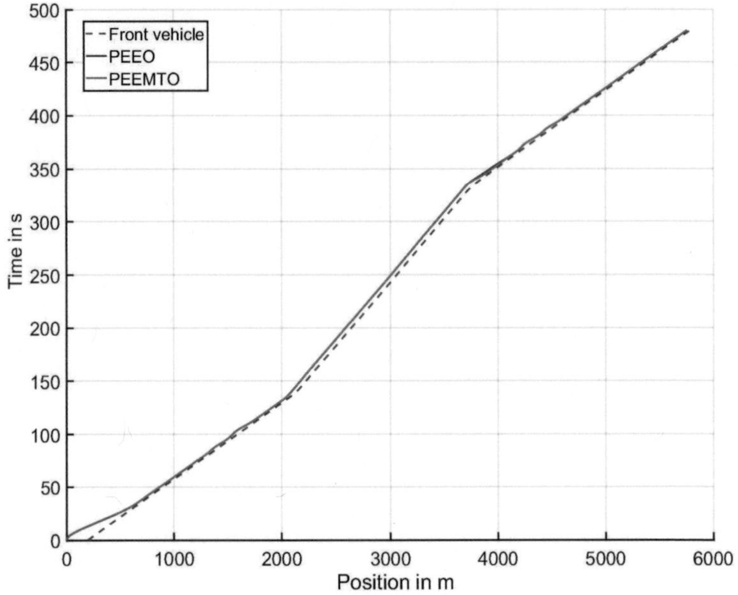

Figure 5.43: Scenario with slow front vehicle. Trajectories of position and time for the front vehicle, PEEO, and PEEMTO.

The results are shown in Figure 5.42 and Figure 5.43. As illustrated in Figure 5.42, the slow vehicle has a strong impact on both PEEO and PEEMTO. There are several road sections, on which PEEO and PEEMTO used higher velocities in previous examples. Now the velocity is often kept at 50 $\frac{\text{km}}{\text{h}}$. PEEO and PEEMTO now have very similar results and PEEO is able to maintain the comfort constraints for the entire scenario. As the slow front vehicle slows down the ego-vehicle, the velocity of PEEO is sufficiently low ahead of strong curves. Figure 5.43 shows the trajectories of PEEMTO, PEEO, and the front vehicle with respect to position and time. As the results of PEEMTO and PEEO are almost the same, their trajectories overlap each other. PEEMTO shifts to the second gear at the beginning of the scenario as there is less velocity variation compared to the previous examples. The number of gear shifts is drastically reduced for PEEO.

In this example, PEEO executes seven gear shifts, while PEEMTO shifts three times. Due to more gear shifts, PEEO still has a 10 % higher combined cost than PEEMTO. PEEMTO has a 1.5 % higher energy consumption than PEEO because gear level adaptation can reduce energy consumption at the cost of higher transmission wear. The travel duration is almost exactly the same.

Fast front vehicle

If the front vehicle has a higher velocity or is sufficiently far away, PEEMTO may still have enough freedom to adopt the most energy-efficient trajectory. In this example, the front vehicle shall choose a cruise velocity of 70 $\frac{\mathrm{km}}{\mathrm{h}}$, unless the speed limit is lower. The driver parameters of the other vehicle are only randomly chosen once and used for both PEEMTO and PEEO.

The results are shown in Figures 5.44 to 5.46. As the optimal velocity trajectory of PEEMTO is mostly lower than 70 $\frac{\mathrm{km}}{\mathrm{h}}$, the optimization leads to the same result as in the scenario without other vehicles. PEEO is still affected by the front vehicle as its velocity exceeds 70 $\frac{\mathrm{km}}{\mathrm{h}}$ on multiple occasions.

The distance between the ego-vehicle and the front vehicle is relatively large as both vehicles travel through the village of Bergwald. This is because PEEO chooses to slow down well ahead of the village entrance due to curvature and slope. The front vehicle only slows down as the speed limit begins to decrease. As the speed limit within the village is 30 $\frac{\mathrm{km}}{\mathrm{h}}$, PEEO cannot catch up with the front vehicle.

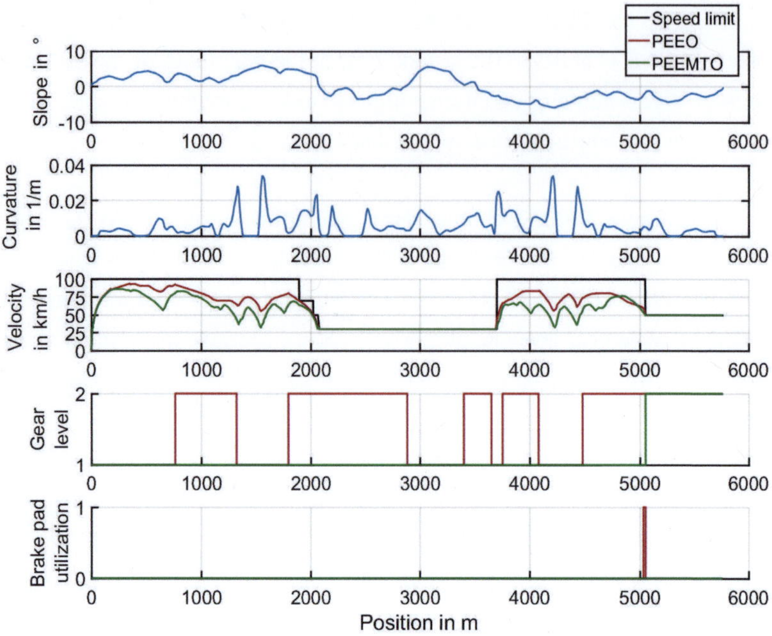

Figure 5.44: Scenario with fast front vehicle. Optimization results of velocity, gear level, and brake pad utilization with respect to position for PEEO, and PEEMTO. Similar results may overlap each other in the illustration.

As the ego-vehicle and the front vehicle approach the bottom of the hill, PEEO actually decides to use the brake pads at approximately 5100 m. As shown in Figure 5.45, the ego-vehicle guided by PEEO comes relatively close to the front vehicle during that moment with a distance of less than 20m at the closest point. The situation is difficult because the speed limit drops from 100 $\frac{\text{km}}{\text{h}}$ to 50 $\frac{\text{km}}{\text{h}}$. The road slope is negative and the driver parameters of the front vehicle are randomly chosen with the exception of the desired cruise velocity. As PEEMTO and PEEO both use the SDM, which assumes default driver parameters, PEEO is not able to precisely predict the velocity trajectory of the front vehicle. The utilization of brake pads could have been avoided if PEEO had decided to shift to the first gear level. But in this case,

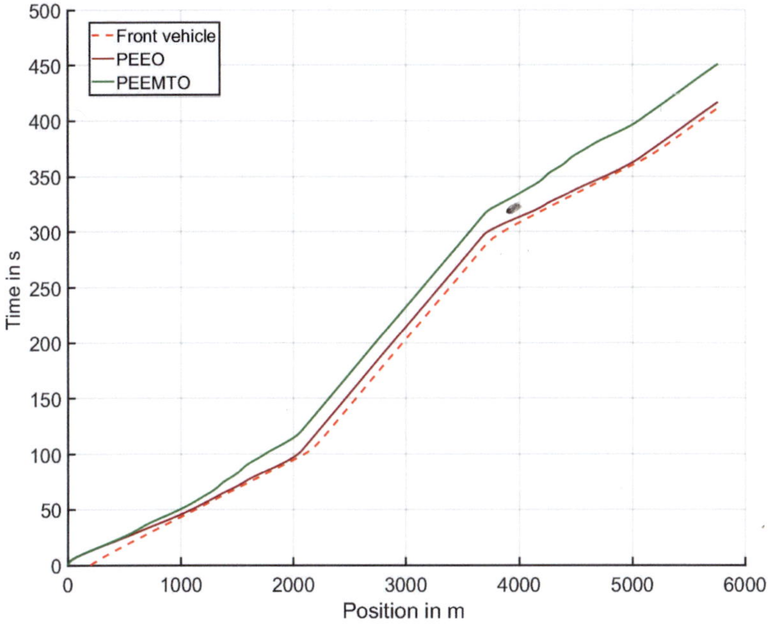

Figure 5.45: Scenario with fast front vehicle. Trajectories of position and time for the front vehicle, PEEO, and PEEMTO.

PEEO decides to use the brake pads instead. As illustrated in Figure 5.46, the engine torque reaches the minimum of -103 Nm during the utilization of brake pads. As mentioned in section 4.3.3, the gear shift cost is higher than the brake pad cost. Thus, if the vehicle only has to use the brake pads during a short moment, the action is likely to be better than changing the gear level. This is especially true if the gear level has to be changed back in the long run.

In this scenario, PEEO has a 16.6 % higher energy consumption and performs 9 times more gear shifts than PEEMTO. PEEMTO has 8.2 % longer travel duration. Adding in the brake pad utilization, PEEO has a 20.6 % higher combined cost than PEEMTO.

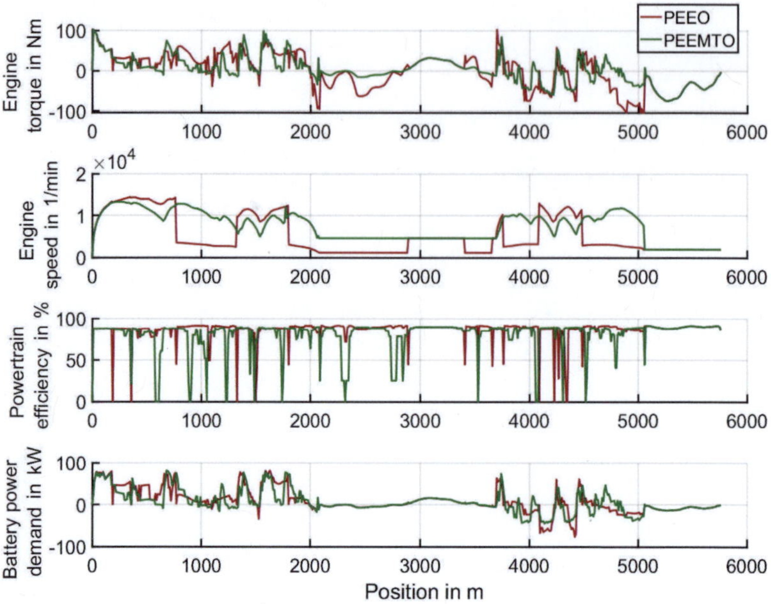

Figure 5.46: Scenario with fast front vehicle. Optimization results of engine torque, engine speed, powertrain efficiency, and battery power demand with respect to time for PEEO, and PEEMTO. Similar results may overlap each other in the illustration.

5.6 Other vehicles and lane changes

In this scenario, the optimization of incorporating other vehicles and lane changes is evaluated. The contenders are the ego-vehicle driver, PEEO, and PEEMTO. A short and almost straight section of the German motorway A8 west of Munich is used as an example (see Figure 5.48). The maximum slope is below 0.2°. The route has three lanes. There is no speed limit. Thus, the recommended cruise velocity of $130\frac{\text{km}}{\text{h}}$ is used as the desired velocity for the ego-vehicle driver.

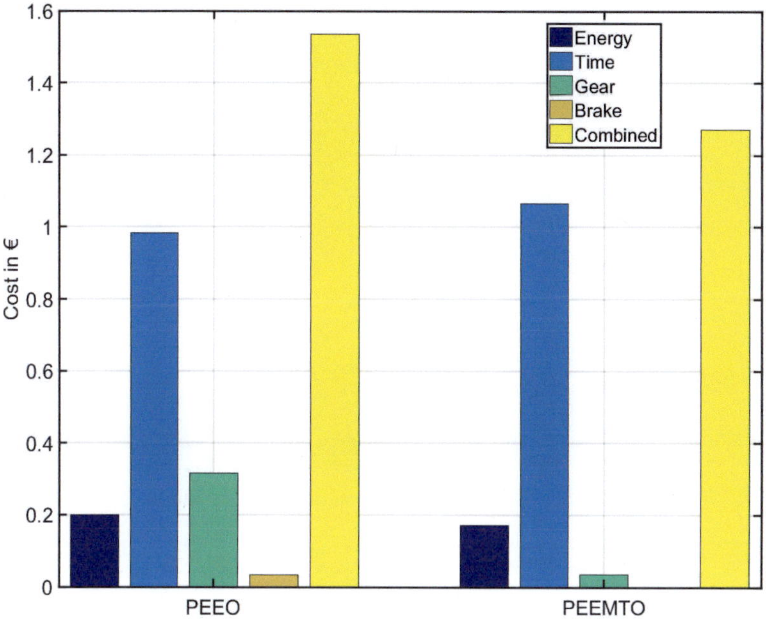

Figure 5.47: Scenario with fast front vehicle. Resulting costs of PEEO and PEEMTO at the end of the experiment.

Apart from the ego-vehicle, eight other vehicles are inserted. The preferred lanes, preferred cruise velocities, and start positions of the different vehicles are given in Table 5.1. The other driver model parameters of the other vehicles are randomly chosen as described in section A.3.3. Once selected, these parameters remain the same for all scenarios in order to improve comparability.

An abstract illustration of the vehicles at the beginning of the scenario is shown in Figure 5.49. The fast vehicles are put at the rear and the slow vehicles at the front. All vehicles favor the lanes, they are moving on at the beginning of the scenario. The other vehicles shall all try to make way for

Figure 5.48: A8 route. Section of A8 highway west of the city of Munic. Yellow arrows show the direction of travel. The image has been obtained from Google Earth.

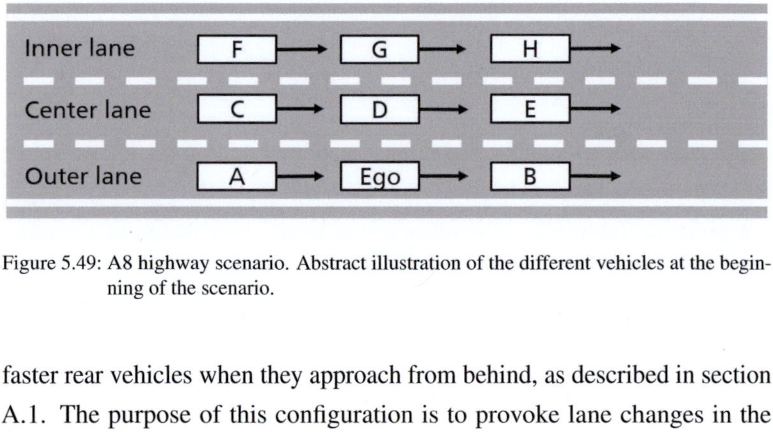

Figure 5.49: A8 highway scenario. Abstract illustration of the different vehicles at the beginning of the scenario.

faster rear vehicles when they approach from behind, as described in section A.1. The purpose of this configuration is to provoke lane changes in the experiment. The ego-vehicle starts at 100 m in the outer lane, at 80 $\frac{\text{km}}{\text{h}}$, and uses the second gear level. At the beginning of the scenario, there is a gap of 100 m between all vehicles in the same lane.

Table 5.1: Vehicle starting conditions. The start velocities and start lanes of the other vehicles are also their preferred cruise velocity and lanes respectively.

Vehicle	Start velocity in $\frac{km}{h}$	Start position in m	Start lane
Ego-vehicle	80	100	Outer lane
Vehicle A	80	0	Outer lane
Vehicle B	130	200	Outer lane
Vehicle C	160	0	Center lane
Vehicle D	130	100	Center lane
Vehicle E	100	200	Center lane
Vehicle F	200	0	Inner lane
Vehicle G	160	100	Inner lane
Vehicle H	130	200	Inner lane

The results are shown in Figures 5.50 to 5.57. As the ego-vehicle and the other vehicles may influence each other, there are several figures that only refer to the outcome of either the ego-vehicle driver, PEEO, or PEEMTO. Only Figure 5.50 and Figure 5.57 refer to all contenders. Figures 5.53 to 5.52 show the trajectories referring to position, lane choice, and time, while Figures 5.56 to 5.55 show an enlarged section of the lane changes.

As shown in Figure 5.50, none of the contenders have to shift gears or use the brake pads.

The results of PEEO are shown in Figures 5.50, 5.51, and 5.54. PEEO does not perform lane changes. It initially reduces the gap between the ego-vehicle and vehicle B. It then maintains the velocity of 80 $\frac{km}{h}$ and stays behind vehicle B for the rest of the scenario.

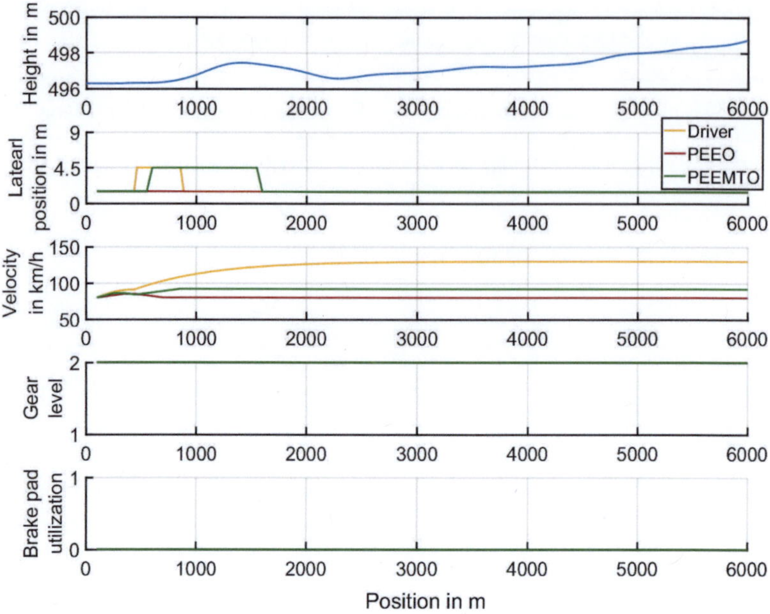

Figure 5.50: A8 highway scenario. Trajectories of the ego-vehicle driver, PEEO, and PEEMTO.

The results of the ego-vehicle driver are shown in Figures 5.50, 5.52, and 5.55. The ego-vehicle driver initially accelerates, then briefly maintains the velocity, and waits for a feasible gap in the center lane. As vehicle A is behind the ego-vehicle, it is able to initiate the lane change earlier than the ego-vehicle. After vehicle A has driven past the ego-vehicle, the ego-vehicle driver changes to the center lane. As the ego-vehicle driver changes the lane, the distance to the rear of vehicle A is less than 30 m. Thus, the distance is initially rather small. As the distance to vehicle A is increased over time, the ego-vehicle driver is able to gradually increase the velocity. The ego-vehicle driver eventually changes back to the outer lane, once the ego-vehicle has driven past vehicle B and continues at 130 $\frac{\text{km}}{\text{h}}$.

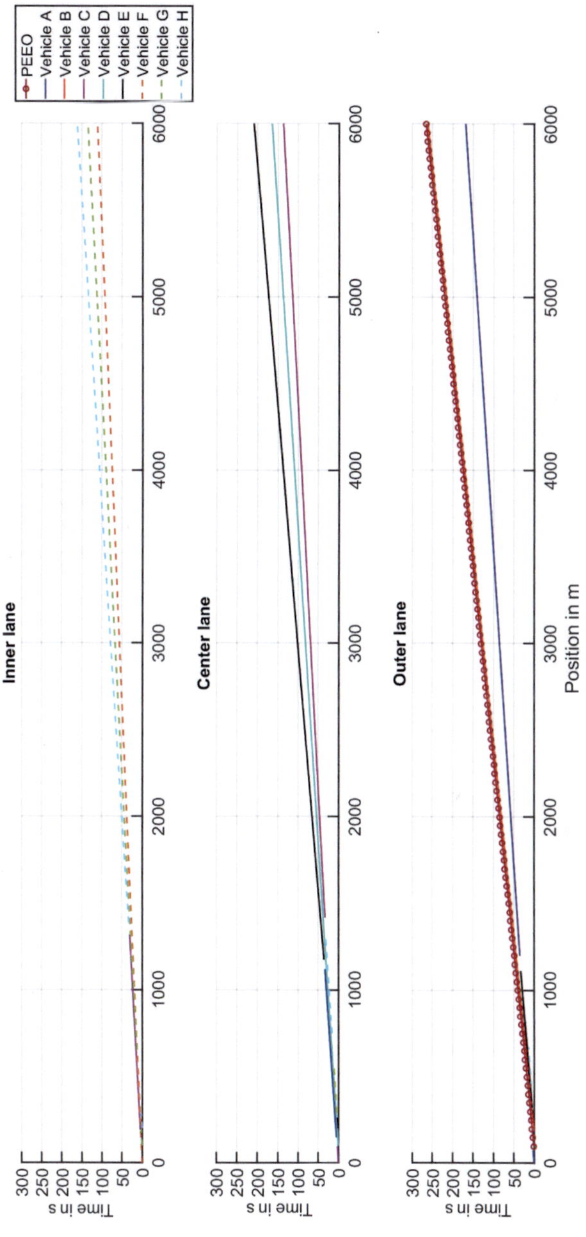

Figure 5.51: A8 highway scenario. Trajectories of PEEO and the other vehicles in the inner, center, and outer lane.

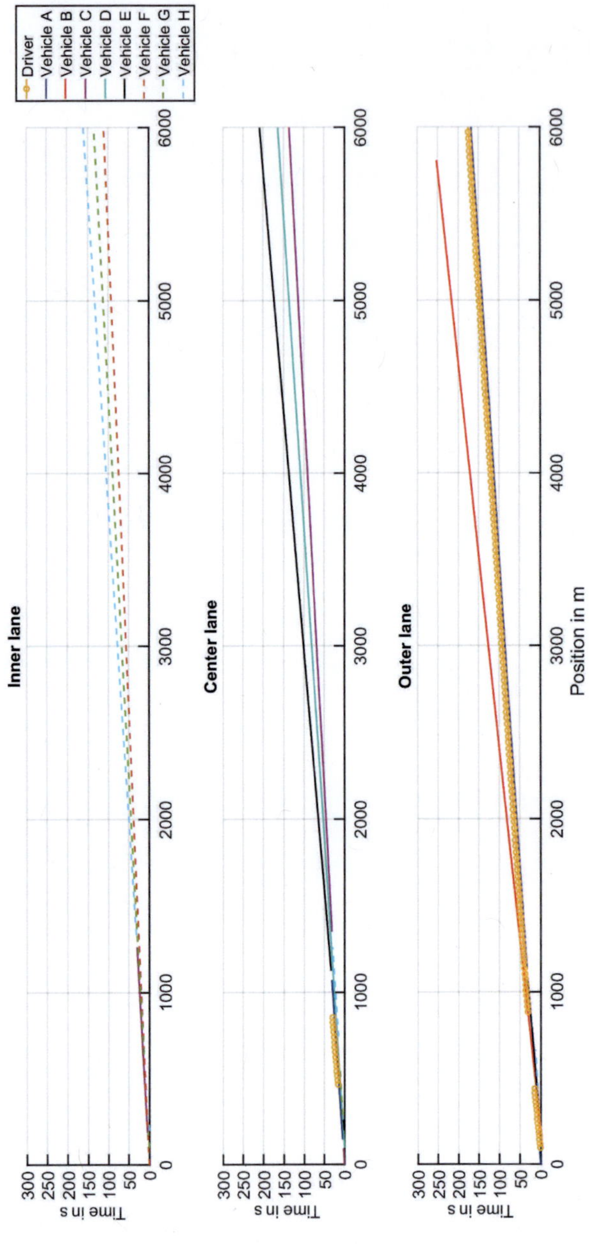

Figure 5.52: A8 highway scenario. Trajectories of the ego-vehicle driver and the other vehicles in the inner, center, and outer lane.

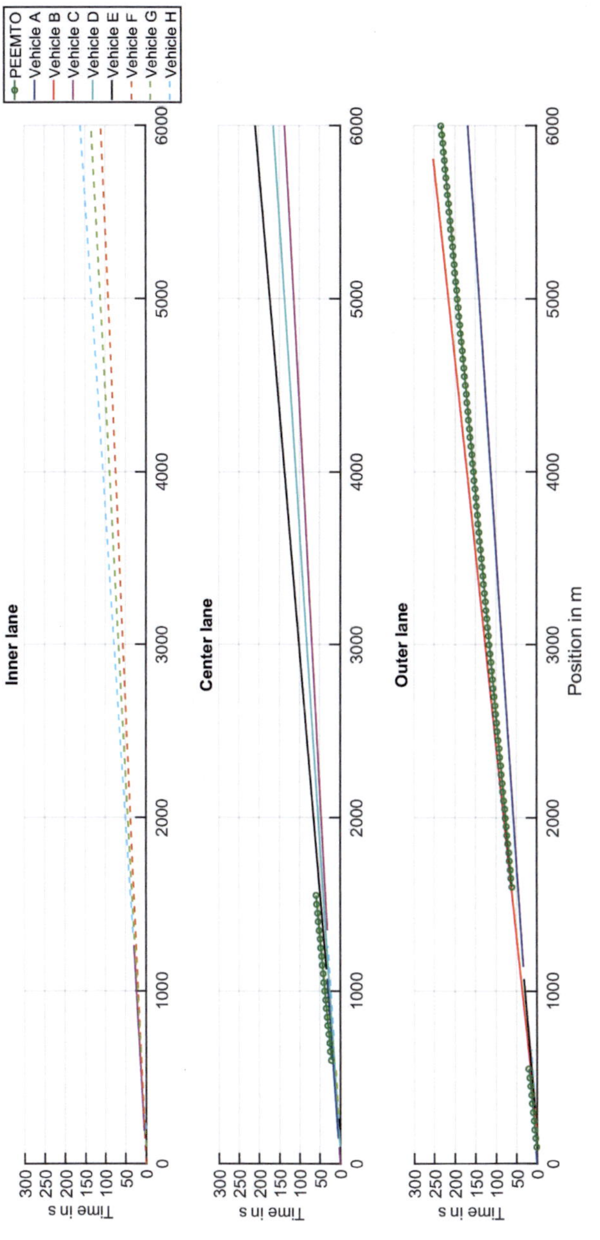

Figure 5.53: A8 highway scenario. Trajectories of PEEMTO and the other vehicles in the inner, center, and outer lane.

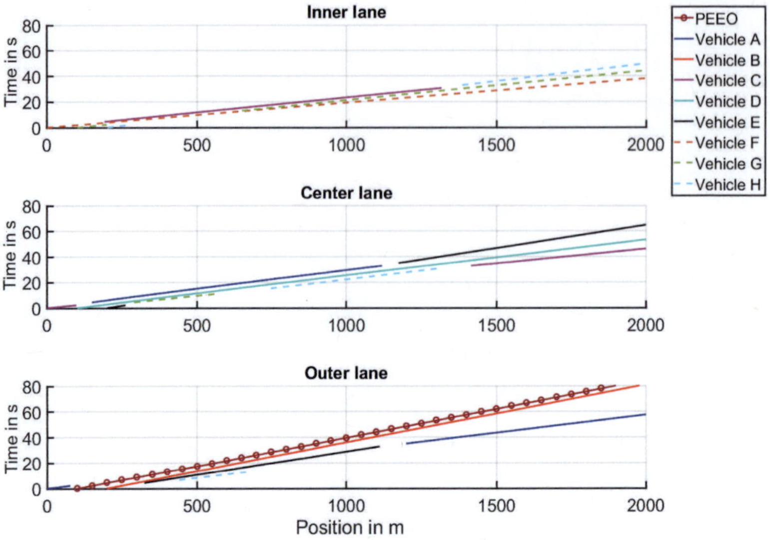

Figure 5.54: A8 highway scenario. Enlarged view of the trajectories of PEEO and the other vehicles in the inner, center, and outer lane.

The results of PEEMTO are shown in Figures 5.50, 5.53, and 5.56. PEEMTO initially anticipates that vehicle C and vehicle D in the center lane will soon overtake the ego-vehicle and create an opportunity to change to the center lane. PEEMTO is not aware that vehicle A plans to overtake the ego-vehicle. After vehicle A has performed the lane change and starts to approach from behind, PEEMTO decides to abandon plans for an early lane change. Note that the ego-vehicle driver performs the lane change earlier than PEEMTO. PEEMTO waits until vehicle A is further ahead before performing the lane change. This example shows that it is possible for a human driver to temporarily outperform PEEMTO through a more aggressive drive style. With default optimization parameters, PEEMTO uses a defensive strategy towards other vehicles and may sometimes miss opportunities to maximize energy efficiency.

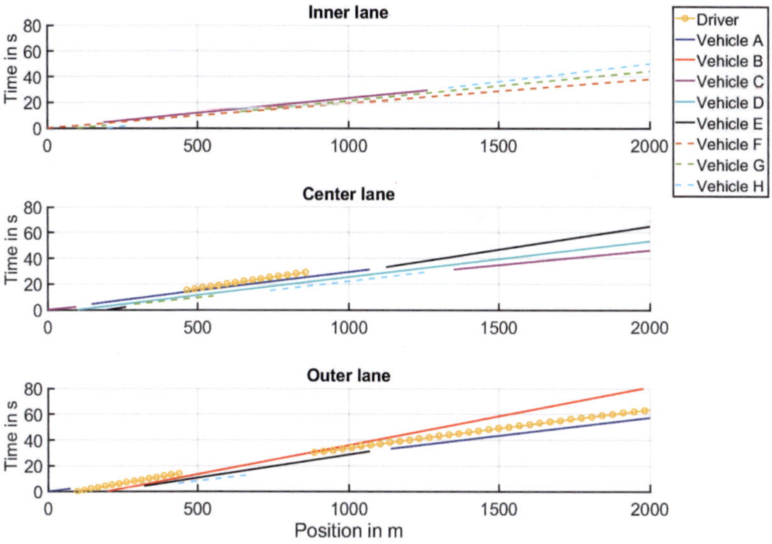

Figure 5.55: A8 highway scenario. Enlarged view of the trajectories of the ego-vehicle driver and the other vehicles in the inner, center, and outer lane.

The scenario ends with a stable outcome. In the end, the fast vehicles are at the front and the slow vehicles at the rear. Every vehicle is moving at its favored velocity and on its favorite lane. There are no more lane changes.

Figure 5.57 shows the resulting costs. The ego-vehicle driver chooses 130 $\frac{\mathrm{km}}{\mathrm{h}}$ as the preferred cruise velocity. PEEO follows the slow predecessor at 80 $\frac{\mathrm{km}}{\mathrm{h}}$, while PEEMTO is eventually able to reach the optimal cruise velocity of 92 $\frac{\mathrm{km}}{\mathrm{h}}$. The ego-vehicle driver has a 146.3 % higher energy consumption than PEEMTO. The travel duration of PEEMTO is 30.7 % longer than that of the ego-vehicle driver. The ego-vehicle driver has a 28.8 % higher combined cost than PEEMTO. PEEMTO has a 33.4 % higher energy consumption than PEEO. The travel duration of PEEO is 15.3 % longer than that of PEEMTO. PEEO has a 2.9 % higher combined cost than PEEMTO. If the contenders maintain their cruise velocities, PEEMTO will consume 37 % more energy

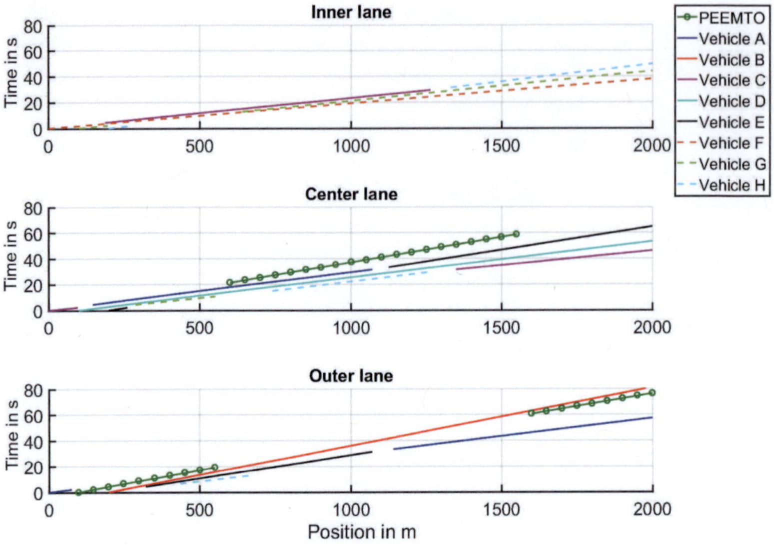

Figure 5.56: A8 highway scenario. Enlarged view of the trajectories of PEEMTO and the other vehicles in the inner, center, and outer lane.

than PEEO and the combined cost of PEEO will be 3.3 % larger. The ego-vehicle driver will consume 154 % more energy and lead to a 23.3 % higher combined cost than PEEMTO.

5.7 Traffic lights

To give the reader a general understanding, how PEEMTO performs in an urban environment with traffic lights, a real-world route is chosen. The route refers to the Ostring, which is a road in the eastern part of the city of Karlsruhe. The chosen route is shown in Figure 5.58.

The north to south direction of the road is used. The speed limit is initially 50 $\frac{\text{km}}{\text{h}}$ before increasing to 60 $\frac{\text{km}}{\text{h}}$ after the fourth traffic light. The route considered in the experiment can have up to three lanes. In the case of three

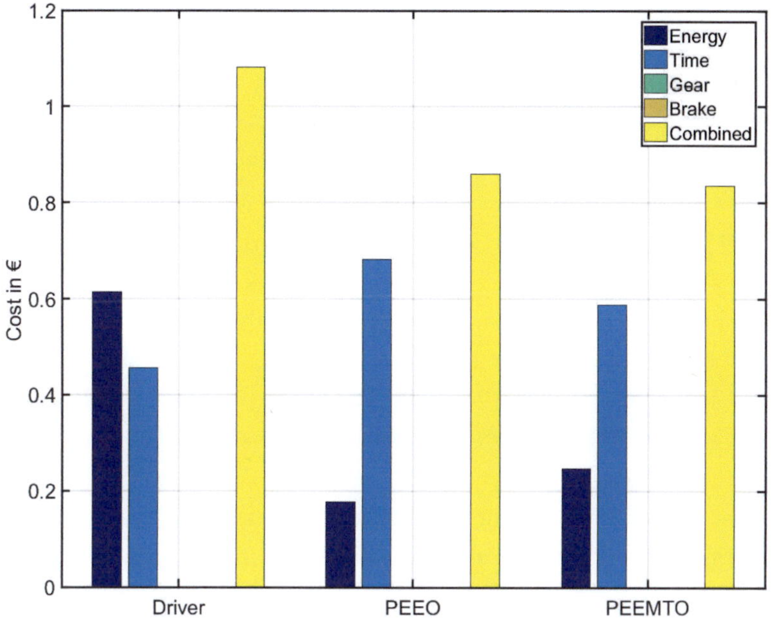

Figure 5.57: A8 highway scenario. Resulting costs of all contenders at the end of the experiment.

lanes, the inner lane is only used at intersections and only allows the vehicles on it to turn left at the intersection. In this example, the vehicles on the road shall not leave the route. Thus, the inner left-turn lanes are not regarded. At the time of writing, the two outermost lanes both offer the opportunity to travel straight ahead along the entire route. The experiment includes the first four traffic lights on the chosen route. There is a fifth traffic light approximately 650 m ahead of the end of the route. It stays in the green phase most of the time and only occasionally changes to the red phase if there are vehicles in the side street waiting to move onto the main road. In the scenario, it is assumed that the fifth traffic light remains in the green phase. The sixth traffic light is at the very end of the route and not further regarded. The comfort constraint is imposed in all scenarios.

5.7.1 Traffic lights without other vehicles

In the first scenario, as shown in Figures 5.59 to 5.61, the ego-vehicle is initially not moving. The start time of 0 s shall also be the time when the first traffic light turns red. The scenario is challenging because the traffic lights are not sufficiently synchronized to allow vehicles to pass through them uninterrupted.

The first traffic light appears after approximately 450 m. The first red phase, as shown in Figure 5.60, is 61 s long. Due to the long red phase, it is not possible to pass through it at 50 $\frac{\text{km}}{\text{h}}$. The results of PEEO and PEEMTO are the same. They both use the same regular horizon length of 250 m. As illustrated in Figure 5.60, the ego-vehicle driver, PEEO, and PEEMTO all come to a full stop at the first traffic light and wait. PEEO and PEEMTO decelerate approximately 80 m to 90 m ahead of the traffic light and therefore earlier than the ego-vehicle driver. This is different compared to the simple deceleration example of Figure 5.24 in section 5.3.2, in which PEEMTO tries to arrive at the destination early. In the current scenario, there is no advantage in travel duration if the vehicle arrives at a red traffic light early. Therefore, starting the deceleration earlier can be more favorable.

The next traffic light is approximately at 680 m with a significantly longer green phase. All contenders are able to pass the second traffic light without stopping although some temporary deceleration is required.

PEEO and PEEMTO are able to maintain their velocity and pass by the third traffic light without interruption. The ego-vehicle driver has a lower acceleration than PEEMTO and has to stop at the third traffic light. This leads to two more gear shifts than in the case of PEEO and PEEMTO.

Figure 5.58: Ostring route. Yellow arrows show the direction of travel. The image has been obtained from Google Earth.

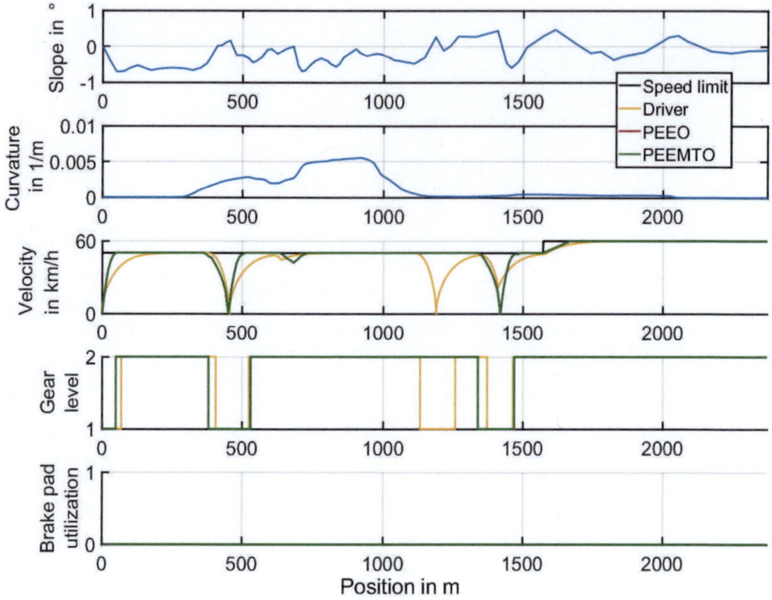

Figure 5.59: Optimization results of scenario in section 5.7.1. Similar results may overlap each other.

But as the fourth traffic light has a long red phase of 67 s, PEEO and PEEMTO have to stop and wait. The ego-vehicle driver does not come to a complete full stop but has to greatly decelerate, which leads to two additional gear shifts. Thus in this example, the travel duration of the ego-vehicle driver is actually only 0.6 % longer than that of PEEMTO. The ego-vehicle driver has a 1.17 % higher energy consumption than PEEMTO. This can be attributed to the third traffic light that stops the ego-vehicle driver, but not PEEMTO. But as discussed in section 5.3.1, PEEMTO with the default optimization parameters tolerates a higher energy consumption during acceleration in order to decrease travel duration. Therefore, the percental saving is small.

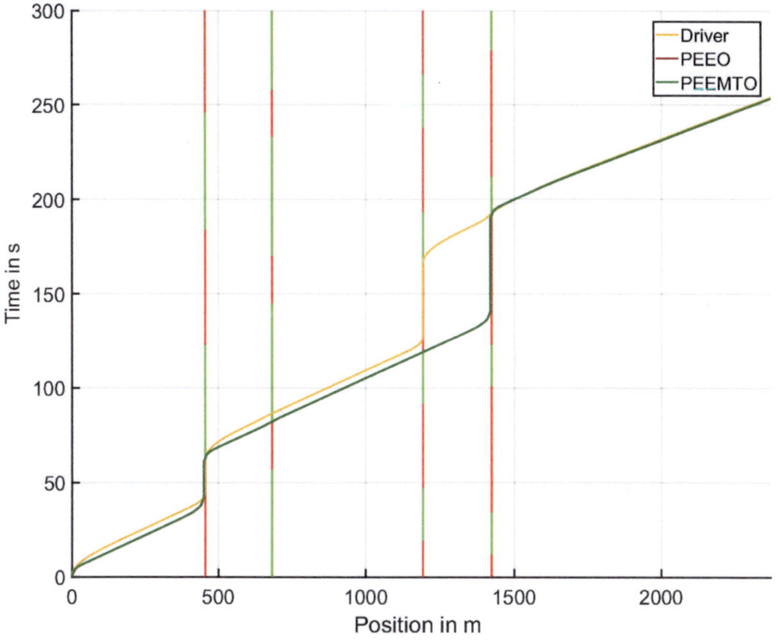

Figure 5.60: Optimization results of scenario in section 5.7.1. The illustration shows different time trajectories with respect to position. The yellow traffic light phases are incorporated into the green traffic light phases. Subtle velocity variations may not be conspicuous in the trajectory illustration. Similar results may overlap each other.

The contribution of the energy consumption cost is also small compared to the travel duration and the gear shift cost. None of the contenders have to use the brake pads. In this example, the ego-vehicle driver has a 9 % higher overall cost than PEEMTO because two more gear shifts are performed. Although PEEMTO uses the LRAHE and PEEO does not, only the regular horizon includes traffic lights. Therefore, the results of PEEMTO and PEEO are the same.

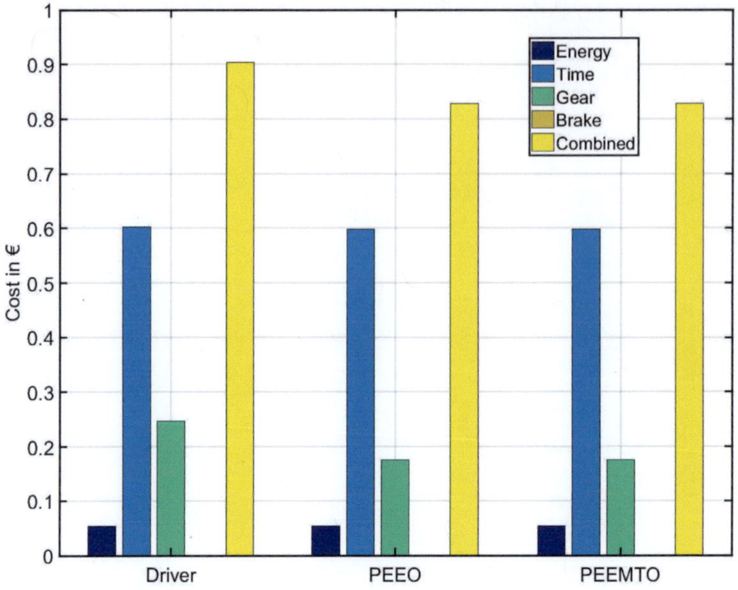

Figure 5.61: Resulting cost components of scenario in section 5.7.1.

5.7.2 Implicit discretization and optimality

As illustrated in the previous example, PEEMTO accelerates to the speed limit, although there is no chance for the ego-vehicle to pass by the first traffic light during a green phase. As illustrated in Figures 5.2 and 5.3, a cruise velocity of 10 $\frac{\mathrm{km}}{\mathrm{h}}$ leads to a smaller energy consumption than a cruise velocity of 50 $\frac{\mathrm{km}}{\mathrm{h}}$. In fact, the latter leads to a 75 % higher energy consumption than the former. As long as the red traffic light cannot be avoided, both fast and slow velocity trajectories lead to the same travel duration because the ego-vehicle has to wait for the red phase to end. Therefore, it is actually better for PEEMTO to choose a very low velocity and slowly approach the red traffic light. This strategy was already mentioned in section 4.11. Although PEEMTO starts the deceleration process earlier than the ego-vehicle driver, the fact remains unchanged that it does accelerate to the speed limit.

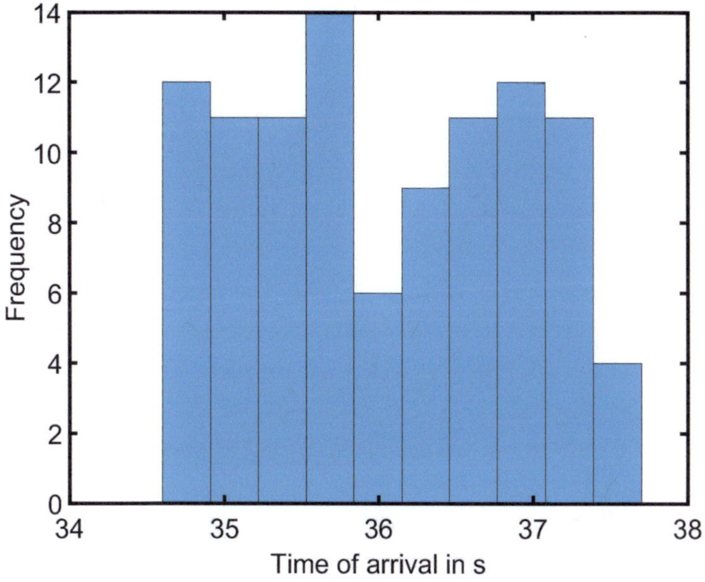

Figure 5.62: Histogram regarding the time of arrival of the different states at the first red traffic light of the scenario in section 5.7.1. The different time values only refer to the decision stage that includes the first traffic light.

The reason for the relatively high velocity and the early arrival of the ego-vehicle at the red traffic light is the implicit discretization of time as discussed in section 4.8. The previous traffic light scenario shall be used for a more detailed explanation. Let $\mathbf{X}_i$ be the decision stage, at which the ego-vehicle stops and waits for the first red traffic light to change to the green phase. Let $\mathbf{X}_i$ be already fully evaluated. This means that all feasible states within $\mathbf{X}_i$ are associated with certain discrete points in time through implicit discretization. A histogram of these discrete time values is shown in Figure 5.62. As illustrated in the histogram, the time values of the different states are within a time frame of 34 and 38 seconds in this example. Thus, the width of the time frame is between three and four seconds. In comparison, the red phase of the first traffic is 61 s long. The time frame is the result of implicit discretization that allows variation regarding the time of arrival at every decision stage. While it is broad enough to deal with other vehicles at every decision stage, it is too narrow to incorporate long traffic light phases.

The time frame width is relatively narrow compared to traffic light phases because of three reasons. The first reason is that the DP algorithm only becomes aware of the traffic light, once the forward evaluation has truly reached the traffic light. Therefore, it does not consider any traffic light delays on the previous stages. The second reason is that the optimal cruise velocity in the scenario of section 5.7.1 is the speed limit of 50 $\frac{\text{km}}{\text{h}}$. Thus, as long as the forward evaluation has not yet reached the traffic light, state transitions closer to the speed limit are likely to be favored. The third reason is that the implicit discretization of time does not enforce the evaluation of extremely late time values. Therefore, extremely slow velocity trajectories may no longer be part of the search space when the traffic light is finally incorporated into the optimization.

In general, the explicit discretization of all state components should be preferred, if the real-time capability of the optimization can be assured. By incorporating very late time values, PEEMTO would be forced to consider very slow trajectories. But in practice, the explicit and fine discretization of numerous continuous variables is often infeasible due to the increase in computational complexity. As shown in the results of Figure 5.15 and Figure 5.27 in section 5.3.1 and section 5.3.2, if the travel duration is omitted, PEEMTO will still accelerate to the optimal cruise velocity as long as it is unhindered. But it will begin the deceleration significantly earlier if it has to come to stop. Thus, if the traffic light is close by, PEEMTO will not entirely accelerate to the speed limit if the travel duration is omitted.

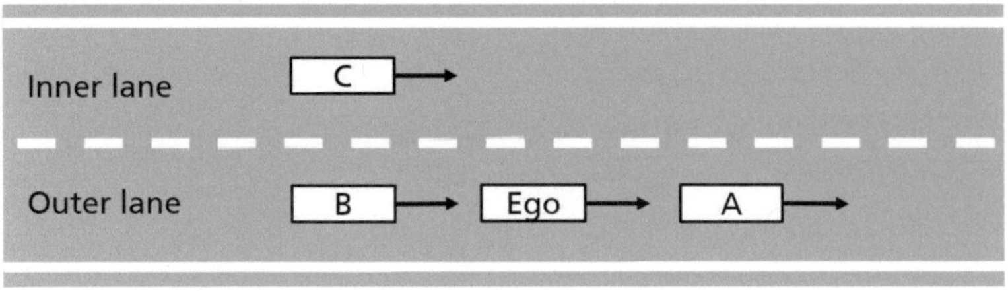

Figure 5.63: Abstract illustration of the different vehicles at the beginning of the first scenario in section 5.7.3.

But if the travel duration is omitted (as a simple heuristic), the original optimization problem is no longer truly addressed. Furthermore, although the implicit discretization may remove very slow trajectories from the search space, the outcome involving higher velocities is actually beneficial towards other vehicles, which otherwise might be involuntarily slowed down by the ego-vehicle. The interests of other vehicles are not explicitly considered in PEEMTO but can be part of future work.

5.7.3 Traffic lights and other vehicles

In the following two scenarios, the impact of both traffic lights and other vehicles on the optimization is evaluated. The phase cycles of the second and fourth traffic light are shifted by several seconds to create a time corridor that allows a vehicle to pass by all traffic lights uninterrupted unless it is blocked by another vehicle. The start time of the simulation is set to 50 s. The ego-vehicle starts at the speed limit of $50\frac{\text{km}}{\text{h}}$ and the second gear level. The starting position is set to 280 m in the outer lane.

Adjacent vehicle behind the ego-vehicle

In the first scenario, there are three other vehicles in the vicinity of the ego-vehicle. The start configuration is shown in Table 5.2. The start velocity

Table 5.2: Vehicle starting conditions at the beginning of the first scenario in section 5.7.3.

Vehicle	Start velocity in $\frac{km}{h}$	Start position in m	Start lane
Ego-vehicle	50	280	Outer lane
Vehicle A	50	380	Outer lane
Vehicle B	50	150	Outer lane
Vehicle C	50	150	Inner lane

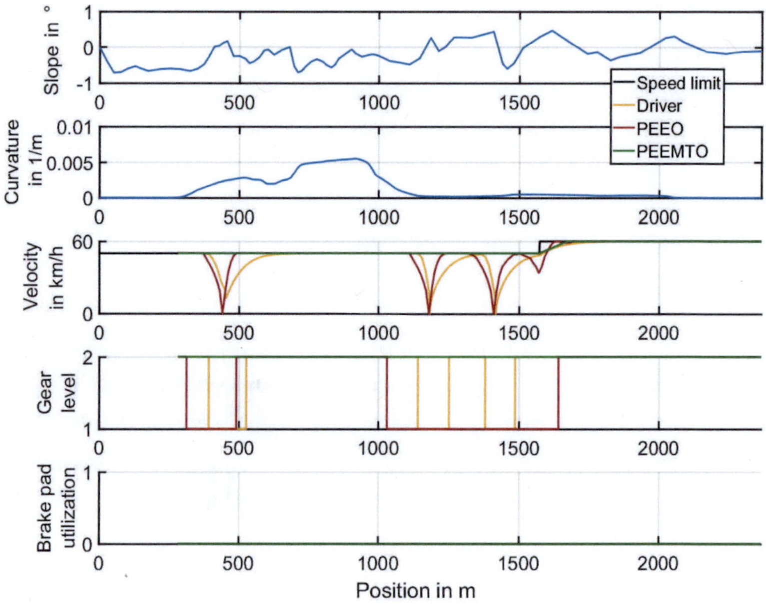

Figure 5.64: Optimization results of the first scenario in section 5.7.3. Similar or identical results may overlap each other.

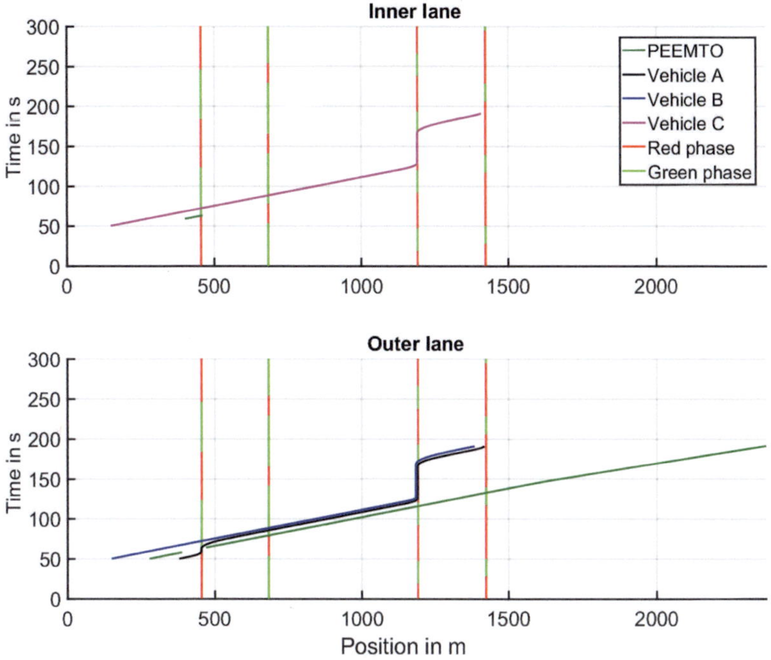

Figure 5.65: Optimization results of PEEMTO. Time trajectory with respect to position. The yellow traffic light phases are incorporated into the green traffic light phases. Subtle velocity variations may not be conspicuous in the trajectory illustration. Similar or identical results may overlap each other.

and the start lanes of the other vehicles shall also be their desired cruise velocity and desired lane. The other driver parameters are set to random values. Once selected, these parameters remain the same for all scenarios in order to improve comparability. An abstract illustration of the initial situation is shown in Figure 5.63. There is initially a front vehicle A, which is 380 m ahead of the ego-vehicle in the same lane. A rear vehicle B is behind the ego-vehicle and starting at 150 m. Vehicle C flanks vehicle B in the inner lane and also starts at 150 m. All vehicles are progressing at the speed limit towards the first traffic light. The results are shown in Figures 5.64 to 5.68.

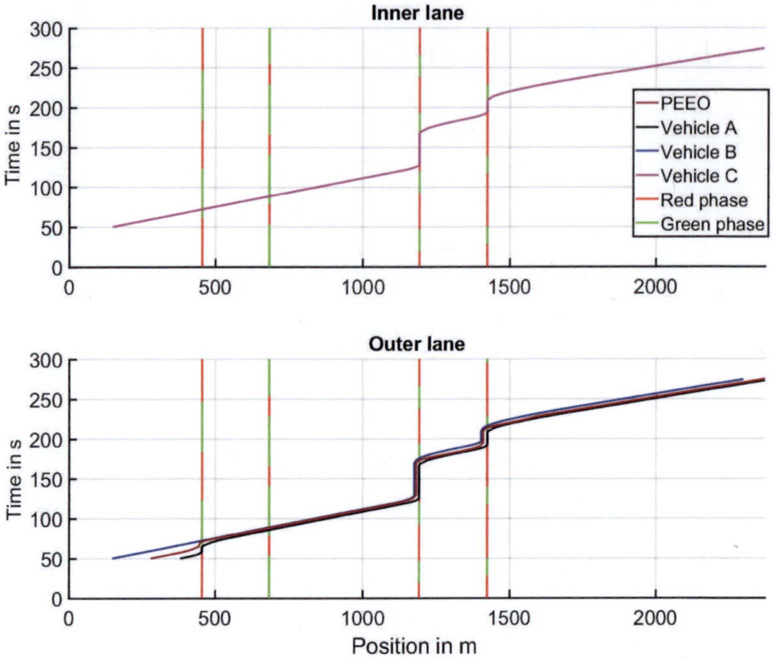

Figure 5.66: Optimization results of PEEO. Time trajectory with respect to position. The yellow traffic light phases are incorporated into the green traffic light phases. Subtle velocity variations may not be conspicuous in the trajectory illustration. Similar or identical results may overlap each other.

As the other vehicles may respond to the ego-vehicle, the trajectories of position and time are shown separately for the ego-vehicle driver, PEEO, and PEEMTO in Figures 5.65 to 5.67.

As shown in Figure 5.65, vehicle A starts to decelerate before the green phase of the first traffic light begins. When approaching the traffic light, PEEMTO changes to the inner lane while vehicle C is still sufficiently far behind. PEEMTO is aware that the traffic light phase will soon change to green and moves towards it without any deceleration. After it has passed by the first traffic light, it changes back to the outer lane and overtakes vehicle A.

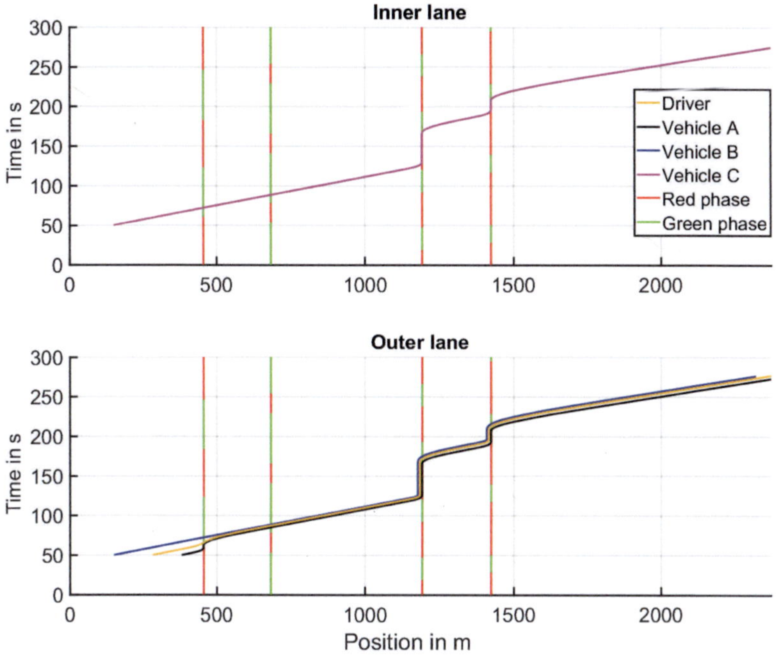

Figure 5.67: Optimization results of the ego-vehicle driver. Time trajectory with respect to position. The yellow traffic light phases are incorporated into the green traffic light phases. Subtle velocity variations may not be conspicuous in the trajectory illustration. Similar or identical results may overlap each other.

The trajectory of PEEO is shown in Figure 5.66. PEEO does not change lanes. It is slowed down by vehicle A. Because both vehicle A and the ego-vehicle lose speed at the first traffic light and because vehicle A has a more gradual acceleration than PEEO, PEEO is not able to pass through the green phase of the third and fourth traffic light.

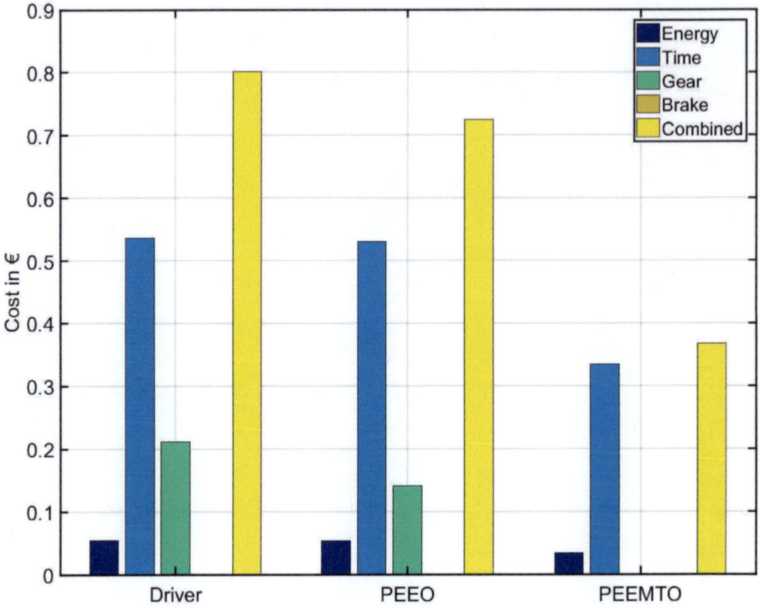

Figure 5.68: Resulting costs of all contenders.

The ego-vehicle driver yields a similar result as shown in Figure 5.67. As the first traffic light is initially red, the lane change incentive is insufficient for the ego-vehicle driver to perform the lane change.

The ego-vehicle driver has a 60 % and PEEO a 58.1 % higher energy consumption than PEEMTO. The ego-vehicle driver has a 60.5 % and PEEO a 58.7 % longer travel duration than PEEMTO. The ego-vehicle driver has a 117.9 % and PEEO a 97 % higher combined cost than PEEMTO.

Adjacent vehicle parallel to the ego-vehicle

The second scenario is very similar to the first one. The only difference is that vehicle C starts alongside the ego-vehicle, i.e., at 280m. The new start configuration is shown in Figure 5.69 and Table 5.3.

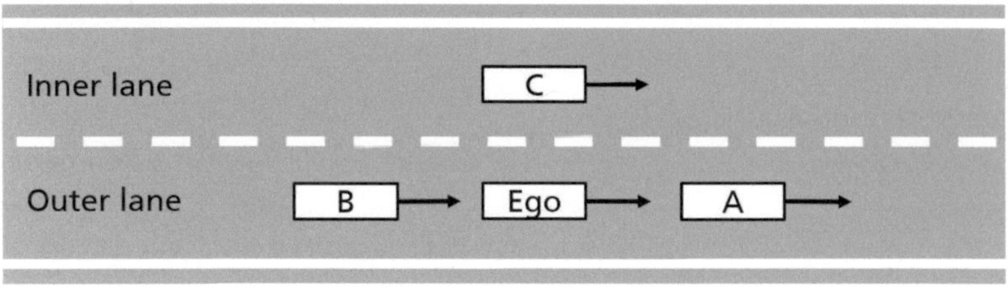

Figure 5.69: Abstract illustration of the different vehicles at the beginning of the scenario.

Table 5.3: Vehicle starting conditions of second scenario in section 5.7.3

Vehicle	Start velocity in $\frac{\text{km}}{\text{h}}$	Start position in m	Start lane
Ego-vehicle	50	280	Outer lane
Vehicle A	50	380	Outer lane
Vehicle B	50	150	Outer lane
Vehicle C	50	280	Inner lane

Figures 5.70 and 5.65 show the new results. PEEMTO can no longer overtake vehicle A as it is blocked by vehicle C. PEEMTO now yields the same result as PEEO. Note that, although the velocity trajectory of PEEMTO is similar to that of the ego-vehicle driver, it makes fewer gear shifts between the third and fourth traffic light. This is because the regular horizon length of 250 m incorporates traffic lights that are close to each other. As PEEMTO realizes that it has to stop at the third and fourth traffic light, it decides not to shift to the second gear level between the two traffic lights. In this example, the ego-vehicle driver has a 1.2 % higher energy consumption, a 1.1 % longer travel duration and two more gear shifts than PEEMTO. The ego-vehicle driver has a 10.6 % higher combined cost than PEEMTO.

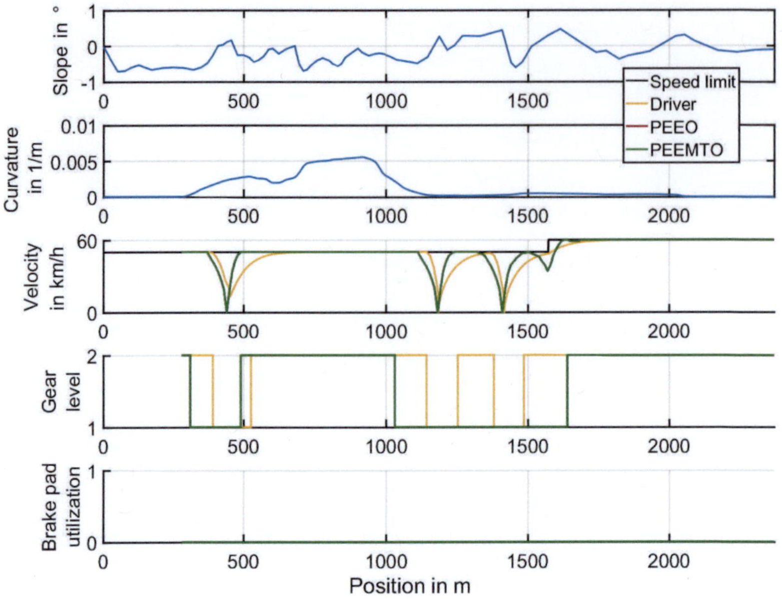

Figure 5.70: Optimization results of the second scenario in section 5.7.3. Similar or identical results may overlap each other.

This example shows that the optimization result in urban scenarios heavily depends on the situation. Sometimes significant improvements can be achieved. But sometimes a single vehicle on an unfavorable trajectory is sufficient to constrain the optimization. If the optimization is heavily constrained by dynamic obstacles, it may still be able to lead to small improvements through efficient acceleration and deceleration. Theoretically, it is also possible that the optimization performs worse than a human driver if the driver is in a more fortunate scenario or ignores certain regulations. Furthermore, the traffic lights may or may not provide favorable green phase time corridors, which has a very large impact on the outcome. The auxiliary horizon does not have any effect on the discussed urban scenarios.

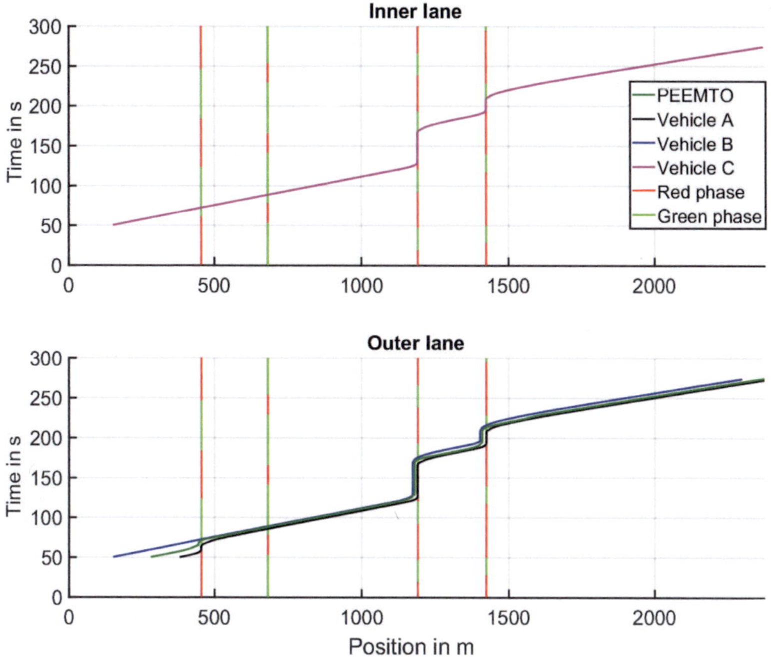

Figure 5.71: Optimization results of the time trajectory with respect to position. The yellow traffic light phases are incorporated into the green traffic light phases. Subtle velocity variations may not be conspicuous in the trajectory illustration. Similar or identical results may overlap each other.

5.8 Random scenarios

The real-world routes consist of urban and highway scenarios. The simulation setup follows the descriptions in section 3.3 and section 3.4. Both directions of the chosen roads are used in the experiments. As discussed in section 3.4.2 and section A.1, zipper merging and lane closures are not evaluated. The evaluated scenarios do not consider recharging of the ego-vehicle. Within the experiments, the length of routes never exceeds 50 km. Thus, recharging is not necessary if the ego-vehicle starts with sufficient initial battery charge. Although the name of the road may change at some point, the routes only follow one road. The selected routes do not contain any sections of curvature or slope that the ego-vehicle driver cannot handle. In other words, the trajectories of the ego-vehicle driver do not exceed the physical limits of the vehicle. The battery SOC at the beginning of the route is always 95 %.

There are 234 scenarios in total. 108 of them refer to highway scenarios while the rest refer to urban scenarios. As discussed in section A.3.2, there are several classes of traffic density in transportation engineering. The evaluated scenarios consider the cases of low traffic density, medium traffic density, and high traffic density. The contenders within the evaluation are PEEMTO, PEEO, and the ego-vehicle driver. Different from the previous scenarios, the driver parameters of the ego-vehicle driver are randomized the same way as the other traffic participants. PEEMTO and PEEO abide by the traffic regulations and always prefer the outer lane. The preferred lane of the other vehicles and the ego-vehicle driver is randomized. Slow vehicles are by definition more likely to choose the outer lane. Further details regarding random vehicle creation are given in section A.3.3. As the other vehicles can be affected by the movement of PEEMTO, PEEO, and the ego-vehicle driver, the three contenders are evaluated separately.

5.8.1 Highway scenarios

The highway scenarios refer to two different sections of the highway A8 between the cities of Ulm und Munic. The sections are illustrated in Figure 5.72. The western road section is 46 km long. The eastern road section is 44.8 km long. There is a gap between them that is occupied by a construction area with lane closures. There is no speed limit, thus the recommended maximum speed is 130 $\frac{\text{km}}{\text{h}}$.

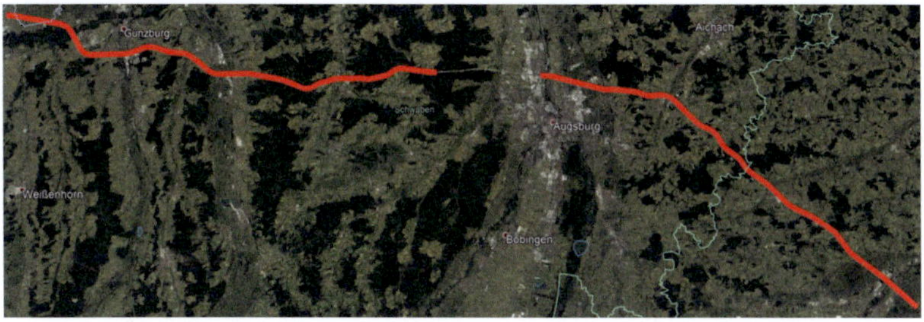

Figure 5.72: Selected western and eastern road sections on the A8 highway. Both directions are used. There are four different routes. The image has been obtained from Google Earth.

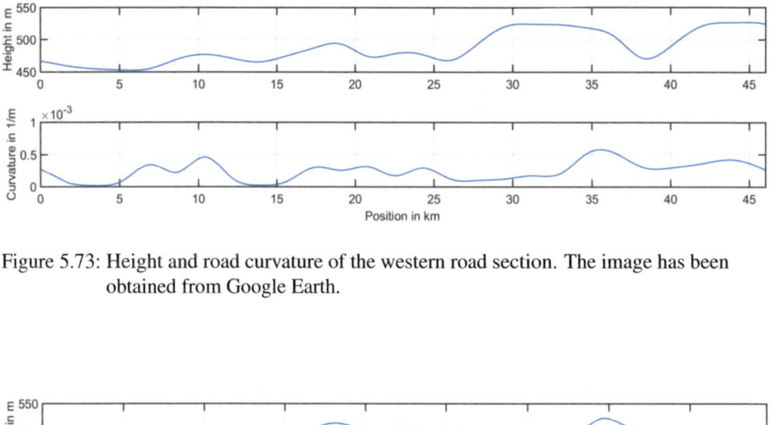

Figure 5.73: Height and road curvature of the western road section. The image has been obtained from Google Earth.

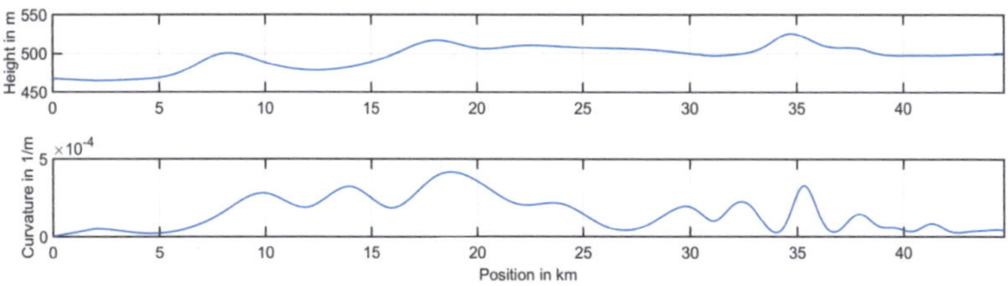

Figure 5.74: Height and road curvature of the eastern road section. The image has been obtained from Google Earth.

Figure 5.73 and 5.74 show the height and the curvature of the road sections. If the west to east direction is used, the end of the route has a higher altitude than the beginning of the route. The slope magnitude is small and does not exceed 1°. The curve radius usually has a length of several kilometers. For very low curvature, the curve estimation of section 3.3 depends the pecision of the route definition.

PEEMTO, PEEO, and the ego-vehicle driver all receive 36 scenarios each. The 36 scenarios in each group are divided into three smaller groups of 12 scenarios, which refer to low traffic density, medium traffic density, and high traffic density respectively. Both road sections can be driven in the west to east or east to west direction. Thus, there are four routes. Each route is driven three times by PEEMTO, PEEO, and the ego-vehicle driver. As the routes have different lengths, the illustrations refer to average velocities and costs over 1 km. The results are shown in Figures 5.75 to 5.80.

The parameters of the ego-vehicle driver are chosen according to the description given in section A.3.3. There shall always be two aggressive ego-vehicle drivers and two defensive ego-vehicle drivers for every type of traffic density. The starting situation shall be initially randomly chosen but used for all contenders in the same type of scenario. Once the simulation starts, vehicles are inserted and removed randomly. Thus, PEEMTO, PEEO, and the ego-vehicle driver never face exactly the same situations although the start situation is identical.

Velocity

Figure 5.75 shows the average velocity distribution from the highway experiments for PEEMTO, PEEO, and the ego-vehicle driver (rows), separated with respect to low traffic density, medium traffic density, and high traffic density (columns).

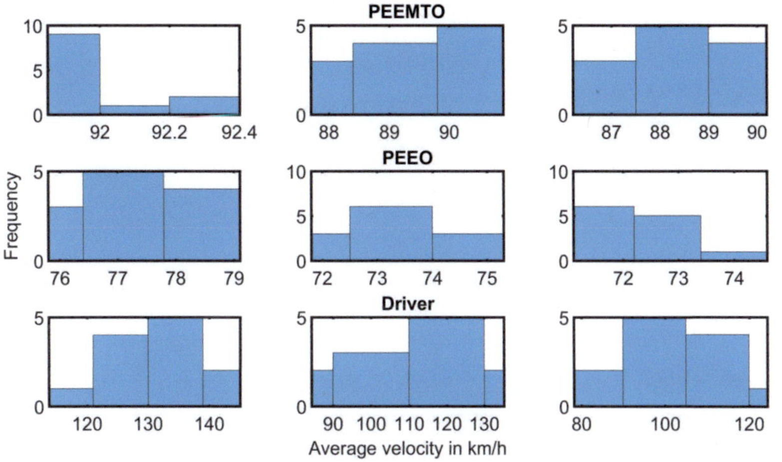

Figure 5.75: Distributions of average velocities. Rows top to bottom: PEEMTO, PEEO, ego-vehicle driver. Columns left to right: low traffic density, medium traffic density, high traffic density.

In the case of PEEMTO, higher average velocity close to the optimal cruise velocity of 92 $\frac{\text{km}}{\text{h}}$ is more likely in case of low traffic density. The ego-vehicle is also less likely to meet a slow front vehicle. If the ego-vehicle does meet a slow front vehicle, there are more likely to be overtaking opportunities. Note that in scenarios, in which the ego-vehicle travels from east to west, the average velocity may even be slightly higher than the optimal cruise velocity because the starting position has a higher altitude than the end of the route. Conversely, if the ego-vehicle travels from west to east, the average velocity can be slightly lower than the optimal cruise velocity. Conversely, high traffic density leads to fewer opportunities for lane changes and the average velocity is lower because of slow front vehicles that cannot be easily overtaken. Furthermore, PEEMTO tries to keep to the outer lane and is therefore likely to be slowed down by slower vehicles in dense traffic. The average velocities are likely to be more diverse because the movement of the ego-vehicle is more heavily affected by other vehicles.

As PEEO does not consider lane changes, the ego-vehicle is blocked as soon as it approaches a slow front vehicle in the same lane. In general, the average velocity of PEEO depends on the question if and when it meets slow or very slow front vehicles. As discussed in section A.3.3, a truck has a default desired velocity of 80 $\frac{\text{km}}{\text{h}}$. But as the random creation of vehicles can also lead to desired velocities of less than 80 $\frac{\text{km}}{\text{h}}$, the ego-vehicle guided by PEEO will slow down accordingly if it meets an extremely slow vehicle. Due to the route distance of almost 50 km, even low and medium traffic densities may eventually yield extremely slow vehicles. As discussed in section A.3.3, the minimum velocity of a defensive truck driver can be as low as 70 $\frac{\text{km}}{\text{h}}$. In general, low traffic density still leads to higher cruise velocities because it is less likely to encounter extremely slow vehicles. The contrary is true for scenarios with high traffic density.

The average velocity of the ego-vehicle driver is generally higher than that of PEEMTO and PEEO. This is due to the default choice of the desired velocity as described in section A.3.3. It is at or close to 130 $\frac{\text{km}}{\text{h}}$ for highways without speed limits. In the case of low traffic density, the ego-vehicle driver is usually able to travel at the desired velocity. Therefore, the velocity distribution for low traffic density is essentially the same as the random definition of desired velocities as discussed in section A.3.3. Due to different ego-vehicle drivers with different attitudes, the velocity distribution is less concentrated compared to PEEMTO. As mentioned earlier, there are always two aggressive ego-vehicle drivers and two defensive ego-vehicle drivers for each class of traffic density. As in the case of PEEMTO and PEEO, high traffic density also reduces the overall cruise velocity of the ego-vehicle driver. The aggressive ego-vehicle drivers may still progress at a relatively high average velocity, while the defensive ego-vehicle drivers are more likely to follow slow vehicles.

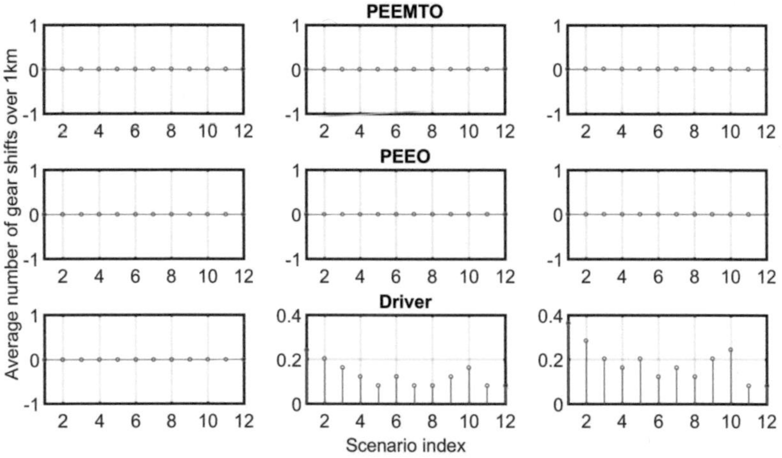

Figure 5.76: Average number of gear shifts over one kilometer. Rows top to bottom: PEEMTO compared to PEEO, PEEMTO compared to the ego-vehicle driver. Columns left to right: low traffic density, medium traffic density, high traffic density.

Gear shifts and brake pad utilization

In most cases, recuperation at the highest gear level is sufficient to slow down the vehicle. But if the ego-vehicle encounters a situation in which abrupt deceleration is necessary, gear shifts and brake pads may be used. Possible situations include aggressive drivers who suddenly appear ahead of the ego-vehicle with little spatial gap between them. But, in general, gear shifts and brake pad utilizations are rare. Figure 5.76 and Figure 5.77 show the average number of gear shifts and the average number of brake pad utilizations respectively in every scenario and in every traffic density. Histograms are not used because the gear shift and brake actions are scarce.

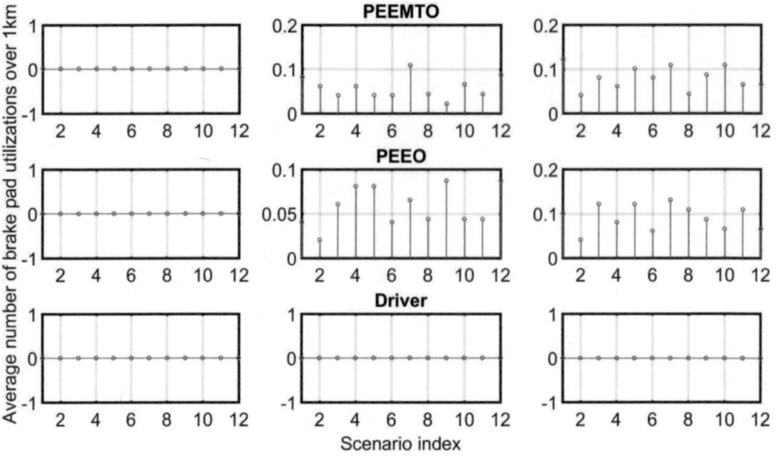

Figure 5.77: Average number of brake pad utilizations over one kilometer. Rows top to bottom: PEEMTO compared to PEEO, PEEMTO compared to the ego-vehicle driver. Columns left to right: low traffic density, medium traffic density, high traffic density.

PEEMTO and PEEO do not shift gears in any of the scenarios as they always prefer to use the brake pads if they need to slow down quickly. As discussed in section 4.3.3, the transmission wear cost is higher than the brake pad wear cost. Furthermore, once the ego-vehicle slows down, it is likely to eventually accelerate back to a higher velocity. Therefore, if gear shifts are used, it is likely that a downshift is followed by an upshift, i.e., there are often two gear shifts in quick succession. The brake pad utilization of PEEMTO and PEEO only occurs in medium and high traffic density scenarios.

The ego-vehicle driver prefers gear shifts due to the kick-down mechanism of the automated transmission as described in section A.2.2. Note that this preference depends on the automated transmission. If there is no kick-down mechanism for rapid deceleration, the ego-vehicle driver may also prefer the brake pads. The ego-vehicle driver only leads to gear shifts in medium and

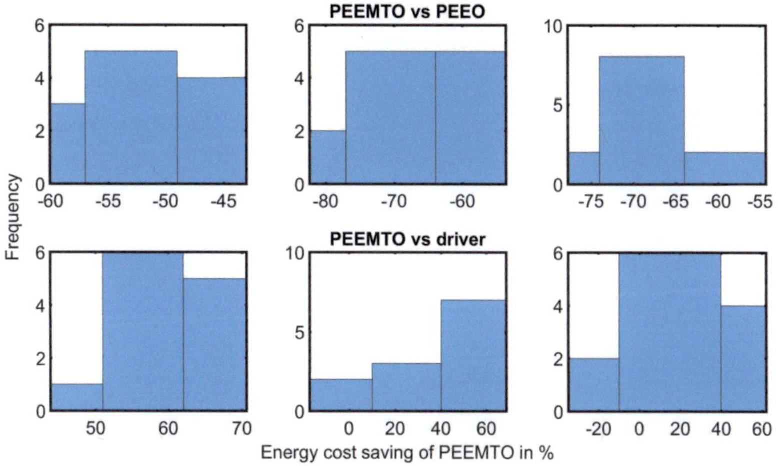

Figure 5.78: Energy consumption cost of PEEMTO compared to PEEO and the ego-vehicle driver. Positive percental values mean PEEMTO leads to smaller costs. Negative percental values mean PEEMTO leads to higher costs. Rows top to bottom: PEEMTO compared to PEEO, PEEMTO compared to the ego-vehicle driver. Columns left to right: low traffic density, medium traffic density, high traffic density.

high traffic density scenarios. The ego-vehicle driver never uses the brake pads in the evaluated scenarios.

Energy consumption cost

Figure 5.78 shows the energy consumption cost of PEEMTO compared to PEEO and the ego-vehicle driver for different traffic densities. Positive percental values mean that PEEMTO leads to smaller costs. Negative percental values mean PEEMTO leads to higher costs. The average cost savings and the value range are shown in Table 5.78. As discussed at the beginning of this chapter, the numeric result depends on the way the percentage computation is conducted. Different to previous sections, this section always works with the percental savings of PEEMTO compared to PEEO and the ego-vehicle driver even if it is negative.

Table 5.4: Energy consumption cost saving of PEEMTO compared to PEEO and the ego-vehicle driver for different traffic densities. Positive percental values mean PEEMTO leads to smaller costs. Negative percental values mean PEEMTO leads to higher costs. Mean and value range are denoted in %.

Compared to	Low density	Medium density	High density
to PEEO	-53,	-66.4,	-68.3,
in % (mean, range)	-60 to -43	-82.4 to -53.6	-77.8 to -54.3
to ego-vehicle driver	61,	43,	28.2,
in % (mean, range)	43.8 to 70.6	-17.2 to 68.6	-35.1 to 62

Energy consumption on highways is heavily influenced by velocity. PEEMTO generally consumes more energy than PEEO. The additional energy consumption can be higher for high traffic density because PEEO is slowed down more heavily by very slow vehicles. Compared to the ego-vehicle driver, PEEMTO usually consumes less energy, especially for low traffic density because the ego-vehicle driver is likely to prefer a higher desired velocity. In very few cases, very defensive ego-vehicle drivers may consume less energy than PEEMTO because they decide to stay behind slow vehicles.

Travel duration cost

Figure 5.79 shows the travel duration cost of PEEMTO compared to PEEO and the ego-vehicle driver for different traffic densities. Positive percental values mean that PEEMTO leads to smaller costs. Negative percental values mean PEEMTO leads to higher costs. The average cost savings and the value range are shown in Table 5.79. The travel duration has an inverse relationship to the average velocity. PEEMTO generally leads to travel time savings compared to PEEO and is usually slower than the ego-vehicle driver.

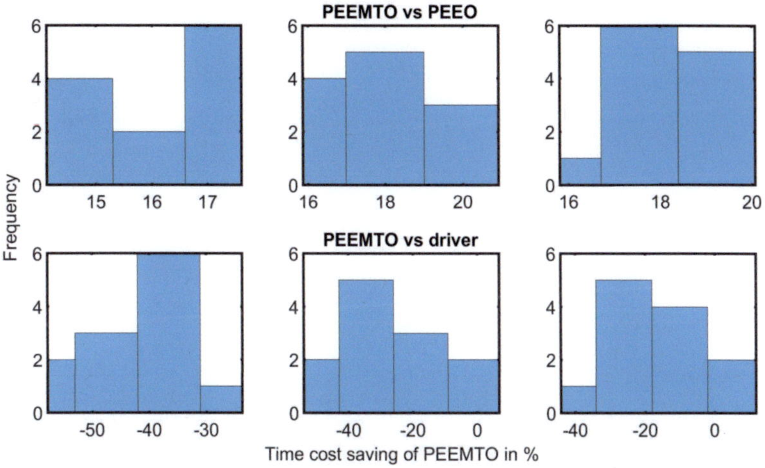

Figure 5.79: Travel duration cost of PEEMTO compared to PEEO and the ego-vehicle driver. Positive percental values mean PEEMTO leads to smaller costs. Negative percental values mean PEEMTO leads to higher costs. Rows top to bottom: PEEMTO compared to PEEO, PEEMTO compared to the ego-vehicle driver. Columns left to right: low traffic density, medium traffic density, high traffic density.

Table 5.5: Travel duration cost saving of PEEMTO compared to PEEO and the ego-vehicle driver for different traffic densities. Positive percental values mean PEEMTO leads to smaller costs. Negative percental values mean PEEMTO leads to higher costs. Mean and value range are denoted in %.

Compared	Low density	Medium density	High density
to PEEO	16.2,	18,	18.1,
in % (mean, range)	14.1 to 17.6	15.9 to 20.9	15.8 to 20.1
to ego-vehicle driver	-42.2,	-28.7,	-17.1,
in % (mean, range)	-57.8 to -23.7	-54.2 to 6.7	-44.1 to 11.6

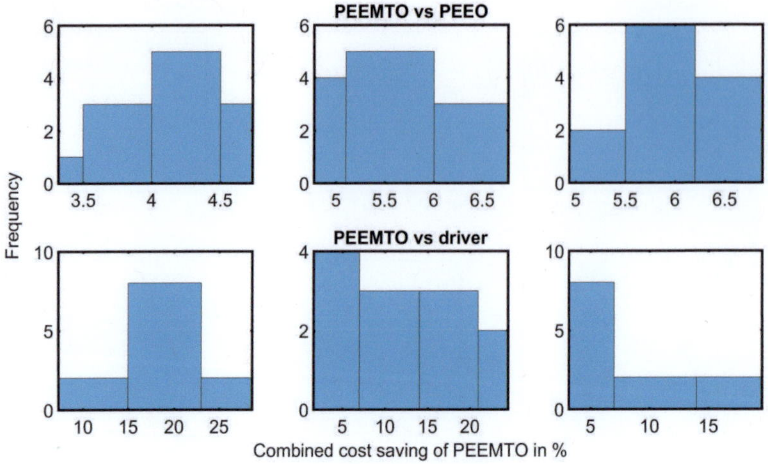

Figure 5.80: Combined cost of PEEMTO compared to PEEO and the ego-vehicle driver. Positive percental values mean PEEMTO leads to smaller costs. Negative percental values mean PEEMTO leads to higher costs. Rows top to bottom: PEEMTO compared to PEEO, PEEMTO compared to the ego-vehicle driver. Columns left to right: low traffic density, medium traffic density, high traffic density.

Combined cost

Figure 5.80 shows the combined cost of PEEMTO compared to PEEO and the ego-vehicle driver for different traffic densities. Positive percental values mean that PEEMTO leads to smaller costs. Negative percental values mean PEEMTO leads to higher costs. The average cost savings and the value range are shown in Table 5.80.

The percental savings are highest compared to the ego-vehicle driver because of higher average velocity. The higher travel duration costs of PEEO is responsible for higher combined costs than PEEMTO despite lower energy consumption. Note that the savings of PEEMTO compared to PEEO are slightly higher for medium and high traffic density. This is due to the lower average velocity or rather longer travel duration of PEEO because

Table 5.6: Combined cost saving of PEEMTO compared to PEEO and the ego-vehicle driver for different traffic densities. Positive percental values mean PEEMTO leads to smaller costs. Negative percental values mean PEEMTO leads to higher costs. Mean and value range are denoted in %.

Compared	Low density	Medium density	High density
to PEEO	4.2,	5.5,	6,
in % (mean, range)	3.3 to 4.7	4.7 to 6.8	4.9 to 6.9
to ego-vehicle driver	19.2,	12.1,	7.3,
in % (mean, range)	7.3 to 28.6	1.5 to 24.4	3.2 to 19.5

the ego-vehicle is more likely to encounter a very slow vehicle at higher traffic densities. As discussed in section 5.2.2, the energy consumption cost becomes larger than the travel duration cost beyond 118 $\frac{\text{km}}{\text{h}}$ at minimum GLC. In general, the results are situation dependent. Therefore, PEEO and the ego-vehicle driver can theoretically have lower costs if the situation is different. But in the highway scenarios, PEEMTO always leads to smaller combined costs.

In the highway scenarios, the auxiliary horizon does not seem to have any significant impact on the results. This can be attributed to the fact that the chosen routes do not have abrupt changes in road slope and road curvature. Based on the evaluated scenarios in this thesis, it can be assumed that the auxiliary horizon is primarily beneficial in mountainous scenarios.

5.8.2 Urban scenarios

The urban scenarios refer to two roads in the city Karlsruhe. They are illustrated in Figure 5.81. The western road is the Adenauerring and the eastern road is the Ostring. The properties of the Ostring road were already introduced in section 5.7.

Figure 5.81: Selected urban road sections in the city Karlsruhe. There are two different routes. The Adenauerring route is to the west. The Ostring route is to the east. The yellow arrows denote the direction of travel. The image has been obtained from Google Earth.

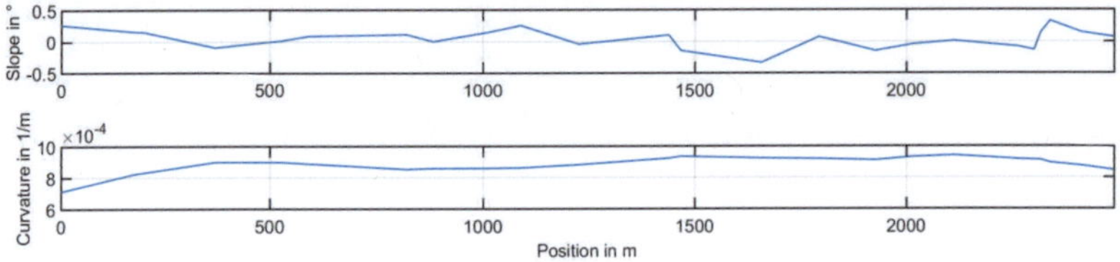

Figure 5.82: Slope and curvature of the Adenauerring route. The slope and curvature of the Ostring route was presented in Figure 5.59.

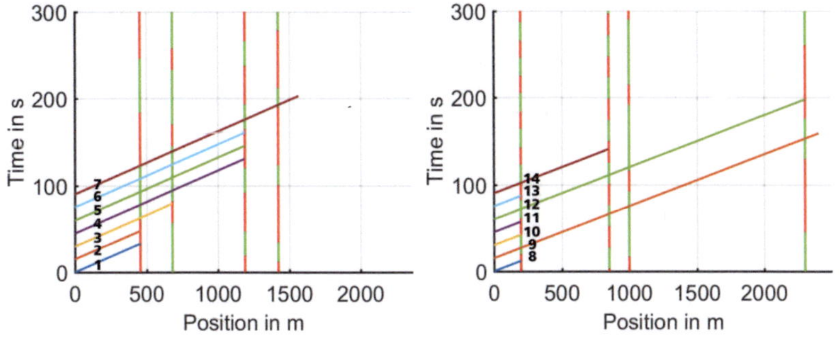

Figure 5.83: Left: Traffic light phases in the Ostring route. Right: Traffic light phases in the Adenauerring route. The start times are set within a range of 0 s to 90 s at 0 s, 15 s, 30 s, etc. The illustrated linear trajectories show how far the ego-vehicle can move for different start times until it is stopped by a red phase. Each start time represents one scenario. The scenario index is displayed next to the corresponding start time.

Figure 5.82 shows the slope and the curvature of the Adenauerring route. The slope magnitude stays below 0.5°. The road curvature radius is approximately 1,100 m long. The speed limit is 60 $\frac{\text{km}}{\text{h}}$.

The contenders PEEMTO, PEEO, and the ego-vehicle driver all receive 42 scenarios each. The 42 scenarios in each group are divided into three smaller groups of 14 scenarios, which refer to low traffic density, medium traffic density, and high traffic density respectively. Each route is driven seven times by PEEMTO, PEEO, and the ego-vehicle driver. As the routes have different lengths, the illustrations refer to average velocities and costs over 1 km.

There are four traffic lights on each route. Their positions and phases are shown in Figure 5.83. Just as in the Ostring scenarios, the yellow phases are counted as part of the closest green phase. If there is a traffic light at the very beginning or very end of the route, it is omitted. PEEMTO, PEEO, and the ego-vehicle driver all start at the beginning of the route and in the outer lane. There are 7 different start times for each contender in each route to introduce some variation into the experiments. The ego-vehicle always starts at the beginning of the route. The ego-vehicle always starts at the desired or optimal cruise velocity. The start times are set within a range of 0 s to 90 s at 0 s, 15 s, 30 s, etc. The illustrated linear trajectories show how far the ego-vehicle can move for different start times until it is stopped by a red phase. Each start time represents one scenario. The scenario index is displayed next to the corresponding start time. For the given configuration, there is only one trajectory at the speed limit in each route that can pass by all traffic lights without stopping: scenarios 7 and 9.

The parameters of the ego-vehicle driver are chosen according to the description given in section A.3.3. There shall always be one aggressive ego-vehicle driver and one defensive ego-vehicle driver for every route in every traffic density. In scenario 10, the ego-vehicle driver shall always be aggressive in order to include scenarios, in which drivers get benefits for breaking traffic regulations. For the same scenario index in the same traffic density, the starting situation shall be initially randomly chosen but used for all contenders. Once the simulation starts, vehicles are inserted and removed randomly. Thus, PEEMTO, PEEO, and the ego-vehicle driver never face exactly the same situations although the start situation is identical.

Number of stops

Figure 5.84 shows the number of stops in each scenario and in each traffic density. In low traffic density, PEEMTO and the ego-vehicle driver have a maximum of three complete stops at traffic lights. PEEO cannot change lanes and has up to four.

In medium and high traffic density, overtaking becomes more difficult. The contenders have a similar number of stops. The maximum number of stops can be as high as 4 for medium and 5 for high traffic density. Note that the ego-vehicle actually does not stop at every traffic light if there are 4 stops.

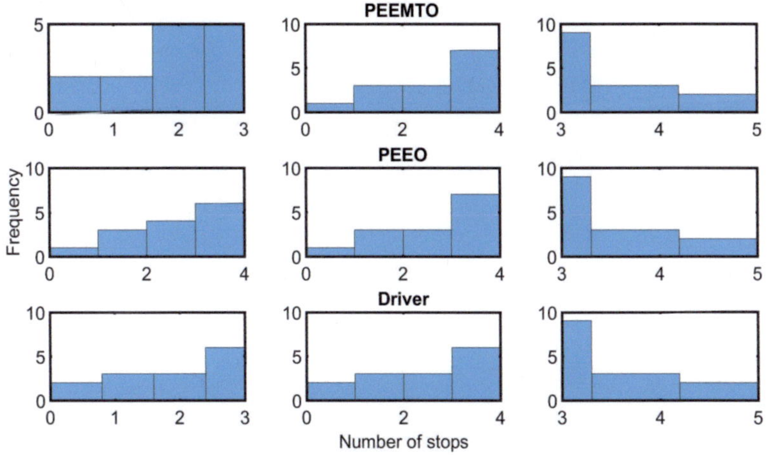

Figure 5.84: Distributions of complete stops. Rows top to bottom: PEEMTO, PEEO, ego-vehicle driver. Columns left to right: low traffic density, medium traffic density, high traffic density.

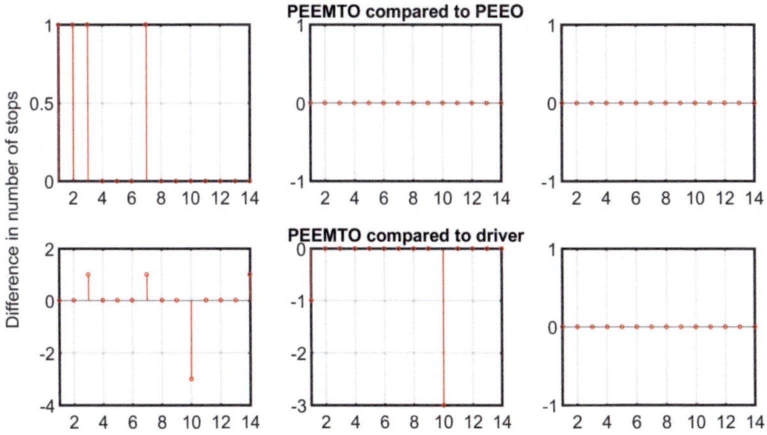

Figure 5.85: Reduction of stops. PEEMTO compared to PEEO and the ego-vehicle driver. A positive difference means PEEMTO leads to fewer stops. A negative difference means PEEMTO leads to more stops. Rows top to bottom: PEEMTO, PEEO, ego-vehicle driver. Columns left to right: low traffic density, medium traffic density, high traffic density.

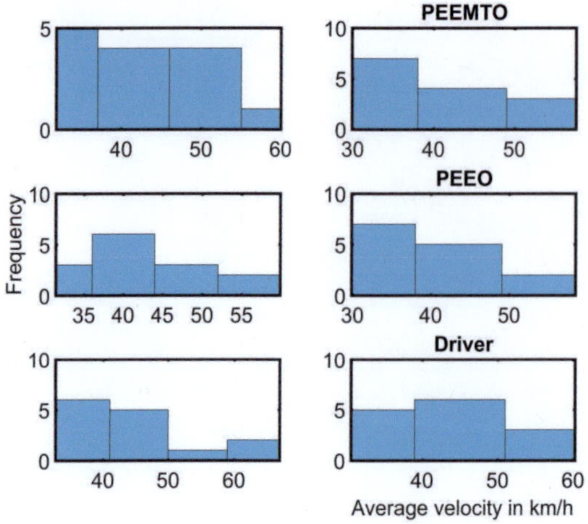

Figure 5.86: Distributions of average velocities. Rows top to bottom: PEEMTO, PEEO, ego-vehicle driver. Columns left to right: low traffic density, medium traffic density, high traffic density.

It is also possible that the ego-vehicle has to stop at the same traffic light several times due to a long vehicle queue in front of it. In general, the number of stops increases with traffic density.

Figure 5.85 illustrates the differences in the number of complete stops of PEEMTO compared to PEEO and the ego-vehicle driver. PEEMTO can avoid stops if the ego-vehicle is moving towards a red traffic light that is about to turn green. This is only possible in low traffic when there is sufficient space to perform lane changes. The ego-vehicle driver can outperform PEEMTO if it is faster than the speed limit or more aggressive during lane changes.

Velocity

Figure 5.86 shows the distributions of the average velocities. The average velocities are broadly spread out due to the traffic lights. The highest velocity of PEEMTO is 60 $\frac{\text{km}}{\text{h}}$, which corresponds to scenario 9 of the Adenauerring route. PEEO can also avoid stops in scenario 9 but is more heavily slowed down by front vehicles. The ego-vehicle driver sometimes has a desired velocity that is higher than the speed limit of 60 $\frac{\mathrm{km}}{\mathrm{h}}$.

In medium traffic density, the average velocity tends to be lower. The velocity distributions of PEEMTO and PEEO have a similar appearance and range. The ego-vehicle driver still tends to be faster.

In high traffic density, the velocity distributions of the contenders all have a similar appearance and range because overtaking is difficult and significant differences are not observed.

Gear shifts

Different to the highway scenarios, gear shifts frequently happen in urban scenarios because vehicles often have to stop at red traffic lights. The gear shift distributions are illustrated in Figure 5.87.
The gear shift distributions of PEEMTO and PEEO always have the same appearance. This is initially surprising because PEEMTO and PEEO do not always have the same number of stops. But as discussed in the last scenario of section 5.7.3, PEEMTO and PEEO do not always shift back to the second gear level when passing a traffic light. If the next traffic light is also within the regular optimization horizon and if its red phase cannot be avoided, the optimization is likely to maintain gear level 1. This same thing happens if the ego-vehicle has to stop at the same traffic light several times due to long vehicle queues.
The number of gear shifts of the ego-vehicle increases with traffic density because the number of stops increases with traffic density. Different to PEEMTO and PEEO, the automated transmission always performs gear shifts during stops. The gear level is set to 1 if the ego-vehicle stops and changed back to 2 if the ego-vehicle accelerates back to a certain velocity.

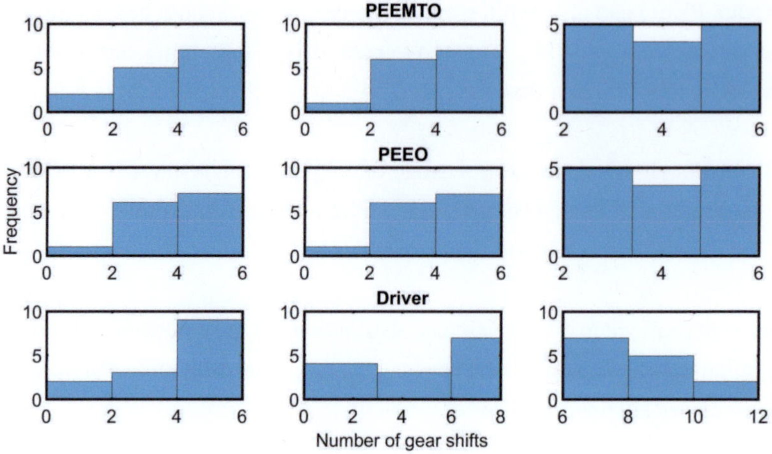

Figure 5.87: Distributions of gear shifts. Rows top to bottom: PEEMTO, PEEO, ego-vehicle driver. Columns left to right: low traffic density, medium traffic density, high traffic density.

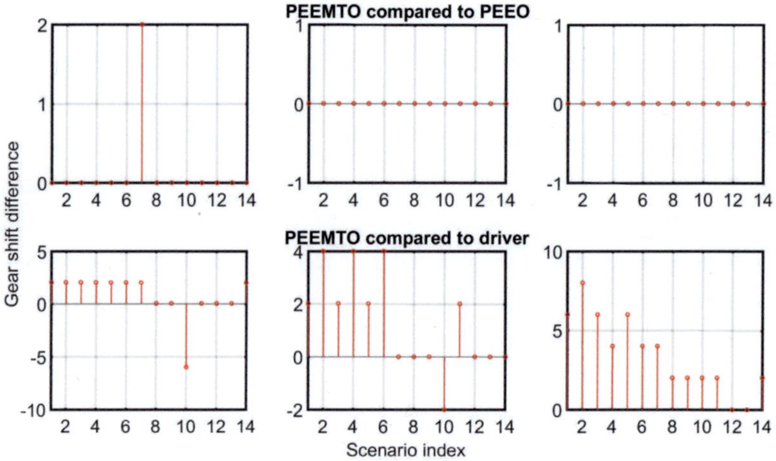

Figure 5.88: Gear shift savings of PEEMTO compared to PEEO and the ego-vehicle driver. Positive values mean PEEMTO has fewer gear shifts. Negative values mean PEEMTO has more gear shifts. Rows top to bottom: PEEMTO, PEEO, ego-vehicle driver. Columns left to right: low traffic density, medium traffic density, high traffic density.

On rare occasions, the automated transmission has to perform additional gear shifts if the ego-vehicle driver must abruptly decelerate because of other vehicles. For further information on the automated transmission, the reader can turn to section A.2.2.
Figure 5.88 shows the difference in gear shifts for every scenario and in every traffic density. Positive numbers denote gear shifts that PEEMTO is able to save in comparison to PEEO or the ego-vehicle driver. Negative numbers denote gear shifts that PEEO and the ego-vehicle driver are able to save in comparison to PEEMTO.
PEEMTO and PEEO are mostly the same with the exception of scenario 7 in low traffic density. In this scenario, PEEMTO is able to drive past the last traffic light after a lane change. In the same scenario, PEEO has to briefly come to a stop at the last traffic light because of front vehicles which stop at the traffic light. Therefore, PEEO performs two 2 more gear shifts than PEEMTO.

PEEMTO is able to outperform the ego-vehicle driver on numerous occasions because the optimization maintains the first gear level if the ego-vehicle has to stop again in the near future. The only exception is scenario 10 in low and medium traffic density. As mentioned earlier, scenario 10 always refers to an aggressive ego-vehicle driver with a higher desired velocity than the speed limit. As the aggressive ego-vehicle driver moves past the first traffic without deceleration, it is possible to pass by all remaining traffic lights without stopping similar to scenario 9. Therefore, the ego-vehicle driver has fewer gear shifts than PEEMTO, which is not allowed to be faster than the speed limit and strictly respects red phases. In scenario 10 with medium traffic density, the ego-vehicle driver performs more gear shifts than in low traffic density because it has to abruptly decelerate on two occasions due to other vehicles. The gear shift savings of PEEMTO are especially high in high traffic density because the ego-vehicle has to stop multiple times at the same traffic lights.

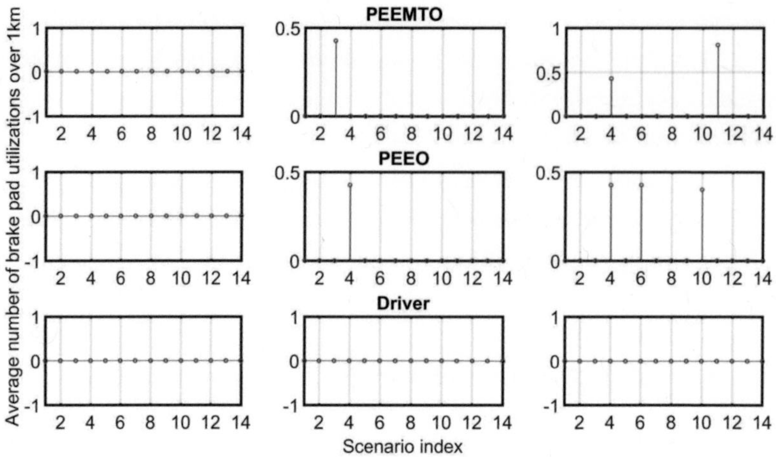

Figure 5.89: Brake pad utilizations. Rows top to bottom: PEEMTO compared to PEEO, PEEMTO compared to the ego-vehicle driver. Columns left to right: low traffic density, medium traffic density, high traffic density.

Brake pad utilization

Similar to the urban scenarios, very few brake pad utilizations are observed. The ego-vehicle driver never needs to use the brake pads. PEEMTO and PEEO only use the brake pads on very few occasions. If brake pads are used, they are only used once or twice in the entire scenario. Due to relatively low urban velocities, decelerations are particularly simple to accomplish. The brake pad utilizations are shown in Figure 5.89 for every scenario and traffic density.

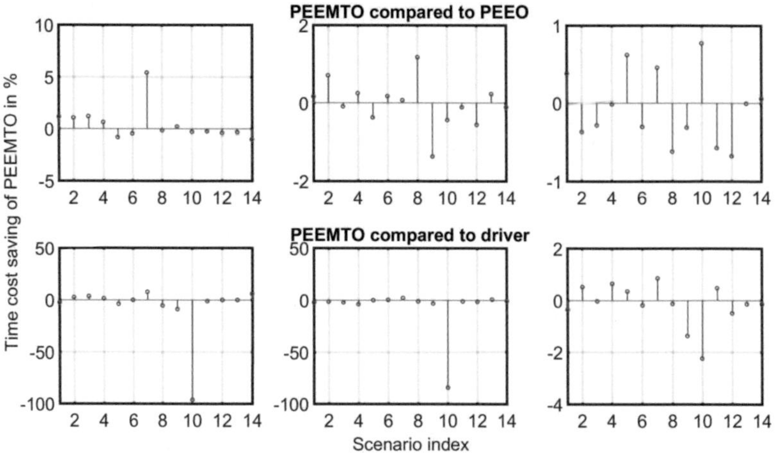

Figure 5.90: Travel duration cost saving of PEEMTO compared to PEEO and the ego-vehicle driver. Positive percental values mean PEEMTO leads to shorter travel durations. Negative percental values mean PEEMTO leads to longer travel durations. Rows top to bottom: PEEMTO compared to PEEO, PEEMTO compared to the ego-vehicle driver. Columns left to right: low traffic density, medium traffic density, high traffic density.

Travel duration cost

Figure 5.90 shows the percental time savings of PEEMTO compared to PEEO and the ego-vehicle driver in every scenario and in every traffic density. The mean and value range of the savings are shown in Table 5.7. For the comparison with the ego-vehicle driver, the median is used because of the extraordinary impact of scenario 10.

In low traffic density, PEEMTO is able to avoid some stops through lane changes and leads to travel duration reductions in several scenarios. The reductions are relatively small. In scenario 7, PEEO only has to stop for a short time at the last traffic light. In scenarios 1 to 3, PEEO stops more often than PEEMTO. But due to the configuration of the traffic light phases, both PEEMTO and PEEO have to eventually stop at the last traffic light in the Ostring route during the same red phase.

Table 5.7: Travel duration cost saving of PEEMTO compared to PEEO and the ego-vehicle driver for different traffic densities. Positive percental values mean PEEMTO leads to smaller costs. Negative percental values mean PEEMTO leads to higher costs. Mean and value range are denoted in %.

Compared	Low density	Medium density	High density
to PEEO	0.41,	-0.02,	-0.06,
in % (mean, range)	-1.03 to 5.41	-1.37 to 1.18	-0.68 to 0.77
to ego-vehicle driver	-0.24,	-1.4,	-0.14,
in % (median, range)	-96.3 to 7.5	-84.6 to 1.9	-2.25 to 0.85

In medium and high traffic density, the difference between PEEMTO and PEEO are minor because PEEMTO is not able to make any lane changes and largely has the same trajectory as PEEO. The results are not entirely the same because different random vehicles lead to some variations.

In the case of the ego-vehicle driver, the aggressive ego-vehicle driver in scenario 10 leads to significantly less travel duration than PEEMTO in low and medium traffic density. This is because the aggressive ego-vehicle driver does not stop at the first traffic light and travels at a higher desired velocity than the speed limit. The differences in high traffic density are relatively minor because the ego-vehicle can be blocked by other vehicles and there are usually few opportunities for lane changes.

Energy consumption cost

The energy consumption cost saving of PEEMTO compared to PEEO and the ego-vehicle driver is shown in Figure 5.91. The mean and value range of the savings are shown in Table 5.8.

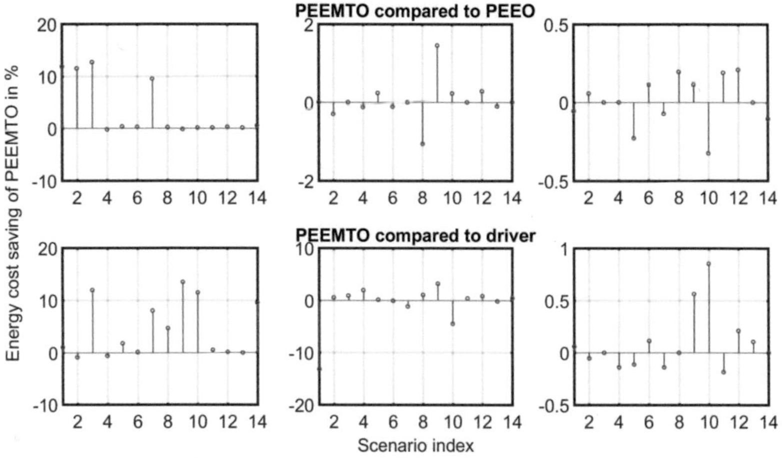

Figure 5.91: Energy consumption cost saving of PEEMTO compared to PEEO and the ego-vehicle driver. Positive percental values mean PEEMTO leads to smaller costs. Negative percental values mean PEEMTO leads to higher costs. Rows top to bottom: PEEMTO compared to PEEO, PEEMTO compared to the ego-vehicle driver. Columns left to right: low traffic density, medium traffic density, high traffic density.

Table 5.8: Energy consumption cost saving of PEEMTO compared to PEEO and the ego-vehicle driver for different traffic densities. Positive percental values mean PEEMTO leads to smaller costs. Negative percental values mean PEEMTO leads to higher costs. Mean and value range are denoted in %.

Compared	Low density	Medium density	High density
to PEEO	3.36,	0.03,	0,
in % (mean, range)	-0.24 to 12.7	-1.07 to 1.45	-0.32 to 0.21
to ego-vehicle driver	4.37,	-0.7,	0.09,
in % (mean, range)	-0.89 to 13.49	-13.25 to 3.2	-0.19 to 0.85

One way to save energy is to avoid stops. Examples include the scenarios 1, 2, 3, and 7 in low traffic density compared to PEEO. Another example is scenario 1 in medium traffic density, in which the ego-vehicle driver has one less stop than PEEMTO.

Another way is to avoid high velocity. In scenario 10 in low traffic density, the ego-vehicle driver does not need to stop and drives past the first traffic light because it is significantly faster than the speed limit, while PEEMTO makes several stops. But PEEMTO still consumes less energy because the ego-vehicle driver moves with a velocity of 67 $\frac{\text{km}}{\text{h}}$, while the average velocity of PEEMTO is below 35 $\frac{\text{km}}{\text{h}}$.

There are also other aspects (e.g., powertrain efficiency) that affect energy consumption, which were already discussed in previous sections.

The differences between PEEMTO and the other contenders decrease in higher traffic densities because lane changes and free movement are more heavily confined.

Combined cost

The combined cost saving of PEEMTO compared to PEEO and the ego-vehicle driver is shown in Figure 5.92. The mean and value range of the savings are shown in Table 5.9. For comparison with the ego-vehicle driver, the median is used because of the extraordinary impact of scenario 10.

In low traffic density and compared to PEEO, PEEMTO primarily reduces the combined cost by avoiding stops. The cost saving in scenario 7 is especially high because PEEMTO is additionally able to avoid 2 gear shifts. In medium and high traffic density, there is not much difference between PEEMTO and PEEO. The small variations are due to randomly created vehicles, which can be different in the experiments of PEEMTO and PEEO. Due to the small variations, the brake pad utilizations of PEEMTO and PEEO have a visible impact.

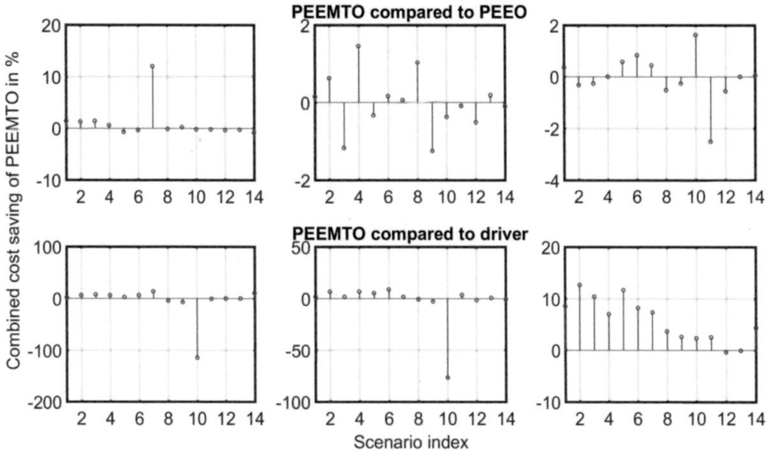

Figure 5.92: Combined cost saving of PEEMTO compared to PEEO and the ego-vehicle driver. Positive percental values mean PEEMTO leads to smaller costs. Negative percental values mean PEEMTO leads to higher costs. Rows top to bottom: PEEMTO compared to PEEO, PEEMTO compared to the ego-vehicle driver. Columns left to right: low traffic density, medium traffic density, high traffic density.

Table 5.9: Combined cost saving of PEEMTO compared to PEEO and the ego-vehicle driver for different traffic densities. Positive percental values mean PEEMTO leads to smaller costs. Negative percental values mean PEEMTO leads to higher costs. Mean and value range are denoted in %.

Compared	Low density	Medium density	High density
to PEEO	0.96,	-0.01,	-0.05,
in % (mean, range)	-0.87 to 12	-1.25 to 1.46	-2.5 to 1.6
to ego-vehicle driver	2.15,	1.52,	5.67,
in % (median, range)	-115 to 13.65	-76.77 to 8.59	-0.4 to 12.65

In low and medium traffic density, the most prominent result is that of the ego-vehicle driver in scenario 10. As the fast ego-vehicle driver does not make any stops, while PEEMTO has to stop several times, the combined cost is significantly lower for the ego-vehicle driver, especially due to the lower travel duration cost and the lower gear shift cost. In the other scenarios, PEEMTO is mostly better. In high traffic density, the combined cost savings of PEEMTO compared to the ego-vehicle driver are quite high. This is primarily due to the many gear shifts that PEEMTO is able to avoid.

The mean and median cost savings in table 5.9 indicate that PEEMTO is often able to lead to some savings compared to PEEO and the ego-vehicle driver or is usually not worse. But the results are, in general, highly situation dependent. If there is not enough space for lane changes, PEEMTO and PEEO largely lead to the same results. The ego-vehicle driver can greatly outperform PEEMTO if it ignores the speed limit or possibly even the beginning of the red phase. In general, PEEMTO performs best if it is able to make lane changes and if it is moving towards a red light that is about to turn green. The differences between the PEEMTO, PEEO, and the ego-vehicle driver diminish with higher traffic density. The strength of PEEMTO in urban scenarios is less reliable than in highway scenarios. As discussed in section 5.7, better usage of low velocity ahead of red traffic lights can further improve the result. Temporary relaxation of the speed limit ahead of traffic lights is another possibility.

5.9 Computation duration and memory demand

The definition of real-time capability depends on the application. For safety-related systems like automotive applications, the update rate of a controller is often very high (e.g., 200 Hz [Fun+12]). PEEMTO computes the optimal long range trajectory that a subsequent controller should use as reference and therefore does not need the same update rate. If no new optimization is available, the controller simply follows the most recently computed trajectory. Nevertheless, PEEMTO must react to changes in the environment, which may be different from the original prediction. In this thesis, an update rate of 10 Hz is defined as real-time capability for PEEMTO.

The scenarios with the highest computational complexity are highways with three lanes and dense traffic. According to [Bai+15a] [Bai+15b] [Bai+15c], a traffic density of 20 vehicles on each lane over 1 km can be interpreted as very high traffic density on highways. Within a horizon length of 250 m, this definition leads to 15 vehicles ahead of the ego-vehicle on a highway with three lanes. With additionally three vehicles behind and two vehicles parallel to the ego-vehicle, PEEMTO has to evaluate 20 other vehicles. The other vehicles shall be evenly distributed over the three lanes.

The experiments in this thesis are conducted on a modern Office-PC with 16 RAM and an Intel i7-4790 CPU at 3.6 GHz with 4 physical cores. The operating system is Windows 10 x64. OpenMP is used to distribute the computation across all available cores with active hyper-threading.

The construction of the state graph takes less than 0.01 s. During the backward procedure of the DP algorithm, the primary task is to follow the chain of optimal predecessors from the last stage to the start state. As every state knows its optimal predecessor after the forward evaluation, the backtracing can be done very quickly. For the given example, the time duration cannot be clearly measured as it is extremely short.

Without hyper-threading and in the ideal case, the computation duration distributed over 4 CPU cores should be 4 times shorter than the same computation task executed on a single CPU core. In this example, if the computation task is not explicitly distributed across all available CPU cores, the operating system still distributes the computational burden across multiple threads but concentrates the workload on one thread. In this case, the computation duration is between 2.318 s and 2.391 s. If the computation task is explicitly distributed across all threads, the computation duration is between 0.785 s and 0.801 s. Compared to the previous case, the computation duration is approximately three times smaller. Thus, the computation duration is still too long for real-time applications on the employed CPU with the default parameter configuration.

In order to decrease computational complexity, it is possible to reduce the discretization precision, the length of the horizon, or evaluate more states through implicit discretization. Indeed, if the velocity discretization is set to 5 $\frac{\text{km}}{\text{h}}$ instead of 1 $\frac{\text{km}}{\text{h}}$, the computation duration is reduced to below 0.1 s within a range of 0.063 s to 0.081 s. Naturally, this means that many velocities drop out of the search space. For the reduced discretization precision, PEEMTO no longer chooses 92 $\frac{\text{km}}{\text{h}}$ as the optimal cruise velocity, but 90 $\frac{\text{km}}{\text{h}}$. In regard to the scenario evaluated in section 5.6, the ego-vehicle driver would still have a 22.3 % and PEEO a 2.3 % higher combined cost than PEEMTO during cruising. Additional reduction in computation duration can be achieved, by using a less computationally complex driver model. If there are no other vehicles, the computation duration sinks to a range of 0.026 s to 0.029 s with a velocity discretization of 5 $\frac{\text{km}}{\text{h}}$. Urban scenarios show a similar picture. For a road with two main lanes, a speed limit of 70 $\frac{\text{km}}{\text{h}}$, and the same number of other vehicles, PEEMTO needs between 0.409 s and

0.517 s. If the velocity discretization is set to 2.5 $\frac{\text{km}}{\text{h}}$ instead of 1 $\frac{\text{km}}{\text{h}}$, the computation duration decreases to a range of 0.082 s to 0.096 s. Furthermore, from the perspective of implementation, additional code optimization for the most time-critical parts can further reduce the computation duration, e.g., by avoiding the use of standard arithmetic libraries.

Another option is to use more potent computation hardware. The highway scenario leads to a computation duration between 0.785 s and 0.801 s while the target duration is 0.1 s. Thus, the current PEEMTO implementation with default optimization parameters requires a CPU with at least 32 physical cores or more to compute the optimization in 0.1 s (e.g., AMD 2990WX). Another possible approach is to create an implementation using GPUs or other hardware platforms that have thousands of computation units.

As discussed in section 4.14, if the state transition costs are precomputed and saved for later use, $(n_\varphi n_\kappa n_v n_G)^2$ elements are created. With the default discretization of Table A.11 and 32 Bit float data type, the elements lead to a memory demand of 156.3 MB for highway scenarios if they are saved in a list without any compression. Additional tables are necessary if different position discretizations are used as described in Table A.11 in the appendix. In comparison, the auxiliary horizon creates little memory demand for each additional stage. Using the default discretization of Table A.11, less than 100 KB is added for each new auxiliary stage.

6 Conclusion

6.1 Summary

In this work, a model predictive motion trajectory optimization for energy-efficient driving has been developed. A novel unified approach is used, which incorporates the vehicle model, static environment elements (i.e., road slope, road curvature, speed limits), and dynamic environment elements, (i.e., traffic lights and other traffic participants). While the focus of the proposed system is on energy-efficient driving, physical feasibility of the computed trajectory, travel safety, and several other aspects are also considered. The optimization goes beyond existing ideas regarding energy-efficient driving optimization by incorporating lane changes and overtaking decisions.

Although the vehicle model refers to an electric vehicle powertrain, the developed optimization can be applied to a wide range of different vehicles. This thesis marks the first time, a model predictive motion trajectory optimization has been applied to an electric vehicle with a transmission.

Monetary costs are proposed, which lead to unambiguous optimization results. Stagewise dynamic programming is used to perform the optimization.

A novel long-range cost estimation using historically accumulated minimum costs has been developed to estimate the long-time optimal behavior of the vehicle beyond the regular finite computation horizon.

In order to decrease the search space, implicit discretization is used. This means that certain continuous state dimensions are not explicitly expanded in the state graph, but rather implicitly computed along different state trajectories.

The evaluation has been conducted in a simulated environment. The simulated routes are based on truly existent roads, i.e., information like road slope, road curvature, speed limits, lanes, and traffic lights is retrieved from the real world. Other vehicles are simulated using established driver models from transportation engineering.

Numerous scenarios show that significant monetary cost reductions can be obtained through the proposed optimization compared to common driver behavior and existing methods of energy-efficient driving optimization.

Additional employment of parallelization on multiple CPU cores moves the algorithm performance into the real time domain.

6.2 Future work

As autonomous and energy-efficient driving cover a very broad field of highly different research areas, this thesis cannot cover all topics. Thus, there are many possible areas, where additional research can be conducted.

The range of current electric vehicles is currently limited compared to vehicles with ICEs. Furthermore, charging the battery can take a long time compared to conventional visits to the gas station. An interesting topic is the optimization of charging station visits along the route. This is also interesting in regard to the auxiliary long-range horizon extension, which can cover very long distances.

A similar topic is time schedule optimization, which deals with appointments, time schedules, time of arrivals, and delays.

The driver models and the prediction of other traffic participants are deterministic in this thesis. Prediction of the behavior of other traffic participants is generally highly challenging. One possible extension is to incorporate probabilistic models, e.g., in the form of hidden Markov models [Zie+16]. Machine learning could also be applied to create adaptive behavior models that may even be driver specific. This would also enable the optimization to include the interests and tolerance of other traffic participants in its decisions.

The optimization regarding traffic lights and traffic light series can be revisited.

Traffic regulations can be at odds with other optimization criteria. An interesting question is if and how certain regulations can be occasionally ignored to improve the result.

The evaluated scenarios all refer to business trips with the private journey of individuals being a special case. Additional scenarios can include autonomous deliveries and taxis.

The proposed optimization has only been evaluated for a limited number of road configurations. Traffic circles, lane merging, complex interaction scenarios, and unavoidable accidents could be additionally considered.

The proposed system relies on a predefined route, which is independently selected from the presented energy efficiency optimization methods. A possible extension is the combination of energy efficiency driving and energy-efficient route selection. Furthermore, path planning and mapping commonly found in robotic applications can also be of interest, e.g., in off-road scenarios.

Cooperative driving based on V2I and V2V can further enhance both energy efficiency and travel safety for a large group of vehicles. Business models centered on this cooperation could be created, e.g., by enabling monetary transactions among different intelligent participants to yield resources, e.g., a specific lane to those members who are willing to purchase them.

The evaluation has been conducted in a simulated environment. Testing the system in real-world traffic is naturally a topic for the future. This includes communicating with real traffic lights and the robust detection of other vehicles. The design of a robust controller that can handle model deviations in the real world is also important to execute the computed state trajectory.

Finally, further decrease in computational complexity can be of interest. Regarding implementation, the execution speed of the algorithm can be further increased by creating an implementation on GPUs.

A Appendix

The appendix provides additional information, but is not necessary to understand the main ideas of this thesis.

A.1 Extended driver model

The ego-vehicle driver (section A.2.2) and the simulation environment (section A.3) use the extended driver model (EDM). The EDM has all the functionalities of the simplified driver model (SDM) as described in section 3.4.2. It also uses the ACC model and can react to traffic lights. Furthermore, lane changes and additional aspects are considered.

A.1.1 Lane changes and MOBIL

Different from the SDM, the EDM shall be able to change lanes. Lane changes are decided by the *minimizing overall braking deceleration induced by lane changes* (MOBIL) model as proposed in [TK13]. The MOBIL concept evaluates the safety criterion of a lane change and the lane change incentive. A descriptive illustration is shown in Figure A.1.

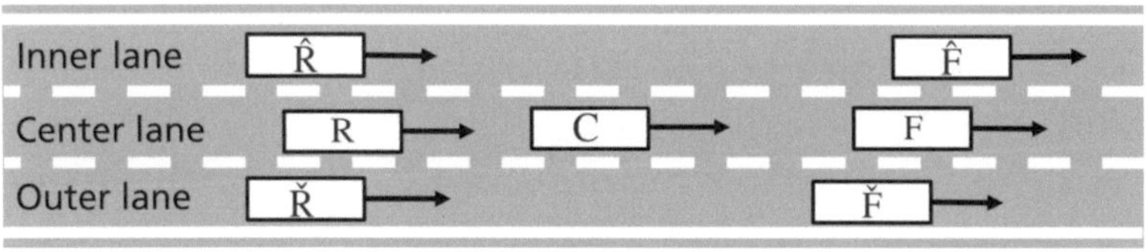

Figure A.1: MOBIL concept.

Without loss of generality, let vehicle C in the center lane be a vehicle that needs to make a lane change decision. The lane change evaluation to the inner lane shall be discussed first. Let $b_{\mathrm{d,safe}}$ be the deceleration limit that vehicle C regards as safe deceleration for a rear vehicle. Let vehicle C assume that vehicle R̂ will adopt the acceleration $\hat{a}_{\hat{\mathrm{R}}}$ if vehicle C changes to the inner lane and places itself in front of vehicle R̂. $\hat{a}_{\hat{\mathrm{R}}}$ of vehicle R̂ is computed through the ACC model as described in section 3.4.2. Note that the MOBIL model assumes that the different vehicles all know each other's driver parameters. Vehicle C assumes that the lane change is safe if $\hat{a}_{\hat{\mathrm{R}}}$ is larger than $-b_{\mathrm{d,safe}}$:

$$\hat{a}_{\hat{\mathrm{R}}} > -b_{\mathrm{d,safe}}. \tag{A.1}$$

If the safety criterion is fulfilled, vehicle C can theoretically perform the lane change. But there has to be an incentive to consider the lane change in the first place. If, for example, there is no other vehicle in front of vehicle C, there is no point in changing to another lane, even if the safety criterion is fulfilled. According to the MOBIL model, the driver should change the lane if the desired velocity has not been reached and if a lane change can enable the driver to apply a higher acceleration $\hat{a}_{\mathrm{C}}$ in the new lane than the current acceleration a_{C} in the current lane. $\hat{a}_{\mathrm{C}}$ is the same as $a_{\mathrm{d,free}}$ for vehicle C if there is no front vehicle in the new lane. If there is a front vehicle F̂ in the new lane, vehicle C must adapt $\hat{a}_{\mathrm{C}}$ to follow the front vehicle using the ACC model. The acceleration gain created by the lane change must be higher than a certain lane change incentive $\Delta a_{\mathrm{d,min}}$. Furthermore, there is an additional bias term $a_{\mathrm{d,bias}}$ that encourages the driver to choose the outer lane. Thus, the MOBIL model respects the keep-right directive. If the acceleration benefit is greater than the sum of $\Delta a_{\mathrm{d,min}}$ and $a_{\mathrm{d,bias}}$, there is sufficient incentive for a lane change to the inner lane. This kind of incentive is the incentive criterion for egoistic drivers:

$$\hat{a}_{\mathrm{C}} - a_{\mathrm{C}} > \Delta a_{\mathrm{d,min}} + a_{\mathrm{d,bias}}. \tag{A.2}$$

The incentive criterion for egoistic drivers is a special case of a more general incentive that also evaluates the benefit for other drivers affected by a lane change of vehicle C. This incentive is called the MOBIL inventive. It adds another term to the previous condition. Let $a_{\hat{R}}$ be the current acceleration of vehicle $\hat{R}$. Let $\hat{a}_{\hat{R}}$ be the new acceleration of vehicle $\hat{R}$ if vehicle C performs the lane change. Let a_R be the current acceleration of vehicle R. Let $\hat{a}_R$ be the new acceleration of vehicle R if vehicle C performs the lane change. How much the acceleration of another vehicle impacts the lane change decision of vehicle C is governed by the politeness factor $\lambda_{d,p}$. For $\lambda_{d,p} = 1$, the driver is highly altruistic. For $\lambda_{d,p} = 0$, the driver is completely egoistic. The MOBIL incentive for a lane change to the inner lane is defined as:

$$\hat{a}_C - a_C + \lambda_{d,p}(\hat{a}_{\hat{R}} - a_{\hat{R}} + \hat{a}_R - a_R) > \Delta a_{d,min} + a_{d,bias}. \tag{A.3}$$

Lane changes to the outer lane are encouraged. With reference to the illustration in Figure A.1, the MOBIL incentive for lane changes to the outer lane is defined as:

$$\check{a}_C - a_C + \lambda_{d,p}(\check{a}_{\check{R}} - a_{\check{R}} + \check{a}_R - a_R) > \Delta a_{d,min} - a_{d,bias}. \tag{A.4}$$

A.1.2 Extensions and alterations

There are several aspects in real-world traffic that the models of [TK13] do not consider.

The MOBIL model has a bias towards the outer lane. But as the reader may know from real-world experience, many drivers may not prefer the outer lane in practice. One reason is to avoid slower trucks, which are obligated to keep to the outer lane on highways if possible. Another reason is to spread out the traffic more evenly across all lanes. Thus, the ego-vehicle driver and the vehicles controlled by the simulation environment shall have a desired lane $l_{d,goal}$ that specifies the favorite lane of a driver. For all lane changes that do not lead towards $l_{\mathrm{d,goal}}$, equation (A.3) is used. For all lane changes that lead towards $l_{\mathrm{d,goal}}$, equation (A.4) is used. Thus, the lane bias $a_{\mathrm{d,bias}}$ now actually refers to the bias towards $l_{\mathrm{d,goal}}$, which is not necessarily the outer lane.

Another observation made in real-world traffic is that some slow drivers may prefer the inner lane or one of the center lanes although they do not wish to move particularly fast. This type of driver will at some point slow down all other rear drivers who are in the same lane and prefer a higher velocity. In the EDM, the slow front vehicle shall try to change to the adjacent right lane if there is a faster rear vehicle approaching from behind. To trigger the evasive lane change of the front vehicle, the rear vehicle must have a desired velocity that is higher than the desired velocity of the front vehicle and the distance between the two vehicles must be smaller than a certain evasion activation distance $\Delta s_{\mathrm{d,evasion}}$. The distance $\Delta s_{\mathrm{d,evasion}}$ shall depend on the speed limit v_{max} and the evasion activation time gap of the front vehicle $\Delta t_{\mathrm{d,evasion}}$. If there is no speed limit, the reference velocity for highways of 130 $\frac{\mathrm{km}}{\mathrm{h}}$ is used:

$$\Delta s_{\mathrm{d,evasion}} = v_{\mathrm{max}} \Delta t_{\mathrm{d,evasion}}. \tag{A.5}$$

In reality, vehicles react to each other simultaneously. If the drivers are all highly altruistic and all want to let others make the first move, deadlocks may be created. The EDM uses the same simplification as the SDM to avoid this problem. The vehicles in the simulation make decisions one by one, following a strict order. The vehicle with the highest longitudinal position value (i.e., the one furthest ahead) makes the first decision. Based on the decision of the first vehicle, the vehicle with the second highest longitudinal position value then makes its decision. This process is repeated for all vehicles. In the illustration of Figure A.1, for example, the order would be F̂, F, F̌, C, R, and finally either R̂ or Ř. As the vehicles R̂ and Ř have the same longitudinal position, the vehicle that makes the decision earlier is randomly chosen.

One of the most complicated maneuvers in traffic simulation is the merging maneuver. This includes zipper merging in lane closures, where two lanes merge into one. According to [TK13], these cooperative maneuvers are notoriously difficult and are only realized in the most elaborate commercial simulators. This thesis does not consider merging maneuvers. The chosen routes evaluated in chapter 5 all exclude road sections with lane closures. In highway sections with acceleration and deceleration lanes, merging dynamics are also omitted. Vehicles in the acceleration lane and their interaction with the vehicles in the outer lane are not simulated. Instead, hitherto non-existing vehicles can be randomly inserted into the outer lane if there is an adjacent acceleration lane. Similarly, vehicles in the outer lane adjacent to a deceleration lane or vehicles in turn lanes can randomly disappear from the simulation.

A.2 Reference systems

This section presents two reference systems that are used to compare to PEEMTO in chapter 5.

A.2.1 Predictive energy efficiency optimization without lane changes

Existing model predictive energy optimization strategies like [Ter09] [Hel10] use sophisticated powertrain models. But interactions with other vehicles to improve energy efficiency are reduced to a minimum. Indeed, if there is a slow vehicle ahead of the ego-vehicle in the same lane, the optimization only follows the slow vehicle without evaluating lane changes. As stated in [Ter09], the author is able to achieve fuel savings of up to 30 % compared to standard cruise controllers if there are no other vehicles on the road. But fuel savings drop to 3 % on average if there are other traffic participants.

Let PEEO be the acronym for predictive energy efficiency optimization without lane changes. Its purpose is to mimic the behavior of existing model predictive energy optimization strategies like [Ter09] [Hel10]. PEEO shall also consider traffic lights the same way as PEEMTO. Indeed, in many ways, PEEO shall be the same as PEEMTO in order to enable direct comparison. There are only two major differences:

- PEEO does not perform lane changes.
- PEEO uses the stationary horizon extension and does not use the long-range auxiliary horizon extension.

A.2.2 Ego-vehicle driver

The second reference system is the ego-vehicle driver that simulates the behavior of a human driver using the EDM model.

Cost computation

Different from the other vehicles in the simulation that accompany the ego-vehicle, the ego-vehicle driver shall produce costs just as PEEMTO. Thus, the results of the ego-vehicle driver can be directly compared to the results of PEEMTO. The ego-vehicle driver uses the same cost formulations, constraints, and vehicle model as PEEMTO. Whenever the driver makes a decision, the results like costs, energy consumption, etc., are subsequently computed from the driver decision using the vehicle model. This also means that feasible results can only be computed if the driver decision does not violate any physical limits of the vehicle. As discussed in section 3.4.2, the driver model does not consider road slope or curvature. Thus, only routes on which the driver decisions produce feasible results can be used for the evaluation in chapter 5.

Automated transmission

As the driver model formulation of [TK13] does not consider gear level changes or any powertrain aspects, a simplified automated transmission control is defined for the EDM. According to [Kle11], a gear change decision of an automated transmission, at least, depends on the current gear level, the current velocity, and the acceleration pedal position.

As mentioned in section 5.2.2, gear level two is regarded as optimal for most cruise velocities, even for low cruise velocities of 30 $\frac{\mathrm{km}}{\mathrm{h}}$. Therefore, the underlying velocity reference for gear shifts is set to 30 $\frac{\mathrm{km}}{\mathrm{h}}$. For stability reasons, the velocity reference cannot be directly used as a threshold function in order to avoid gear shift fluctuations. Instead, two slightly different velocity thresholds 25 $\frac{\mathrm{km}}{\mathrm{h}}$ and 29 $\frac{\mathrm{km}}{\mathrm{h}}$ are used for down-shift and up-shift decisions respectively.

Another functionality encountered in many automated transmissions is the kick-down mechanism. If the driver depresses the acceleration pedal beyond a certain threshold (kick-down), the automated transmission interprets the action as the driver's desire for strong acceleration and reduces the gear level, unless the engine speed ω_e is already too high. A similar kick-down mechanism shall also be used here. As the computation of the acceleration pedal position is not considered in this thesis, the engine torque demand is used to trigger the kick-down reaction. Furthermore, as the REM-2030 transmission only has two gear levels, the kick-down mechanism only works at gear level two. As discussed in section 3.1.1, the REM-2030 EE can supply the maximum engine torque of 103 Nm up to an engine speed of approximately 7,500 $\frac{1}{\mathrm{min}}$. Therefore, if the engine speed does not exceed 7,500 $\frac{1}{\mathrm{min}}$ and if the engine torque demand is above a certain threshold $T_{\mathrm{e,d,max}}(\omega_\mathrm{e})$, the gear level should be reduced independently of velocity. For the purpose of this thesis, $T_{e,d,max}(\omega_e)$ is set to 95 % of the maximum engine torque $T_{e,max}(\omega_e)$:

$$T_{e,d,max}(\omega_e) = 0.95 T_{e,max}(\omega_e). \tag{A.6}$$

The condition for a down-shift during acceleration due to kick-down is therefore:

$$T_e > T_{e,d,max}(\omega_e) \quad \wedge \quad \omega_e \leq 7{,}500 \frac{1}{\text{min}} \quad \wedge \quad G = 2. \tag{A.7}$$

Different from vehicles with ICEs, the EE plays a significantly larger role during deceleration. Therefore, a kick-down mechanism is also defined for very strong generator torque demand. Similar to the kick-down mechanism during acceleration, the gear level should be reduced during deceleration if the engine speed does not exceed 7,500 $\frac{1}{\text{min}}$ and if the engine torque demand is below a certain threshold $T_{e,d,min}(\omega_e)$. Let $T_{e,d,min}(\omega_e)$ be 95 % of the minimum engine torque or the maximum generator torque $T_{e,min}(\omega_e)$:

$$T_{e,d,min}(\omega_e) = 0.95 T_{e,min}(\omega_e). \tag{A.8}$$

The condition for a down-shift during deceleration due to kick-down is therefore:

$$T_e < T_{e,d,min}(\omega_e) \quad \wedge \quad \omega_e \leq 7{,}500 \frac{1}{\text{min}} \quad \wedge \quad G = 2. \tag{A.9}$$

The kick-down mechanism overrules the velocity dependent gear shift.

A.3 Simulation environment

The simulation environment contains all elements in the simulation, i.e., route, ego-vehicle, other vehicles, and traffic lights. The simulation truly moves and changes all elements in the environment. While the states of the other vehicles are changed according to the EDM, the state of the ego-vehicle is changed according to the optimization result of PEEMTO, PEEO, or the ego-vehicle driver. A deviation from the optimization result is not simulated, i.e., the ego-vehicle precisely follows the optimal trajectory.

A.3.1 Traffic lights

For the purpose of this thesis, existing traffic lights along the chosen routes are included in the simulation. While locations of the traffic lights can be easily retrieved from reality, the signal control software is not publicly available. For the purpose of this thesis, local real-world measurements of the red, green, and yellow phase durations are collected for every traffic light along the selected routes. The simplified assumption is that the recorded phases are repeated. The measurements of different traffic lights are not conducted at the same time, but rather recorded whenever a measurement is started. In the default configuration, the different traffic light phases shall have the same time separation as in the original measurements. It is possible that in reality the traffic lights are influenced by the traffic flow, pedestrians, and other components, i.e., they would adapt their phase control overtime. PEEMTO is independent of the exact nature of traffic light phase shift mechanics and can deal with all types of traffic lights. Nevertheless, it should be part of future work to either obtain the exact real-world traffic light signal control programs, or truly establish direct communication between the ego-vehicle and the traffic lights.

A.3.2 Traffic density

Chapter 5 uses scenarios with different degrees of traffic density. The underlying question is how many vehicles should be created. According to [Bai+15a] [Bai+15b] [Bai+15c], there are different classes of level of service (LOS), which include the traffic density. The evaluation uses the classes B, C, and D in the random scenarios of section 5.8. The numeric traffic density for each class, with respect to the speed limit is given in Table A.1. The consequences of traffic density for the different classes are:

- A: Very low traffic density, de facto unhindered travel progression.
- B: Low traffic density, influence of other vehicles noticeable.
- C: Medium traffic density, movement depends on other vehicles.
- D: High traffic density, other vehicles have strong influence.
- E: Very high traffic density, sluggish traffic, maximum road traffic capacity reached.
- F: Excessive, traffic jam, traffic capacity of the road exceeded.

Table A.1: Classes of level of service (LOS). Traffic density in vehicles per km, per lane, dependent on speed limit $v_{\max}$.

Class	$v_{\max} \leq 50\,\frac{\text{km}}{\text{h}}$	$v_{\max} = 70\,\frac{\text{km}}{\text{h}}$	$v_{\max} \geq 80\,\frac{\text{km}}{\text{h}}$
A	≤ 7	≤ 6	≤ 3
B	≤ 14	≤ 12	≤ 6
C	≤ 23	≤ 20	≤ 10
D	≤ 34	≤ 30	≤ 15
E	≤ 45	≤ 40	≤ 20
F	> 45	> 40	> 20

A.3.3 Vehicles and random creation

The simulation only considers vehicles that are within a distance range of 2 km ahead and behind the ego-vehicle to decrease the computational burden. This 4 km long section with the ego-vehicle at the center shall be called the ego-world. In general, the ego-world must be significantly larger than the regular horizon length and the sensor range of the ego-vehicle. Other vehicles may enter or exit the route if the road configuration allows it. Opposing traffic and other vehicles that are not related to the route are not simulated. The ego-world confinement is only used for the highway scenarios of section 5.8. In the urban scenarios, the ego-world is the entire route.

The simulation environment generally does not use the default driver parameters given in Table A.5 and Table A.6. Instead, random deviations from the default parameters are generated to simulate different drivers. The random driver parameters are chosen using normal distributions. The mean is usually close or identical to the original default driver parameter while the standard deviation allows some deviation from it. The simulation often uses two normal distributions for a single parameter. The first one only refers to numbers smaller than the mean, while the second one only refers to numbers larger than the mean. Apart from the driver parameters, several other random choices are made with certain probabilities, e.g., the choice of the driver type. There is sometimes also a range of minimum and maximum values that the parameters must not exceed. The choice of the mean, the standard deviation, and other randomization parameters are manually chosen design parameters.

Vehicle classes

The simulation distinguishes between different vehicle classes. There are passenger vehicles and trucks. Passenger vehicles shall all have a length of 5 m, while trucks shall always be 10 m long. If there is no speed limit, the recommended maximum speed for passenger cars is 130 $\frac{\text{km}}{\text{h}}$, while the recommended maximum speed for trucks is only 80 $\frac{\text{km}}{\text{h}}$. A truck shall always choose the outer lane as the desired lane.

Driver types

The simulation also distinguishes between three types of drivers: defensive drivers, normal drivers, and aggressive drivers. The random choice of the parameters is influenced by the driver type. The choice of the desired velocity uses the default desired velocity as a reference, i.e., the chosen desired velocity is usually close to the speed limit or the recommended maximum speed if there is no speed limit. A newly created vehicle has a 70 % chance of having a normal driving style. Thus, the majority of vehicles are controlled by normal drivers, whose model parameters are close to the default parameters. Alternatively, a newly created vehicle shall have a 15 % chance of having an aggressive driving style and a 15 % chance of having a defensive driving style.

The normal driver type has the following characteristics:

- The initially desired lane is likely to be the outer lane on highways.
- The initially desired lane can be any lane except the exit lane on urban roads.
- The desired velocity is likely to be close to the speed limit or the recommended maximum speed.
- The acceleration and deceleration are close to the default EDM behavior.
- There is a 10 % chance that the vehicle creation process leads to a driver, who always moves past a traffic light if the traffic light turns red when the vehicle is only, e.g., 20 m ahead of it.
- The driver is likely to leave sufficient spatial gaps to other vehicles.

The aggressive driver type has the following characteristics:

- The initially desired lane is likely one of the center lanes or the inner lane.

- The desired velocity cannot be lower than the speed limit or the recommended maximum speed and is likely to be higher.
- The acceleration and deceleration are likely to be stronger than the default EDM behavior.
- There is a 50 % chance that the vehicle creation process leads to a driver, who always moves past a traffic light if the traffic light turns red when the vehicle is only, e.g., 20 m ahead of it.
- The driver is likely to only leave small spatial gaps to other vehicles. Nevertheless, the time gap with respect to the rear vehicle shall be at least 0.5 s long to prevent accidents. Note that scenarios with accidents are not considered in the evaluations.

The defensive driver type has the following characteristics:

- The initially desired lane is always the outer lane.
- The desired velocity can never be higher than the speed limit or the recommended maximum speed and is likely to be lower.
- The acceleration and deceleration are likely to be weaker than the default EDM behavior.
- In regard to traffic lights, the driver always follows the default EDM behavior.
- The driver is likely to leave ample spatial gaps to other vehicles.

Additional information regarding parameter choice is given in Tables A.7 to A.10.

The ego-vehicle driver in the random scenarios of section 5.8 is also chosen randomly. In the scenarios of section 5.8, there shall always be a predefined number of aggressive and defensive drivers. Additional information is given in section 5.8.

Start configuration

The start lanes of the other vehicles are chosen the same way as their desired lanes. The start velocities of the other vehicles are chosen to be the same as their desired velocities. The start positions are selected with the goal to evenly distribute the different vehicles.

Random entries of new vehicles

New random vehicles can be created if the desired traffic density within the ego-world is not exceeded. The traffic density may increase or decrease over time. In general, it is not possible to precisely maintain the desired traffic density. In fact, some variation is wanted in the simulation.

On highways, new vehicles may randomly enter the route if there is an acceleration lane next to the outer lane. Furthermore, the simulation does not simulate the movement of other vehicles in the acceleration lane, or the interaction between vehicles in the outer lane and the acceleration lane. Instead, a new vehicle is simply created in the outer lane if there is an opportunity.
Whenever a new acceleration lane enters the ego-world, the simulation decides how many vehicles should enter the route. The assumption is that the traffic density of both the route and the acceleration lane is the same. This leads to the number of vehicles that wish to enter the route depending on the length of the acceleration lane. The simulation identifies the gaps in the outer lane. The vehicles that should enter the route from the acceleration lane are randomly assigned to the gaps. In the ideal case, the simulation is able to insert all vehicles. Naturally, sufficient space in the outer lane is a requirement. As previously discussed, the gap between a newly created vehicle and an existing vehicle depends on the driver type. If it is not possible, the attempt is repeated during the next simulation update until the acceleration lane leaves the ego-world.

Additional vehicles are inserted on the front and rear edges of the ego-world if the desired traffic density is too low (e.g., 15 % lower than desired). Normal and defensive vehicles appear at the front. Normal and aggressive vehicles appear at the rear. The procedure continues until the desired traffic density is reached. This can happen at the same time as new vehicles enter the route from acceleration lanes.

On urban roads, the procedure is similar to highways. But, additionally, intersections can appear. New vehicles can enter the route at intersections during the appropriate traffic light phase. New vehicles are not created if there is not sufficient space on the road. The movement of the vehicles that enter the route through intersections is not simulated.

Random exits of existing vehicles

Existing vehicles randomly decide if they want to leave the route at the next possible exit with a certain amount of probability. The choice is only made once for each new exit opportunity. Once the decision is made, the desired lane may change and certain lanes may have to be avoided depending on the decision and the lane configuration. If a vehicle does not want to leave the route but gets stuck in an exit lane, it will leave the route when the exit lane ends. Vehicles that reach the end of the route always disappear.

A.4 Parameters and discretization

This section presents the default parameters that are often used in this thesis.

Tables A.2, A.3, and A.4 show the parameters of the vehicle model as presented in section 3.1.

Table A.2: Default REM-2030 vehicle parameters

Parameter	Symbol	Value	Unit
Effective cross sectional area	A_{eff}	2.04	m^2
Air drag coefficient	c_{w}	0.33	1
Inertia of all wheels	J_{w}	5.7	kgm^2
Vehicle mass	m	1738	kg
Dynamic wheel radius	r_{w}	0.3	m
Vehicle length	Δl_{ego}	5	m
Linear ground adhesion coefficient	$\mu_{\text{b,lin}}$	2.36	1
Maximum ground adhesion coefficient	$\mu_{\text{b,max}}$	1.18	1
Air density	ρ_{air}	1.205	$\frac{\text{kg}}{\text{m}^3}$
Maximum acceptable tire slip	$\sigma_{\text{b,max}}$	15	%

Tables A.5 and A.6 show the default parameters of the driver model as presented in section 3.4.2 and section A.1. In the case of randomly created vehicles, the default parameters serve as a reference. The randomization parameters are given in Tables A.7 to A.10.

Table A.11 shows the default optimization parameters as presented in chapter 4. The longitudinal position discretization uses a transition duration of one second as a reference, given a certain speed limit. This means that the distance between two decision stages should lead to a travel duration of approximately one second when traveling at the current speed limit. The motivation is derived from gear shifts. As discussed in section 3.1.1, a gear shift is assumed to be finished after one second. Therefore, if a discrete state transition requires approximately one second or longer, it will be possible to change the gear level at every decision stage.

Table A.3: Default REM-2030 powertrain parameters

Parameter	Symbol	Value	Unit
Final drive ratio	i_{f}	4.33	1
Transmission ratios of gears	i_{t}	4, 1	1
Maximum battery cell discharge current	$I_{\mathrm{c,max}}$	20	A
Maximum battery cell charge current	$I_{\mathrm{c,min}}$	-20	A
Engine inertia	J_{e}	0.003	kgm^2
Number of serial battery cells	$n_{\mathrm{bat,s}}$	84	1
Number of parallel battery cells	$n_{\mathrm{bat,p}}$	12	1
Number of gear levels	n_{G}	2	1
Maximum engine power	$P_{\mathrm{e,max}}$	80	kW
Maximum generator power	$P_{\mathrm{e,min}}$	-80	kW
Battery cell capacity	$Q_{\mathrm{c,max}}$	20	Ah
Battery cell internal resistance	$R_{\mathrm{i,c}}$	5	mΩ
Maximum engine torque	$T_{\mathrm{e,max}}$	103	Nm
Maximum generator torque	$T_{\mathrm{e,min}}$	-103	Nm
Maximum battery cell voltage	$V_{\mathrm{c,max}}$	4.2	V
Feasible battery SOC range	-	20-95	%
DC/AC efficiency	η_{DCAC}	98	%
DC/DC efficiency	η_{DCDC}	98	%
Transmission efficiency of gears	η_{t}	95.8, 97	%
Maximum engine rotation speed	$\omega_{\mathrm{e,max}}$	15,000	$\frac{1}{\mathrm{min}}$

Table A.4: Default REM-2030 lateral vehicle dynamics parameters

Parameter	Symbol	Value	Unit
Front cornering stiffness	c_{f}	88,000	$\frac{\mathrm{N}}{\mathrm{rad}}$
Rear cornering stiffness	c_{r}	146,000	$\frac{\mathrm{N}}{\mathrm{rad}}$
Steering ratio	i_{s}	15.9	1
Wheelbase	l	2.69	m
Front wheelbase	l_{f}	1.21	m
Rear wheelbase	l_{r}	1.48	m

Table A.5: Default simplified driver model parameters. There is no default choice for $v_{\mathrm{d,goal}}$.

Parameter	Symbol	Value	Unit
Preferred acceleration	a_{d}	1	$\frac{\mathrm{m}}{\mathrm{s}^2}$
Comfortable deceleration	b_{d}	1.5	$\frac{\mathrm{m}}{\mathrm{s}^2}$
Acceleration exponent	δ_{d}	4	1
Minimal distance	$\Delta s_{\mathrm{d,min}}$	2	m
Desired time gap	Δt_{d}	1	s
Coolness factor	$\lambda_{\mathrm{d,c}}$	0.99	1

Table A.6: Default extended driver model parameters. There is no default choice for $l_{\mathrm{d,goal}}$.

Parameter	Symbol	Value	Unit
Lane bias	$a_{\mathrm{d,bias}}$	0.3	$\frac{\mathrm{m}}{\mathrm{s}^2}$
Safe deceleration	$b_{\mathrm{d,safe}}$	2	$\frac{\mathrm{m}}{\mathrm{s}^2}$
Lane change incentive	$\Delta a_{\mathrm{d,min}}$	0.1	$\frac{\mathrm{m}}{\mathrm{s}^2}$
Evasion activation time gap	$\Delta t_{\mathrm{d,evasion}}$	3	s
Politeness factor	$\lambda_{\mathrm{d,p}}$	0.2	1

Table A.7: Randomization parameter choice for normal driver type. "STD lower" refers to the standard deviation for numbers smaller than the mean. "STD higher" refers to the standard deviation for numbers larger than the mean.

Symbol	Mean	STD lower	STD higher	Unit
a_{d}	1	0.1	0.25	$\frac{\mathrm{m}}{\mathrm{s}^2}$
$a_{\mathrm{d,bias}}$	0.3	0.1	0.1	$\frac{\mathrm{m}}{\mathrm{s}^2}$
b_{d}	1.5	0.25	0.25	$\frac{\mathrm{m}}{\mathrm{s}^2}$
$b_{\mathrm{d,safe}}$	2	0.15	0.25	$\frac{\mathrm{m}}{\mathrm{s}^2}$
$l_{\mathrm{d,goal}}$	0	-	0.5	1
$v_{\mathrm{d,goal}}$	v_{max}	2.5	2.5	$\frac{\mathrm{km}}{\mathrm{h}}$
δ_{d}	4	1	2	1
$\Delta a_{\mathrm{d,min}}$	0.1	0.05	0.1	$\frac{\mathrm{m}}{\mathrm{s}^2}$
$\Delta s_{\mathrm{d,min}}$	2	0.1	1	m
Δt_{d}	1	0.1	1	s
$\Delta t_{\mathrm{d,evasion}}$	2	-	1	s
$\lambda_{\mathrm{d,c}}$	0.99	0.1	0.001	1
$\lambda_{\mathrm{d,p}}$	0.2	0.1	0.1	1

Table A.8: Randomization parameter choice for aggressive driver type. "STD lower" refers to the standard deviation for numbers smaller than the mean. "STD higher" refers to the standard deviation for numbers larger than the mean.

Symbol	Mean	STD lower	STD higher	Unit
a_{d}	1.5	0.25	0.5	$\frac{\mathrm{m}}{\mathrm{s}^2}$
$a_{\mathrm{d,bias}}$	0.5	0.1	0.1	$\frac{\mathrm{m}}{\mathrm{s}^2}$
b_{d}	2	0.15	0.5	$\frac{\mathrm{m}}{\mathrm{s}^2}$
$b_{\mathrm{d,safe}}$	2	0.5	0.5	$\frac{\mathrm{m}}{\mathrm{s}^2}$
$l_{\mathrm{d,goal}}$	0	-	1	1
$v_{\mathrm{d,goal}}$	v_{max}	-	5	$\frac{\mathrm{km}}{\mathrm{h}}$
δ_{d}	4	1	4	1
$\Delta a_{\mathrm{d,min}}$	0.075	0.05	0.1	$\frac{\mathrm{m}}{\mathrm{s}^2}$
$\Delta s_{\mathrm{d,min}}$	2	0.5	1	m
Δt_{d}	1	0.25	0.5	s
$\Delta t_{\mathrm{d,evasion}}$	2	-	1	s
$\lambda_{\mathrm{d,c}}$	0.995	0.001	0.001	1
$\lambda_{\mathrm{d,p}}$	0	-	-	1

Table A.9: Randomization parameter choice for defensive driver type. "STD lower" refers to the standard deviation for numbers smaller than the mean. "STD higher" refers to the standard deviation for numbers larger than the mean.

Symbol	Mean	STD lower	STD higher	Unit
a_{d}	1	0.25	0.1	$\frac{\mathrm{m}}{\mathrm{s}^2}$
$a_{\mathrm{d,bias}}$	0.3	0.1	0.1	$\frac{\mathrm{m}}{\mathrm{s}^2}$
b_{d}	1.25	0.25	0.25	$\frac{\mathrm{m}}{\mathrm{s}^2}$
$b_{\mathrm{d,safe}}$	2.25	0.15	0.5	$\frac{\mathrm{m}}{\mathrm{s}^2}$
$l_{\mathrm{d,goal}}$	0	-	-	1
$v_{\mathrm{d,goal}}$	v_{max}	5	-	$\frac{\mathrm{km}}{\mathrm{h}}$
δ_{d}	4	1	1	1
$\Delta a_{\mathrm{d,min}}$	0.2	0.05	0.15	$\frac{\mathrm{m}}{\mathrm{s}^2}$
$\Delta s_{\mathrm{d,min}}$	2.5	0.25	1	m
Δt_{d}	1.5	0.25	1	s
$\Delta t_{\mathrm{d,evasion}}$	2	-	1	s
$\lambda_{\mathrm{d,c}}$	0.9	0.1	0.001	1
$\lambda_{\mathrm{d,p}}$	0.5	0.1	0.1	1

Table A.10: Driver parameter constraints. If a random number is chosen that is smaller or larger than the constraints, it is redefined as the corresponding minimum or maximum respectively.

Symbol	Minimum	Maximum	Unit
a_{d}	0	4	$\frac{\mathrm{m}}{\mathrm{s}^2}$
$a_{\mathrm{d,bias}}$	0	1	$\frac{\mathrm{m}}{\mathrm{s}^2}$
b_{d}	0.5	4	$\frac{\mathrm{m}}{\mathrm{s}^2}$
$b_{\mathrm{d,safe}}$	0.5	4	$\frac{\mathrm{m}}{\mathrm{s}^2}$
$l_{\mathrm{d,goal}}$	0	l_{max}	1
$v_{\mathrm{d,goal}}$	v_{max}-10	-	$\frac{\mathrm{km}}{\mathrm{h}}$
δ_{d}	1	-	1
$\Delta a_{\mathrm{d,min}}$	0.01	1	$\frac{\mathrm{m}}{\mathrm{s}^2}$
$\Delta s_{\mathrm{d,min}}$	0.5	10	m
Δt_{d}	0.5	3	s
$\Delta t_{\mathrm{d,evasion}}$	2	5	s
$\lambda_{\mathrm{d,c}}$	0	1	1
$\lambda_{\mathrm{d,p}}$	0	1	1

Table A.11: Default optimization parameters and discretization

Parameter	Value	Unit
Start length of auxiliary horizon	1000	m
Length of regular horizon	250	m
Electricity cost	0.2953	$\frac{€}{kWh}$
Minimum gross labor cost	8.5	$\frac{€}{h}$
Gear shift attrition cost	0.035	€
Brake pad attrition cost	0.017	€
Velocity discretization	1	$\frac{km}{h}$
Gear level discretization	1	1
Position discretization for $v_{max} \leq 10\,\frac{km}{h}$	1	m
Position discretization for $10\,\frac{km}{h} < v_{max} < 50\,\frac{km}{h}$	5	m
Position discretization for $50\,\frac{km}{h} \leq v_{max} \leq 70\,\frac{km}{h}$	10	m
Position discretization for $70\,\frac{km}{h} < v_{max} \leq 100\,\frac{km}{h}$	25	m
Position discretization for $v_{max} > 100\,\frac{km}{h}$	50	m
Lateral position discretization, lane width	3	m
Slope discretization	1	$^\circ$
Curve radius discretization	100	m

Glossary

Backtracing

Backtracing is another expression for the backward evaluation process in FBDP, which constructs the optimal path. Backtracing can be done swiftly in FBDP because the vast computational complexity is concentrated in the forward evaluation process.

Ego-vehicle

The ego-vehicle is the vehicle that is guided or controlled by PEEMTO, PEEO, or the ego-vehicle driver.

Ego-vehicle driver

The ego-vehicle driver is a reference system used to compare to PEEMTO. The purpose is to simulate the behavior of a real driver. The ego-vehicle driver controls the ego-vehicle and uses the EDM. It uses a simplified automated transmission. It is able to compute the resulting costs of its actions using the vehicle model but does not perform any energy efficiency optimization.

Ego-world

The ego-world is a limited section of the route that currently surrounds the ego-vehicle. The simulation only simulates other vehicles within this area.

Extended driver model (EDM)

The extended driver model contains all functionalities of the SDM and several additional model extensions, including lane changes. It is used by the ego-vehicle driver and the simulation environment.

Forward evaluation

The FBDP algorithm starts with the construction of the state graph before starting the forward evaluation process. During the process, the costs of state transitions between succeeding decision stages are identified and compared to each other. This evaluation is done for all state transitions over all decision stages. The forward evaluation is followed by backtracing.

Fully evaluated decision stage

A fully evaluated decision stage is a decision stage, whose states already know their optimal predecessor states at the previous decision stage.

Journey

A journey describes the entire track the ego-vehicle has to travel, from the very beginning to the final destination.

Implicit discretization

In order to decrease the search space dimension, certain state dimensions are not explicitly included. Instead, certain state components are computed along different search paths based on the progression of other state components.

Front and rear vehicle

For explanation purposes, let there be two vehicles A and B. If vehicle A is ahead of vehicle B, then vehicle A is a front vehicle from the perspective of vehicle B, and vehicle B is a rear vehicle from the perspective of vehicle A.

Long-range auxiliary horizon extension (LRAHE)

An auxiliary state graph is constructed that grows during the journey until the end of the route. The auxiliary state graph helps the optimization to find the optimal end state at the end of the regular state graph. The auxiliary state graph itself uses the SHE at its end if it has not yet reached the end of the route.

Predictive energy-efficient motion trajectory optimization (PEEMTO)

PEEMTO is the model predictive trajectory optimization developed in this thesis. It computes the optimal state trajectory regarding energy-efficient driving. It does not compute the control trajectory. It considers lane changes and uses the LRAHE.

Predictive energy efficiency optimization without lane changes (PEEO)

PEEO is a reference system used to compare to PEEMTO. It represents existing model predictive optimization strategies used for energy-efficient driving. PEEO is very similar to PEEMTO. But it does not consider lane changes and only uses the SHE.

Principle of optimality (PO)

"An optimal policy has the property that whatever the initial state and initial decision are, the remaining decisions must constitute an optimal policy with regard to the state resulting from the first decision." [Bel54]

Road

A road refers to the entire physical road with a single road name and includes opposite lanes, acceleration lanes, exit lanes, etc. The route is sometimes only a part of the road and may sometimes consist of several different roads. The lanes of the road that divert the ego-vehicle from the route are not part of the route.

Route

A route can incorporate the entire journey or only a part of it. The optimization only considers the route. If the route is only a part of the journey, a human driver has to take over control at the end of the route.

Simplified driver model (SDM)

The simplified driver model is based on the established IDM driver model from transportation engineering and several of its extensions. It is used by PEEMTO and PEEO during the forward evaluation.

Stationary horizon extension (SHE)

The stationary horizon extension is used to estimate the optimal behavior at the end of the optimization horizon. It is based on existing approaches.

Bibliography

[ACK12] M. Ardelt, C. Coester, and N. Kaempchen. "Highly Automated Driving on Freeways in Real Traffic Using a Probabilistic Framework". In: *IEEE Transactions on Intelligent Transportation Systems* 13.4 (Dec. 2012), pp. 1576–1585. ISSN: 1524-9050. DOI: 10.1109/TITS.2012.2196273.

[Als+12] M. Alsabaan et al. "Optimization of fuel cost and emissions with vehicular networks at traffic intersections". In: *2012 15th International IEEE Conference on Intelligent Transportation Systems*. Sept. 2012, pp. 613–619. DOI: 10.1109/ITSC.2012.6338697.

[Ame01] American Association of State Highway and Transportation Officials. *A Policy on Geometric Design of Highways and Streets*. 2001. ISBN: 1-56051-156-7.

[Ask+17] A. Askari et al. "Effect of adaptive and cooperative adaptive cruise control on throughput of signalized arterials". In: *2017 IEEE Intelligent Vehicles Symposium (IV)*. June 2017, pp. 1287–1292. DOI: 10.1109/IVS.2017.7995889.

[AW11] M. Ardelt and P. Waldmann. "Hybrides Steuerungs- und Regelungskonzept für das hochautomatisiertes Fahren auf Autobahnen". In: *Automatisierungstechnik* 59.12 (2011).

[Bah+14] M. Bahram et al. "A prediction-based reactive driving strategy for highly automated driving function on freeways". In: *2014 IEEE Intelligent Vehicles Symposium Proceedings*. June 2014, pp. 400–406. DOI: 10.1109/IVS.2014.6856503.

[Bai+15a] M. M. Baier et al. *Handbuch für die Bemessung von Straßenverkehrsanlagen HBS Teil A Autobahnen.* Forschungsgesellschaft für Straßen- und Verkehrswesen. 2015.

[Bai+15b] M. M. Baier et al. *Handbuch für die Bemessung von Straßenverkehrsanlagen HBS Teil L Landstraßen.* Forschungsgesellschaft für Straßen- und Verkehrswesen. 2015.

[Bai+15c] M. M. Baier et al. *Handbuch für die Bemessung von Straßenverkehrsanlagen HBS Teil S Stadtstraßen.* Forschungsgesellschaft für Straßen- und Verkehrswesen. 2015.

[Bär+11] T. Bär et al. "Probabilistic driving style determination by means of a situation based analysis of the vehicle data". In: *2011 14th International IEEE Conference on Intelligent Transportation Systems (ITSC).* Oct. 2011, pp. 1698–1703. DOI: `10.1109/ITSC.2011.6082924`.

[BB12] B. Breuer and K. H. Bill. *Bremsenhandbuch.* 4th ed. Springer Vieweg, 2012. ISBN: 978-3-8348-1796-9. DOI: `10.1007/978-3-8348-2225-3`.

[Bel54] R. Bellman. "The theory of dynamic programming". In: *Bulletin of the American Mathematical Society* (1954). DOI: `10.1090/S0002-9904-1954-09848-8`.

[Ben+15] P. Bender et al. "The combinatorial aspect of motion planning: Maneuver variants in structured environments". In: *2015 IEEE Intelligent Vehicles Symposium (IV).* June 2015, pp. 1386–1392. DOI: `10.1109/IVS.2015.7225909`.

[Ber05] Dimitri P. Bertsekas. *Dynamic Programming and Optimal Control.* 3rd ed. Vol. 1. Athena Scientific, 2005.

[Ber07] Dimitri P. Bertsekas. *Dynamic Programming and Optimal Control.* 3rd ed. Vol. 2. 2007.

[Bos16] Bosch GmbH. *The Bosch active gas pedal: gentle vibration can lighten pressure on the gas pedal and warn of wrong-way drivers*. 2016. URL: https://ua.bosch-automotive.com/en/news_and_extras/newsroom/the_bosch_active_gas_pedal_1/standard_page_1__with_marginal_column_6 (visited on 10/16/2017).

[Bun18] Bundesnetzagentur. *Informationen zum Haushaltskundenpreis für Strom und Gas*. 2018. URL: https://www.bundesnetzagentur.de/DE/Sachgebiete/ElektrizitaetundGas/Verbraucher/PreiseRechnTarife/preiseundRechnungen-node.html (visited on 05/23/2018).

[BZK05] B. Bakker, Z. Zivkovic, and B. Krose. "Hierarchical dynamic programming for robot path planning". In: *2005 IEEE/RSJ International Conference on Intelligent Robots and Systems*. Aug. 2005, pp. 2756–2761. DOI: 10.1109/IROS.2005.1545548.

[Con15] Continental AG. *Predictive Assistance: Continental Presents Adaptive Cruise Control with eHorizon*. 2015. URL: https://www.continental-corporation.com/en/press/press-releases/predictive-assistance--continental-presents-adaptive-cruise-control-with-ehorizon-14712 (visited on 08/09/2018).

[CPR10] A. Casavola, G. Prodi, and G. Rocca. "Efficient gear shifting strategies for green driving policies". In: *Proceedings of the 2010 American Control Conference*. June 2010, pp. 4331–4336. DOI: 10.1109/ACC.2010.5530832.

[DDK00] I. De Vlieger, D. De Keukeleere, and J. G. Kretzschmar. "Environmental effects of driving behaviour and congestion related to passenger cars". In: *Atmospheric Environment* 34 (2000), pp. 4649–4655. DOI: 10.1016/S1352-2310(00)00217-X.

[Def04] Defense Advanced Research Projects Agency. *DARPA Grand Challenge 2004*. 2004. URL: http://archive.darpa.mil/grandchallenge04/index.htm (visited on 10/16/2017).

[Def05] Defense Advanced Research Projects Agency. *DARPA Grand Challenge 2005*. 2005. URL: http://archive.darpa.mil/grandchallenge05/gcorg/index.html (visited on 10/16/2017).

[Def07] Defense Advanced Research Projects Agency. *DARPA Grand Challenge 2007*. 2007. URL: http://archive.darpa.mil/grandchallenge/ (visited on 10/16/2017).

[Dij59] E. Dijkstra. "A note on two problems in connexion with graphs". In: *Numerische Mathematik* 1 (1959). DOI: 10.1007/BF01386390.

[Eas17] East Software Coders. *ECO-Driving Speedometer*. 2017. URL: https://play.google.com/store/apps/details?id=com.eastcoders.speedometer (visited on 10/16/2017).

[Eff16] Efficient Drivers. *Fuel Economy for Torque Pro*. 2016. URL: https://play.google.com/store/apps/details?id=org.prowl.fuelEconomy&hl=de (visited on 10/16/2017).

[Ene17] Energy Saving Trust. *Advising fuel efficient driving techniques for your fleet*. 2017. URL: http://www.energysavingtrust.org.uk/business/transport/subsidised-ecodriving-training (visited on 10/16/2017).

[EU12] T. Emter and T. Ulrich. "Fusion of geometrical and visual information for localization and mapping in outdoor environments". In: *2012 Ubiquitous Positioning, Indoor Navigation, and Location Based Service (UPINLBS)*. Oct. 2012, pp. 1–5. DOI: 10.1109/UPINLBS.2012.6409748.

[FCA17] FCA Italy S.p.A. *eco:Drive*. 2017. URL: `https://play.google.com/store/apps/details?id=com.fiat.ecodrive` (visited on 10/16/2017).

[Fre11] C. Frese. "Planung kooperativer Fahrmanöver". ISBN 978-3-86644-798-1, ISSN 1863-6489. PhD thesis. Karlsruher Schriften zur Anthropomatik, Band 10, KIT Scientific Publishing, Karlsruhe Institute of Technology, 2011.

[Fun+12] J. Funke et al. "Up to the limits: Autonomous Audi TTS". In: *2012 IEEE Intelligent Vehicles Symposium*. June 2012, pp. 541–547. DOI: `10.1109/IVS.2012.6232212`.

[Gar10] Garmin Ltd. *Garmin Eco Route*. 2010. URL: `https://www.garmin.com/de/ecoroutehd/` (visited on 10/16/2017).

[Ger10] German Aerospace Center. *TanDEM-X*. 2010. URL: `https://www.dlr.de/dlr/en/desktopdefault.aspx/tabid-10378/566_read-426/#/gallery/345` (visited on 05/28/2018).

[Goo17] Google Inc. *Google Elevation API*. 2017. URL: `https://developers.google.com/maps/documentation/elevation/intro` (visited on 10/16/2017).

[GS05] L. Guzzella and A. Sciarretta. *Vehicle Propulsion Systems*. 2nd. Springer, 2005.

[Hak14] K. L. Haken. *Grundlagen der Kraftfahrzeugtechnik*. Hanser Verlag, 2014.

[HB11] A. A. H. Hussein and I. Batarseh. "An overview of generic battery models". In: *2011 IEEE Power and Energy Society General Meeting*. July 2011, pp. 1–6. DOI: `10.1109/PES.2011.6039674`.

[Hel10] E. Hellström. "Look-ahead Control of Heavy Vehicles". PhD thesis. Linköping University, 2010.

[Her17] Here Technologies. *Unlocking the power of location intelligence.* 2017. URL: `https://www.here.com/products/mapping/map-data` (visited on 10/16/2017).

[Hoo88] J. Hooker. "Optimal driving for single vehicle fuel economy". In: *Transportation Research* 22A (1988), pp. 183–201.

[HRR83] J. Hooker, A. Rose, and G. Roberts. "Optimal control of automobiles for fuel economy". In: *Transportation Research* 17 (1983), pp. 146–167.

[HRR85] J. Hooker, A. Rose, and G. Roberts. *Fuel efficient driving strategies*. Tech. rep. Carnegie-Mellon University, 1985.

[HT08] C. Hong and A. H. Tewfik. "Efficient Updating of Biological Sequence Analysis". In: *IEEE Journal of Selected Topics in Signal Processing* 2.3 (June 2008), pp. 365–377. ISSN: 1932-4553. DOI: `10.1109/JSTSP.2008.924382`.

[HT09] C. Hong and A. H. Tewfik. "Heuristic Reusable Dynamic Programming: Efficient Updates of Local Sequence Alignment". In: *IEEE/ACM Transactions on Computational Biology and Bioinformatics* 6.4 (Oct. 2009), pp. 570–582. ISSN: 1545-5963. DOI: `10.1109/TCBB.2009.30`.

[Hua+08] W. Huang et al. "Using 3D road geometry to optimize heavy truck fuel efficiency". In: *2008 11th International IEEE Conference on Intelligent Transportation Systems*. Oct. 2008, pp. 334–339. DOI: `10.1109/ITSC.2008.4732656`.

[Int17] Intermap Technologies. *Intermap Next Map Powerful Elevation Data*. 2017. URL: `http://www.intermap.com/data/nextmap` (visited on 10/16/2017).

[Jan18] H. Janker. *Straßenverkehrsrecht*. Vol. 56. dtv Verlagsgesellschaft, June 22, 2018. ISBN: 978-3406580390.

[Jin+16] Q. Jin et al. "Power-Based Optimal Longitudinal Control for a Connected Eco-Driving System". In: *IEEE Transactions on Intelligent Transportation Systems* 17.10 (Oct. 2016), pp. 2900–2910. ISSN: 1524-9050. DOI: 10.1109/TITS.2016.2535439.

[Joy16] JoyNow! *EcoDrive Free Speedometer*. 2016. URL: https://play.google.com/store/apps/details?id=com.joynow.ecodrivefree (visited on 10/16/2017).

[JSV08] J. Jaffar, A. E. Santosa, and R. Voicu. "Efficient Memoization for Dynamic Programming with Ad-Hoc Constraints". In: *Association for the Advancement of Artificial Intelligence* (2008).

[Keu+09] T. Keulen et al. "Predictive Cruise Control in Hybrid Electric Vehicles". In: *World Electric Vehicle Journal* 3 (2009), pp. 1–11.

[Keu+10] T. van Keulen et al. "Velocity trajectory optimization in Hybrid Electric trucks". In: *Proceedings of the 2010 American Control Conference*. June 2010, pp. 5074–5079. DOI: 10.1109/ACC.2010.5530695.

[Kle11] W. Klement. *Fahrzeuggetriebe*. Hanser, 2011.

[KN10] U. Kiencke and L. Nielsen. *Automotive Control Systems*. Springer, 2010.

[Koh+11] R. Kohlhaas et al. "Anticipatory energy saving assistant for approaching slower vehicles". In: *2011 14th International IEEE Conference on Intelligent Transportation Systems (ITSC)*. Oct. 2011, pp. 1966–1971. DOI: 10.1109/ITSC.2011.6083148.

[Koh+13] R. Kohlhaas et al. "Towards driving autonomously: Autonomous cruise control in urban environments". In: *2013 IEEE Intelligent Vehicles Symposium (IV)*. June 2013, pp. 116–121. DOI: 10.1109/IVS.2013.6629457.

[Koh+14] R. Kohlhaas et al. “Semantic state space for high-level maneuver planning in structured traffic scenes”. In: *17th International IEEE Conference on Intelligent Transportation Systems (ITSC)*. Oct. 2014, pp. 1060–1065. DOI: 10.1109/ITSC.2014.6957828.

[KR13] R. K. Kamalanathsharma and H. A. Rakha. “Multi-stage dynamic programming algorithm for eco-speed control at traffic signalized intersections”. In: *16th International IEEE Conference on Intelligent Transportation Systems (ITSC 2013)*. Oct. 2013, pp. 2094–2099. DOI: 10.1109/ITSC.2013.6728538.

[Kuh+16] F. Kuhnt et al. “Robust environment perception for the Audi Autonomous Driving Cup”. In: *2016 IEEE 19th International Conference on Intelligent Transportation Systems (ITSC)*. Nov. 2016, pp. 1424–1431. DOI: 10.1109/ITSC.2016.7795744.

[Kun+12] H. B. Kuntze et al. “SENEKA - sensor network with mobile robots for disaster management”. In: *2012 IEEE Conference on Technologies for Homeland Security (HST)*. Nov. 2012, pp. 406–410. DOI: 10.1109/THS.2012.6459883.

[KVD13] C. Klöffer, M. Veigel, and M. Doppelbauer. “Fahrzyklusbasierte Auslegung eines DC/DC-Wandlers zur wirkungsgradoptimalen Anpassung der Zwischenkreisspannung”. In: *Internationaler ETG-Kongress 2013*. VDE Verlag, 2013. ISBN: 978-3-8007-3550-1.

[Lav+07] R. Laver et al. *Useful Life of Transit Buses and Vans*. FTA VA-26-7229-07.1. U.S. Department of Transportation Federal Transit Administration, 2007.

[LaV06] S. M. LaValle. *Planning Algorithms*. Cambridge University Press, 2006.

[Liu15] J. Liu. "Driving Volatility in Instantaneous Driving Behaviors: Studies Using Large-Scale Trajectory Data". PhD thesis. University of Tennessee, 2015.

[Lun10a] J. Lunze. *Regelungstechnik 1*. 8th ed. Springer, 2010.

[Lun10b] J. Lunze. *Regelungstechnik 2*. 6th ed. Springer, 2010.

[MA12] A. A. Malikopoulos and J. P. Aguilar. "Optimization of driving styles for fuel economy improvement". In: *2012 15th International IEEE Conference on Intelligent Transportation Systems*. Sept. 2012, pp. 194–199. DOI: 10.1109/ITSC.2012.6338607.

[MG93] V. Monastyrsky and I. Golownykh. "Rapid computation of optimal control for vehicles". In: *Transportation Research* 27B.3 (1993), pp. 219–227.

[MN14] G. Mousavi and M. Nikdel. "Various battery models for various simulation studies and applications". In: *Renewable and Sustainable Energy Reviews* 32.C (2014), pp. 477–485. URL: http://EconPapers.repec.org/RePEc:eee:rensus:v:32:y:2014:i:c:p:477-485.

[Mok+16] Z. Mokrani et al. "Energy management of battery-PEM Fuel cells Hybrid energy storage system for electric vehicle". In: *2016 International Renewable and Sustainable Energy Conference (IRSEC)*. Nov. 2016, pp. 985–990. DOI: 10.1109/IRSEC.2016.7984073.

[MW15] M. Mitschke and H. Wallentowitz. *Dynamik der Kraftfahrzeuge*. Springer Vieweg, 2015.

[Nat00] National Aeronautics and Space Administration. *NASA SRTM*. 2000. URL: http://www2.jpl.nasa.gov/srtm/ (visited on 10/16/2017).

[Nat17] Natural Resources Canada. *Fuel-efficient Driving Techniques*. 2017. URL: http://www.nrcan.gc.ca/energy/efficiency/transportation/cars-light-trucks/fuel-efficient-driving-techniques/7507 (visited on 10/16/2017).

[NBL07] H. Naunheimer, B. Bertsche, and G. Lechner. *Fahrzeuggetriebe*. Springer, 2007.

[NGZ11] D. Nienhüser, T. Gumpp, and J. M. Zöllner. "Relevance estimation of traffic elements using Markov logic networks". In: *2011 14th International IEEE Conference on Intelligent Transportation Systems (ITSC)*. Oct. 2011, pp. 1659–1664. DOI: 10.1109/ITSC.2011.6082903.

[Nie+12] D. Nienhüser et al. "Energy Efficient Driving and Operation Strategies Based on Situation Awareness and Reasoning". In: *it Information Technology* (2012).

[Nie14] D. Nienhüser. "Kontextsensitive Erkennung und Interpretation fahrrelevanter statischer Verkehrselemente". PhD thesis. Karlsruhe Institut für Technologie, 2014.

[NW06] J. Nocedal and S. Wright. *Numerical Optimization*. Springer, 2006.

[PB17] A. Petrowski and S. Ben-Hamida. *Evolutionary Algorithms*. John Wiley and Sons, 2017.

[PEF13a] J. Petereit, T. Emter, and C. Frey. "Combined Trajectory Generation and Path Planning for Mobile Robots Using Lattices with Hybrid Dimensionality". In: *International Conference on Robot Intelligence Technology and Applications 2013*. 2013.

[PEF13b] J. Petereit, T. Emter, and C. Frey. "Mobile Robot Motion Planning in Multi-Resolution Lattices with Hybrid Dimensionality". In: *IFAC Symposium on Intelligent Autonomous Vehicles 2013*. 2013.

[PEF13c] J. Petereit, T. Emter, and C. W. Frey. "Safe mobile robot motion planning for waypoint sequences in a dynamic environment". In: *2013 IEEE International Conference on Industrial Technology (ICIT)*. Feb. 2013, pp. 181–186. DOI: 10.1109/ICIT.2013.6505669.

[Pér+10] J. Pérez et al. "Design and implementation of a neuro-fuzzy system for longitudinal control of autonomous vehicles". In: *International Conference on Fuzzy Systems*. July 2010, pp. 1–6. DOI: 10.1109/FUZZY.2010.5584208.

[Pet16] J. Petereit. "Adaptive State X Time Lattices: A Contribution to Mobile Robot Motion Planning in Unstructured Dynamic Environments". PhD thesis. Karlsruher Schriften zur Anthropomatik, Band 27, KIT Scientific Publishing, Karlsruhe Institute of Technology, 2016.

[PKS09] B. Passenber, P. Kock, and O. Stursberg. "Combined Time and Fuel Optimal Driving of Trucks based on a Hybrid Model". In: *European Control Conference 2009*. 2009, pp. 4955–4960.

[Plo+12] J. Ploeg et al. "Introduction to the Special Issue on the 2011 Grand Cooperative Driving Challenge". In: *IEEE Transactions on Intelligent Transportation Systems* 13.3 (Sept. 2012), pp. 989–993. ISSN: 1524-9050. DOI: 10.1109/TITS.2012.2210636.

[Por+13] C. Porter et al. *Effects of Travel Reduction and Efficient Driving on Transportation: Energy Use and Greenhouse Gas Emissions*. Tech. rep. National Renewable Energy Laboratory (Golden, CO) and Cambridge Systematics for the U.S. Department of Energy, 2013.

[Qi+17] X. Qi et al. "Deep reinforcement learning-based vehicle energy efficiency autonomous learning system". In: *2017 IEEE Intelli-*

gent Vehicles Symposium (IV). June 2017, pp. 1228–1233. DOI: 10.1109/IVS.2017.7995880.

[REM15] REM 2030. *regional eco mobility 2030*. 2015. URL: http://www.rem2030.de/ (visited on 10/16/2017).

[RK11] H. Rakha and R. K. Kamalanathsharma. “Eco-driving at signalized intersections using V2I communication”. In: *2011 14th International IEEE Conference on Intelligent Transportation Systems (ITSC)*. Oct. 2011, pp. 341–346. DOI: 10.1109/ITSC.2011.6083084.

[Ros10] T. Ross. *Fuzzy Logic*. John Wiley & Sons, 2010.

[Ruf+14a] M. Ruf et al. “A Continuous Approach to Autonomous Driving”. In: *Conference Vehicle and Infrastructure Safety Improvement in Adverse Conditions and Night Driving 2014*. 2014.

[Ruf+14b] M. Ruf et al. “Situation Prediction And Reaction Control (SPARC)”. In: *9. Workshop Fahrerassistenzsysteme*. 2014.

[Ruf+15a] M. Ruf et al. “Comparison of Local vs. Global Optimization for Trajectory Planning in Automated Driving”. In: *10. Workshop Fahrerassistenzsysteme*. 2015.

[Ruf+15b] M. Ruf et al. “Global Trajectory Optimization on Multilane Roads”. In: *2015 IEEE 18th International Conference on Intelligent Transportation Systems*. Sept. 2015, pp. 1908–1914. DOI: 10.1109/ITSC.2015.309.

[Rus+03] C. Rusu et al. “Classical geometrical approach to circle fitting review and new developments”. In: *Journal of Electronic Imaging* (2003), pp. 179–193.

[Sah+07] P. Sahlholm et al. “Automated speed selection for heavy duty vehicles”. In: *International Association of Vehicle System Dynamics Symposium*. 2007.

[SC86a] R. Smith and P. Cheeseman. "On the Representation and Estimation of Spatial Uncertainty". In: *International Journal of Robotics Research* (1986).

[SC86b] R. Smith and P. Cheeseman. "On the Representation and Estimation of Spatial Uncertainty". In: *Conference on Uncertainty in Arificial Intelligence 1986*. 1986.

[Sch12] T. Schamm. *Schlussbericht zum BMBF-Verbundprojekt Energieeffizientes Fahren 2014 (EFA2014) Phase 1 Teilvorhaben: Erkennung, Modellierung und Interpretation semistatischer und dynamischer Objekte*. Tech. rep. Forschungszentrum für Informatik Karlsruhe, 2012.

[Sch14] T. Schamm. "Modellbasierter Ansatz zur probabilistischen Interpretation von Fahrsituationen". PhD thesis. Karlsruhe Institut für Technologie, 2014.

[SFY07] F. Syed, D. Filev, and H. Ying. "Applied intelligent systems: blending fuzzy logic with conventional control". In: *Fuzzy Information Processing Society* (2007), pp. 395–414.

[SHB10] D. Schamm, M. Hiller, and R. Bardini. *Modellbildung und Simulation der Dynamik von Kraftfahrzeugen*. Springer Verlag, 2010.

[SL77] A. Schwarzkopf and R. Leipnic. "Control of highway vehicles for minimum fuel consumption over varying terrain". In: *Transportation Research* 11 (4 1977), pp. 279–286.

[Sma+14] N. Smajlovic et al. *EFA 2014 Energieeffizientes Fahren 2014 Phase 2 Teilvorhaben BMW*. Tech. rep. Bayrische Motoren Werke AG, 2014.

[SMB11] P. Schuricht, O. Michler, and B. Bäker. "Efficiency-increasing driver assistance at signalized intersections using predictive traffic state estimation". In: *2011 14th International IEEE Conference on Intelligent Transportation Systems (ITSC)*. Oct. 2011, pp. 347–352. DOI: 10.1109/ITSC.2011.6083111.

[Sni06] M. Sniedovich. "Dijkstra's algorithm revisited: the dynamic programming connexion". In: *Control and Cybernetics 2006* 35.3 (2006).

[SR09] M. A. Symmons and G. Rose. "Ecodrive training delivers substantial fuel savings for heavy vehicle drivers". In: *PROCEEDINGS of the Fifth International Driving Symposium on Human Factors in Driver Assessment, Training and Vehicle Design*. 2009.

[SRD09] M. Symmons, G. Rose, and G. Van Doorn. *Ecodrive as a road safety tool for Australian conditions*. Australian Government Department of Infrastructure, Transport, Regional Development and Local Government, 2009.

[Sta17] Statistisches Bundesamt. *Verdienste auf einen Blick*. 2017. URL: https://www.destatis.de/DE/Publikationen/Thematisch/VerdiensteArbeitskosten/Arbeitnehmerverdienste/BroschuereVerdiensteBlick0160013179004.pdf (visited on 05/28/2018).

[Str06] Forschungsgesellschaft für Straßen- und Verkehrswesen. *Hinweise zur mikroskopischen Verkehrsflusssimulation Grundlagen und Anwendungen*. 2006.

[Sug15] M. Sugiyama. *Statistical Reinforcement Learning: Modern Machine Learning Approaches*. CRC Press Taylor & Francis Group, 2015.

[SZ12] C. Stiller and J. Ziegler. "3D perception and planning for self-driving and cooperative automobiles". In: *International Multi-Conference on Systems, Signals & Devices*. Mar. 2012, pp. 1–7. DOI: 10.1109/SSD.2012.6198130.

[Ter09] S. Terwen. "Vorausschauende Längsregelung schwerer Lastkraftwagen". PhD thesis. Schriften des Instituts für Regelungs- und Steuerungssysteme, Band 6, KIT Scientific Publishing, Karlsruhe Institute of Technology, 2009.

[Thr+06] S. Thrun et al. "Stanley: The Robot That Won the DARPA Grand Challenge: Research Articles". In: *J. Robot. Syst.* 23.9 (Sept. 2006), pp. 661–692. ISSN: 0741-2223. DOI: 10.1002/rob.v23:9. URL: http://dx.doi.org/10.1002/rob.v23:9.

[Tie+12] T. Tielert et al. "Can V2X communication help electric vehicles save energy?" In: *2012 12th International Conference on ITS Telecommunications*. Nov. 2012, pp. 232–237. DOI: 10.1109/ITST.2012.6425172.

[TK13] M. Treiber and A. Kesting. *Traffic Flow Dynamics*. Springer, 2013.

[Urm+07] C. Urmson et al. *Tartan Racing: A Multi-Modal Approach to the DARPA Urban Challenge*. Tech. rep. CMU-RI-TR-. Pittsburgh, PA: Carnegie Mellon University, Apr. 2007.

[US 17] U.S. Department of Energy. *Gas Mileage Tips*. 2017. URL: https://www.fueleconomy.gov/feg/drive.shtml (visited on 10/16/2017).

[VB16] R. S. Vadamalu and C. Beidl. "Online MPC based PHEV Energy Management using conic interior-point methods". In: *2016 IEEE Intelligent Vehicles Symposium (IV)*. June 2016, pp. 466–471. DOI: 10.1109/IVS.2016.7535427.

[Wah15] H. Wahl. "Optimale Regelung eines prädiktiven Energiemanagements von Hybridfahrzeugen". PhD thesis. Karlsruher Schriftenreihe Fahrzeugsystemtechnik, Band 43, KIT Scientific Publishing, Karlsruhe Institute of Technology, 2015.

[Wan+17] Y. Wang et al. "Google Earth elevation data extraction and accuracy assessment for transportation applications". In: *PLoS ONE* (Apr. 26, 2017).

[Wer+10] M. Werling et al. "Optimal trajectory generation for dynamic street scenarios in a Frenét Frame". In: *2010 IEEE International Conference on Robotics and Automation*. May 2010, pp. 987–993. DOI: 10.1109/ROBOT.2010.5509799.

[Wer+12] M. Werling et al. "Optimal trajectories for time-critical street scenarios using discretized terminal manifolds". In: *The International Journal of Robotics Research 2012* (2012).

[Wil12] A. Wilde. *EFA 2014 Energieeffizientes Fahren 2014 Phase 1 Teilvorhaben BMW*. Tech. rep. Bayrische Motoren Werke AG, 2012.

[Win+15] H. Winner et al. *Handbuch Fahrerassistenzsysteme: Grundlagen, Komponenten und Systeme für aktive Sicherheit und Komfort (ATZ/MTZ-Fachbuch)*. Springer Vieweg, 2015.

[Woo16] P. Woock. "Umgebungskartenschätzung aus Sidescan-Sonardaten für ein autonomes Unterwasserfahrzeug". ISBN 978-3-7315-0541-9, ISSN 1863-6489. PhD thesis. Karlsruher Schriften zur Anthropomatik, Band 26, KIT Scientific Publishing, Karlsruhe Institute of Technology, 2016. DOI: 10.5445/KSP/1000055793.

[Xia+12] H. Xia et al. "Field operational testing of ECO-approach technology at a fixed-time signalized intersection". In: *2012 15th International IEEE Conference on Intelligent Transportation*

Systems. Sept. 2012, pp. 188–193. DOI: 10.1109/ITSC.2012.6338888.

[ZF15] A. Zube and C. Frese. "Collision Avoidance for Human-Robot Interaction Distinguishing between Static and Dynamic Obstacles". In: *International Workshop on Human-Friendly Robotics 2015*. 2015.

[Zie+14a] J. Ziegler et al. "Trajectory planning for Bertha - A local, continuous method". In: *2014 IEEE Intelligent Vehicles Symposium Proceedings*. June 2014, pp. 450–457. DOI: 10.1109/IVS.2014.6856581.

[Zie+14b] J Ziegler et al. "Kartengestütztes automatisiertes Fahren auf der Bertha-Benz-Route von Mannheim nach Pforzheim". In: *9. Workshop Fahrerassistenzsysteme*. 2014.

[Zie+15] J. Ziehn et al. "Correspondence between variational methods and Hidden Markov Models". In: *2015 IEEE Intelligent Vehicles Symposium (IV)*. June 2015, pp. 380–385. DOI: 10.1109/IVS.2015.7225715.

[Zie+16] J. R. Ziehn et al. "A tractable interaction model for trajectory planning in automated driving". In: *2016 IEEE 19th International Conference on Intelligent Transportation Systems (ITSC)*. Nov. 2016, pp. 1410–1417. DOI: 10.1109/ITSC.2016.7795742.

[Zof+16] M. R. Zofka et al. "Simulation framework for the development of autonomous small scale vehicles". In: *2016 IEEE International Conference on Simulation, Modeling, and Programming for Autonomous Robots (SIMPAR)*. Dec. 2016, pp. 318–324. DOI: 10.1109/SIMPAR.2016.7862413.

[ZS09] J. Ziegler and C. Stiller. "Spatiotemporal state lattices for fast trajectory planning in dynamic on-road driving scenarios". In: *2009 IEEE/RSJ International Conference on Intelligent Robots and Systems*. Oct. 2009, pp. 1879–1884. DOI: 10.1109/IROS.2009.5354448.

[ZW08] J. Ziegler and M. Werling. "Navigating car-like robots in unstructured environments using an obstacle sensitive cost function". In: *2008 IEEE Intelligent Vehicles Symposium*. June 2008, pp. 787–791. DOI: 10.1109/IVS.2008.4621302.

[ZXL16] F. Zhang, J. Xi, and R. Langari. "An adaptive equivalent consumption minimization strategy for parallel hybrid electric vehicle based on Fuzzy PI". In: *2016 IEEE Intelligent Vehicles Symposium (IV)*. June 2016, pp. 460–465. DOI: 10.1109/IVS.2016.7535426.

List of publications

[GF12a] T. Guan and C. Frey. "EXPERT A driver assistance system for fuel efficient driving". In: *3rd International Conference on Machine Control and Guidance*. Mar. 2012.

[GF12b] T. Guan and C. W. Frey. "Fuel efficiency driver assistance system for manufacturer independent solutions". In: *2012 15th International IEEE Conference on Intelligent Transportation Systems*. Sept. 2012, pp. 212–217. DOI: 10.1109/ITSC.2012.6338685.

[GF12c] T. Guan and C. W. Frey. "Model adaptive driver assistance system to increase fuel savings". In: *2012 IEEE International Conference on Vehicular Electronics and Safety (ICVES 2012)*. July 2012, pp. 312–317. DOI: 10.1109/ICVES.2012.6294306.

[GF13] T. Guan and C. W. Frey. "Predictive fuel efficiency optimization using traffic light timings and fuel consumption model". In: *16th International IEEE Conference on Intelligent Transportation Systems (ITSC 2013)*. Oct. 2013, pp. 1553–1558. DOI: 10.1109/ITSC.2013.6728451.

[CGF14] O. Chevrant-Breton, T. Guan, and C. W. Frey. "Search space reduction in dynamic programming using monotonic heuristics in the context of model predictive optimization". In: *17th International IEEE Conference on Intelligent Transportation Systems (ITSC)*. Oct. 2014, pp. 2113–2118. DOI: 10.1109/ITSC.2014.6958015.

[GF14] T. Guan and C. W. Frey. "Using ensemble of decision trees with SVM nodes to learn the behaviour of a transmission control software". In: *17th International IEEE Conference on Intelligent Transportation Systems (ITSC)*. Oct. 2014, pp. 1323–1328. DOI: 10.1109/ITSC.2014.6957870.

[Gua15] T. Guan. "Geschwindigkeitsprofil Optimierung des REM-2030 Elektrofahrzeugs im Vergleich zum REM-2030 Fahrprofil". In: *Symposium REM 2030*. 2015.

[GF15] T. Guan and C. W. Frey. "Reuse historic costs in dynamic programming to reduce computational complexity in the context of model predictive optimization". In: *2015 IEEE International Conference on Vehicular Electronics and Safety (ICVES)*. Nov. 2015, pp. 256–263. DOI: 10.1109/ICVES.2015.7396927.

[GF16a] T. Guan and C. W. Frey. "Predictive energy efficiency optimization of an electric vehicle using information about traffic light sequences and other vehicles". In: *2016 IEEE 19th International Conference on Intelligent Transportation Systems (ITSC)*. Nov. 2016, pp. 919–926. DOI: 10.1109/ITSC.2016.7795665.

[GF16b] T. Guan and C. W. Frey. "Predictive energy efficiency optimization of an electric vehicle using traffic light sequence information". In: *2016 IEEE International Conference on Vehicular Electronics and Safety (ICVES)*. July 2016, pp. 1–6. DOI: 10.1109/ICVES.2016.7548168.

[GF16c] T. Guan and C. W. Frey. "Unified predictive fuel efficiency optimization using traffic light sequence information". In: *2016 IEEE Intelligent Vehicles Symposium (IV)*. June 2016, pp. 1103–1108. DOI: 10.1109/IVS.2016.7535527.

[GF17] T. Guan and C. W. Frey. "Improvement of predictive energy efficiency optimization using long distance horizon estimation".

In: *2017 IEEE Intelligent Vehicles Symposium (IV)*. June 2017, pp. 1249–1255. DOI: 10.1109/IVS.2017.7995883.

Curriculum Vitae

Personal information

Name	Tianyi Guan
Date of birth	April 13th 1983
City of birth	Changchun

Academic studies

2010	Graduate school graduation from University Stuttgart Certificate: Diplom Ingenieur in Electrical Engineering and Information Technology

Professional activity

Since October 2010	Scientific associate at Fraunhofer Institute of Optronics, System Technologies, and Image Exploitation IOSB

Karlsruher Schriftenreihe zur Anthropomatik (ISSN 1863-6489)

Herausgeber: Prof. Dr.-Ing. habil. Jürgen Beyerer

Band 1 Jürgen Geisler
Leistung des Menschen am Bildschirmarbeitsplatz. 2006
ISBN 3-86644-070-7

Band 2 Elisabeth Peinsipp-Byma
Leistungserhöhung durch Assistenz in interaktiven Systemen zur Szenenanalyse. 2007
ISBN 978-3-86644-149-1

Band 3 Jürgen Geisler, Jürgen Beyerer (Hrsg.)
Mensch-Maschine-Systeme. 2010
ISBN 978-3-86644-457-7

Band 4 Jürgen Beyerer, Marco Huber (Hrsg.)
Proceedings of the 2009 Joint Workshop of Fraunhofer IOSB and Institute for Anthropomatics, Vision and Fusion Laboratory. 2010
ISBN 978-3-86644-469-0

Band 5 Thomas Usländer
Service-oriented design of environmental information systems. 2010
ISBN 978-3-86644-499-7

Band 6 Giulio Milighetti
Multisensorielle diskret-kontinuierliche Überwachung und Regelung humanoider Roboter. 2010
ISBN 978-3-86644-568-0

Band 7 Jürgen Beyerer, Marco Huber (Hrsg.)
Proceedings of the 2010 Joint Workshop of Fraunhofer IOSB and Institute for Anthropomatics, Vision and Fusion Laboratory. 2011
ISBN 978-3-86644-609-0

Band 8 Eduardo Monari
Dynamische Sensorselektion zur auftragsorientierten Objektverfolgung in Kameranetzwerken. 2011
ISBN 978-3-86644-729-5

Die Bände sind unter www.ksp.kit.edu als PDF frei verfügbar oder als Druckausgabe bestellbar.

Band 9 Thomas Bader
Multimodale Interaktion in Multi-Display-Umgebungen. 2011
ISBN 3-86644-760-8

Band 10 Christian Frese
Planung kooperativer Fahrmanöver für kognitive Automobile. 2012
ISBN 978-3-86644-798-1

Band 11 Jürgen Beyerer, Alexey Pak (Hrsg.)
Proceedings of the 2011 Joint Workshop of Fraunhofer IOSB and Institute for Anthropomatics, Vision and Fusion Laboratory. 2012
ISBN 978-3-86644-855-1

Band 12 Miriam Schleipen
Adaptivität und Interoperabilität von Manufacturing Execution Systemen (MES). 2013
ISBN 978-3-86644-955-8

Band 13 Jürgen Beyerer, Alexey Pak (Hrsg.)
Proceedings of the 2012 Joint Workshop of Fraunhofer IOSB and Institute for Anthropomatics, Vision and Fusion Laboratory. 2013
ISBN 978-3-86644-988-6

Band 14 Hauke-Hendrik Vagts
Privatheit und Datenschutz in der intelligenten Überwachung: Ein datenschutzgewährendes System, entworfen nach dem „Privacy by Design" Prinzip. 2013
ISBN 978-3-7315-0041-4

Band 15 Christian Kühnert
Data-driven Methods for Fault Localization in Process Technology. 2013
ISBN 978-3-7315-0098-8

Band 16 Alexander Bauer
Probabilistische Szenenmodelle für die Luftbildauswertung. 2014
ISBN 978-3-7315-0167-1

Band 17 Jürgen Beyerer, Alexey Pak (Hrsg.)
Proceedings of the 2013 Joint Workshop of Fraunhofer IOSB and Institute for Anthropomatics, Vision and Fusion Laboratory. 2014
ISBN 978-3-7315-0212-8

Die Bände sind unter www.ksp.kit.edu als PDF frei verfügbar oder als Druckausgabe bestellbar.

Band 18 Michael Teutsch
Moving Object Detection and Segmentation for Remote Aerial Video Surveillance. 2015
ISBN 978-3-7315-0320-0

Band 19 Marco Huber
Nonlinear Gaussian Filtering: Theory, Algorithms, and Applications. 2015
ISBN 978-3-7315-0338-5

Band 20 Jürgen Beyerer, Alexey Pak (Hrsg.)
Proceedings of the 2014 Joint Workshop of Fraunhofer IOSB and Institute for Anthropomatics, Vision and Fusion Laboratory. 2014
ISBN 978-3-7315-0401-6

Band 21 Todor Dimitrov
Permanente Optimierung dynamischer Probleme der Fertigungssteuerung unter Einbeziehung von Benutzerinteraktionen. 2015
ISBN 978-3-7315-0426-9

Band 22 Benjamin Kühn
Interessengetriebene audiovisuelle Szenenexploration. 2016
ISBN 978-3-7315-0457-3

Band 23 Yvonne Fischer
Wissensbasierte probabilistische Modellierung für die Situationsanalyse am Beispiel der maritimen Überwachung. 2016
ISBN 978-3-7315-0460-3

Band 24 Jürgen Beyerer, Alexey Pak (Hrsg.)
Proceedings of the 2015 Joint Workshop of Fraunhofer IOSB and Institute for Anthropomatics, Vision and Fusion Laboratory. 2016
ISBN 978-3-7315-0519-8

Band 25 Pascal Birnstill
Privacy-Respecting Smart Video Surveillance Based on Usage Control Enforcement. 2016
ISBN 978-3-7315-0538-9

Band 26 Philipp Woock
Umgebungskartenschätzung aus Sidescan-Sonardaten für ein autonomes Unterwasserfahrzeug. 2016
ISBN 978-3-7315-0541-9

Band 27 Janko Petereit
Adaptive State × Time Lattices: A Contribution to Mobile Robot Motion Planning in Unstructured Dynamic Environments. 2017
ISBN 978-3-7315-0580-8

Band 28 Erik Ludwig Krempel
Steigerung der Akzeptanz von intelligenter Videoüberwachung in öffentlichen Räumen. 2017
ISBN 978-3-7315-0598-3

Band 29 Jürgen Moßgraber
Ein Rahmenwerk für die Architektur von Frühwarnsystemen. 2017
ISBN 978-3-7315-0638-6

Band 30 Andrey Belkin
World Modeling for Intelligent Autonomous Systems. 2017
ISBN 978-3-7315-0641-6

Band 31 Chettapong Janya-Anurak
Framework for Analysis and Identification of Nonlinear Distributed Parameter Systems using Bayesian Uncertainty Quantification based on Generalized Polynomial Chaos. 2017
ISBN 978-3-7315-0642-3

Band 32 David Münch
Begriffliche Situationsanalyse aus Videodaten bei unvollständiger und fehlerhafter Information. 2017
ISBN 978-3-7315-0644-7

Band 33 Jürgen Beyerer, Alexey Pak (Eds.)
Proceedings of the 2016 Joint Workshop of Fraunhofer IOSB and Institute for Anthropomatics, Vision and Fusion Laboratory. 2017
ISBN 978-3-7315-0678-2

Band 34 Jürgen Beyerer, Alexey Pak and Miro Taphanel (Eds.)
Proceedings of the 2017 Joint Workshop of Fraunhofer IOSB and Institute for Anthropomatics, Vision and Fusion Laboratory. 2018
ISBN 978-3-7315-0779-6

Band 35 Michael Grinberg
Feature-Based Probabilistic Data Association for Video-Based Multi-Object Tracking. 2018
ISBN 978-3-7315-0781-9

Band 36 Christian Herrmann
Video-to-Video Face Recognition for Low-Quality Surveillance Data. 2018
ISBN 978-3-7315-0799-4

Band 37 Chengchao Qu
Facial Texture Super-Resolution by Fitting 3D Face Models. 2018
ISBN 978-3-7315-0828-1

Band 38 Miriam Ruf
Geometrie und Topologie von Trajektorienoptimierung für vollautomatisches Fahren. 2018
ISBN 978-3-7315-0832-8

Band 39 Angelika Zube
Bewegungsregelung mobiler Manipulatoren für die Mensch-Roboter-Interaktion mittels kartesischer modellprädiktiver Regelung. 2018
ISBN 978-3-7315-0855-7

Band 40 Jürgen Beyerer and Miro Taphanel (Eds.)
Proceedings of the 2018 Joint Workshop of Fraunhofer IOSB and Institute for Anthropomatics, Vision and Fusion Laboratory. 2019
ISBN 978-3-7315-0936-3

Band 41 Marco Thomas Gewohn
Ein methodischer Beitrag zur hybriden Regelung der Produktionsqualität in der Fahrzeugmontage. 2019
ISBN 978-3-7315-0893-9

Band 42 Tianyi Guan
Predictive energy-efficient motion trajectory optimization of electric vehicles. 2019
ISBN 978-3-7315-0978-3

Die Bände sind unter www.ksp.kit.edu als PDF frei verfügbar oder als Druckausgabe bestellbar.